BARNACLE PARP'S GUIDE TO
GARDEN & YARD POWER TOOLS

BARNACLE PARP'S GUIDE TO
GARDEN & YARD POWER TOOLS

Selection, Maintenance & Repair
BY WALTER HALL

 Rodale Press, Emmaus, Pennsylvania

Printed in the United States of America on recycled paper,
containing a high percentage of de-inked fiber.

Book design by Jerry O'Brien

Illustrations by John Carlance

Library of Congress Cataloging in Publication Data

Hall, Walter, 1940–
    Barnacle Parp's guide to garden and yard power tools.

    Includes index.
    1. Garden tools. 2. Power lawn mowers. 3. Power
tools. I. Title.
SB454.8.H34   1983   681'.7631   82–20527
ISBN 0–87857–446–8 hardcover
ISBN 0–87857–447–6 paperback

2   4   6   8   10   9   7   5   3   1 hardcover
2   4   6   8   10   9   7   5   3   1 paperback

For
Robert and Vivian Jonas

Contents

Introduction

It was late summer, and no one in Creede, Colorado, had any idea where I might find the elusive character known locally as Barnacle Parp. He hadn't started his fall wood gathering yet, so he wouldn't be up on Pool Table Mountain with his chain saw. A number of people had looked for him, hoping he would tune, repair, or sharpen their saws before the season began, but they had concluded that they'd have to wait. It was the worst time of the year for fishing, so he wasn't up Rat Creek, everyone was sure. All of the summer repairs to his cabin were finished, including the new roof, well, and septic system, so he wasn't out with Pappy Fairchild digging with the backhoe or dozing with the cat. It was too early for hunting, and he had already made his "culture venture" trips to several northern cities, so he was probably in the area somewhere—some cool place in the woods.

I am a writer. Actually, I am a poet. I write books like this one primarily because they give me an income and allow me to live in the woods. But I am not truly a woodsman, at least not like Parp. Parp can travel for months in the woods on a couple of pounds of cornmeal and a few fish hooks. I, however, have to take along freeze-dried dinners, and I would quickly return to town if I found that I had forgotten my washcloth.

It was unlikely that I would find Parp in the vast wilderness that surrounds Creede like the flesh of a dinosaur around a poison dart. But I had to try. I wanted to do this book and felt the need to consult Father Mechanic, wherever he might be. So I took two days to load my pack with extra compasses, tin cups, matches, soap, an enormous supply of aluminum-foil-wrapped food, and all the other things Parp laughs at

when we have one of our rare, shared camps in the high country.

The first day I made almost 7 miles. At noon on the second day, I descended a slope on the other side of the Great Divide and staggered gasping into Parp's camp at an abandoned shepherd's cabin in a certain valley in the San Juans. I had guessed right.

As soon as I could talk, I explained to Parp the reasons for my search and intrusion. In his years in these woods, Parp had done it all. He had owned a chain saw shop and outdoor power equipment service center in Lake City. He had gardened tomatoes, spuds, and certain interesting herbs at very high altitudes. He had helped to keep Pappy Fairchild's heavy equipment operating when it was nothing more than a quilt of welded patches. He had also taught me about all sorts of machines, everything from lawn mowers to tractors. Thanks to Parp's tutoring, I'd had some success sharpening chain saws, overhauling log splitters, and tuning up tillers. But to write a really authoritative guide to outdoor power equipment, I would need Parp over my shoulder as I wrote, and in the shop as I checked everything twice.

Well, Parp said okay, but he predicted that his own desires, obligations, and habits would cause the project to extend through several seasons. We would work together and select, use, maintain, and repair each separate tool extensively through its own appropriate function and season. We would not hurry this book, said Parp, because too many gardeners, ranchers, and woodspeople would depend on its accuracy. In retrospect, I guess it took even longer than Parp thought it would.

A glance at the Table of Contents will tell you that all but Part One of this book is arranged according to groups of tools—those used in the yard or on the grounds, those used in the garden or on the farm, and those used in the woodlot or in the forest. Part One is devoted to the small gasoline engines most commonly used to power the outdoor equipment discussed in the rest of the book.

As you may have guessed, this nonfiction work includes a number of characters who may or may not be completely or partially fictional. They are Pappy Fairchild, Parp's neighbor and friend and only surviving original resident of Old Creede (as a teenager, Pappy built the first water system for the original town, which was not located at the site of the present Creede); Love-of-His-Life, a close friend of Parp's; Ish Stewart, a legendary fisherman of the San Juans who taught Parp to ice-fish; and, of course, Parp himself, he who was born in a tree house, worked in a logging camp when he was ten, served as cop for the town of Creede, and finally took a correspondence course in professional writing. Other characters may be behind the scenes, but most failed to materialize in the text.

Remember, as Parp says, to always be careful around machinery of any kind: safety first.

PART ONE:
The Force that Drives

CHAPTER ONE:
Air-Cooled, Two-Cycle Engines

The air-cooled, two-cycle engine is far and away the most common type of engine used in backyard tools. Two-cycle engines power lawn mowers, chain saws, brushcutters, weed trimmers, blowers, sprayers, tillers, cultivators, chippers, shredders, air compressors, pumps, and generators. Some of these appliances may use larger, four-cycle engines, especially in heavy-duty models, but two-cycle engines are much more likely to appear in the average backyard. Hence, Parp will begin with two-cycle engines and will devote much space and time describing the theory, use, maintenance, and repair of these engines. They are, after all, the most successful product to date in the long search for ultralightweight power sources. In fact, they have made possible most of the tools presented in this book. They are also an excellent subject for a first course in engine theory and repair procedures.

HOW SMALL ENGINES WORK

Magic— well, says Parp, fire, like electricity, is magic, or close enough. An engine is a way of using fire by trapping it in a small chamber called, appropriately, a combustion chamber. The energy released by the fire is then controlled and directed in order to move parts that move other parts to perform the job at hand. Once you accept the elemental magic of the fire itself, the rest is simple and logical. The energy released by fire is chemical energy, and an engine simply converts this chemical energy into mechanical energy, which is then harnessed and utilized.

All engine-powered backyard tools employ a piston engine that is very similar to an automobile engine. A piston is a movable plug inserted in a cylinder. At the top of this cylinder is a relatively small space called the combustion chamber, and it is in this chamber that fuel is burned to release chemical energy (see Illus. 1–1). Since the cylinder is rigid except for the space occupied by the movable piston, which has just enough space to move, energy released by the burning fuel forces the piston to move. The piston, thrusting downward, then moves a connecting rod. This motion creates circular energy that is transferred to a crankshaft. The crankshaft then turns the blades of a lawn mower or the sprocket of a chain saw.

It's as simple as that, except that all of this burning, pushing, and turning requires bearings, seals, and, above all, a cooling system. It also necessitates a method for the disposing of burned fuel, or exhaust. The original source of fire—a spark plug and an ignition system—adds to the seeming complexity of the unit. All of these additions also bring with them most of the mechanical troubles likely to be encountered and handled by the backyard mechanic. Few of us will ever rebore a cylinder or replace a piston. Many of us *will* replace a spark plug or clean a muffler, and problems with these rather simple components can stop an engine just as quickly as can a run bearing or a thrown rod—and more often.

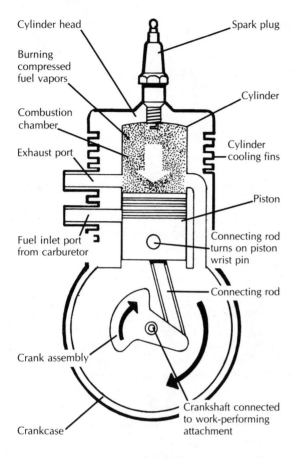

Cylinder head

Spark plug

Burning compressed fuel vapors

Cylinder

Combustion chamber

Cylinder cooling fins

Exhaust port

Piston

Fuel inlet port from carburetor

Connecting rod turns on piston wrist pin

Connecting rod

Crank assembly

Crankshaft connected to work-performing attachment

Crankcase

Illus. 1–1—Parts of a Typical Two-Cycle Engine

THEORY AND OPERATION OF TWO-CYCLE ENGINES

In a two-cycle (or two-stroke) engine, all of the functions, or phases, of the engine's operation are completed during one revolution of the crankshaft, comprising one upward stroke and one downward stroke of the piston. A two-cycle engine is lubricated by oil that is combined with gasoline to produce a two-cycle fuel

mixture. Two-cycle engines can be identified by the absence of an oil tank separate from the gasoline tank. Backyard tools such as chain saws do have a separate oil tank, but it is for bar and chain oil or work-performing attachment lubrication, not for engine lubrication. If removed from the chain saw, the engine would not have a separate oil tank.

Both four- and two-cycle engines develop power by burning a highly combustible, vaporized mixture of gasoline and air. Two-cycle fuel also includes a carefully measured amount of oil that's added to protect moving parts through lubrication. The vaporized fuel mixture is burned in the combustion chamber, above the cylinder and below the cylinder head.

In a two-cycle engine, all engine functions—fuel intake, fuel combustion, exhaust release, and engine lubrication—must occur during one revolution, or in one up-and-down movement of the piston. Thus, more than one operation is performed during each piston stroke. For now, we'll ignore just how the vaporized fuel mixture is introduced into the combustion chamber. We'll just accept that it's there.

As you engage the engine's starter and turn the crankshaft, the piston rises in the cylinder. As it moves upward, it greatly compresses the vaporized fuel mixture trapped in the combustion chamber. At exactly the same time, another shot of vaporized fuel/air mixture is drawn into the crankcase of the engine by the low pressure caused by the ascending piston.

When the piston is near the uppermost limit of its travel, a precisely timed electrical charge travels through the ignition cable to the spark plug, which is threaded into the cylinder head. As the voltage jumps across the terminals of the spark plug, it sparks. This spark ignites the vaporized fuel mixture, which burns very rapidly. This, of course, forces the piston to travel downward, under power. As the piston travels downward, it uncovers two ports. One port allows the exhaust gas to escape; the other allows a

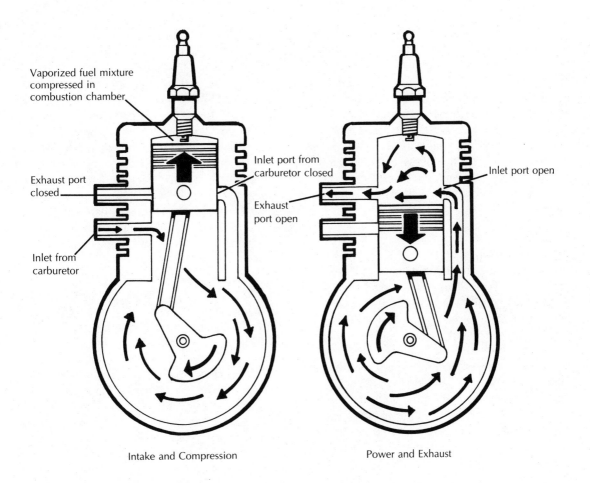

Vaporized fuel mixture compressed in combustion chamber

Inlet port from carburetor closed

Inlet port open

Exhaust port closed

Exhaust port open

Inlet from carburetor

Intake and Compression

Power and Exhaust

Illus. 1–2—Phases of a Typical Piston-Ported. Two-Cycle Engine

During the intake and compression phases (left), the upstroke of the piston compresses the fuel vapor above it in the combustion chamber while creating low pressure in the crankcase that draws in fuel vapors from the carburetor. In the power and exhaust phases (right), the piston's downstroke closes the inlet port from the carburetor and opens the inlet port to the combustion chamber, thus forcing fuel into it. The exhaust port also opens, and the fuel vapor forces the exhaust out.

fresh charge of vaporized fuel air mixture to take the place of the escaping exhaust. Thus, the engine has performed all necessary functions in a single revolution and will continue to do so until it runs out of fuel, is turned off, or experiences a mechanical failure.

Two-Cycle Fuel Systems

When you buy a new power tool, such as a chain saw or an engine-powered brushcutter, you encounter numerous warnings that gasoline must be mixed with an approved engine oil, called two-cycle engine oil, before filling the fuel tank. Usually, a sticker near the fuel tank tells you exactly what the mixture must be. If not, your owner's manual contains this essential information. Parp assumes you've mixed your fuel properly and have just filled the fuel tank. Now let's go through the major functions of the fuel system in order to understand how it works. This understanding is critical in discovering what the problem is when the fuel system fails to function properly. We'll start on the outside and follow the fuel mixture as it travels through the engine.

The Fuel Tank

One reason that two-cycle engines are commonly used in portable backyard tools is that these tools must be operable in all positions. If the fuel and oil tanks had to be in a certain position relative to the engine to keep their respective fluids separate, you would not be able to operate a chain saw at an extreme angle. Since two-cycle engines are lubricated by oil mixed with the fuel, they don't need a separate oil tank. Now, the only remaining problem is how to get the fuel/oil mixture to flow evenly into the crankcase regardless of the position of the fuel tank relative to the engine. Clearly, a gravity-fed system will not work. Thus, a fuel pump is essential. We'll soon cover details of the fuel pump and its operation, but for now let's just look at a problem caused by the presence of a fuel pump.

When you fill your fuel tank, the fuel going in replaces most of the air in the tank. If the cap placed on the fuel tank keeps it airtight, the action of the fuel pump drawing fuel into the engine would create a vacuum in the tank. This would soon make it impossible for the fuel pump to operate properly, and the engine would die of fuel starvation. So, all fuel tanks have special caps called breather caps. These vented caps allow air to enter the fuel tank as fuel is used, in order to maintain enough pressure in the tank to force fuel into the carburetor. If the breather

cap is clogged with grease, sawdust, or debris of any kind, the engine will not run properly—often not at all. A loose cap, or one with a large hole, is obviously dangerous. Less obviously, such a cap will allow the volatile portion of the fuel to evaporate, which causes fuel to go stale and leaves a residue like gum or varnish that causes hard starts and, eventually, engine damage. So, the cap on your fuel tank must be the correct cap; it must be kept free of clogging grease and dirt; and it must be in good operating condition. A clogged fuel tank cap is a common cause of poor engine performance and should be one of the first items checked when an engine is not performing properly.

How Fuel Moves

We have already seen that a low-pressure area is created in the crankcase and lower cylinder as the piston travels upward. This low-pressure area, or partial vacuum, is the prime mover of the fuel in the fuel system.

Since the breather cap on your fuel tank allows air from the atmosphere to enter the tank and prevent a vacuum, the pressure on the fuel in the tank is the same as atmospheric pressure. When a low-pressure area is created in the crankcase, the higher atmospheric pressure in the fuel tank forces the fuel to travel in the direction of the crankcase. The engine fuel system is, of course, designed in such a way that the fuel cannot go elsewhere.

The Carburetor

The fuel, however, does not pass directly into the crankcase from the fuel tank. It must first pass through a portion of the carburetor. The carburetor's function is to mix air with the incoming fuel in exactly the right proportion for the engine's needs. It is here that the fuel is vaporized.

The Choke

One part of a carburetor is designed to accept some air from the atmosphere. When the piston travels upward and creates a low-pressure area in the crankcase, air is drawn into the carburetor. The flow of this air is regulated by a plate that opens and closes; it is called the choke. The choke determines the size of the carburetor's air passage and, therefore, the amount of air flowing into the carburetor to be mixed with the fuel. The passage that feeds air to the carburetor is called the air horn.

The Venturi

As the airflow is sucked through the air horn by the low pressure in the crankcase, it passes through a venturi, or sudden narrowing of the air passage. This causes the airflow to increase in speed and decrease in pressure (known as the Venturi principle). At this point, a fuel jet connects the fuel supply with the venturi air passage. Since the fuel is under atmospheric pressure, and since the pressure of the incoming air flow is lessened by the venturi, the airflow across the fuel jet draws out fuel in the form of little drops. These fuel drops then mix with the rapidly moving airflow and are vaporized. This principle is commonly seen in atomizers, such as those on perfume bottles or window-cleaner sprays.

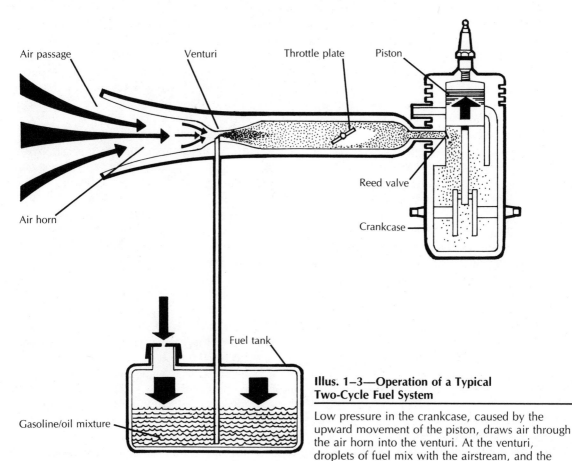

Air passage — Venturi — Throttle plate — Piston — Air horn — Reed valve — Crankcase — Fuel tank — Gasoline/oil mixture

Illus. 1–3—Operation of a Typical Two-Cycle Fuel System

Low pressure in the crankcase, caused by the upward movement of the piston, draws air through the air horn into the venturi. At the venturi, droplets of fuel mix with the airstream, and the vaporized fuel mixture is drawn past the open throttle plate into the crankcase.

The Throttle

The throttle plate works in much the same way as the choke plate, but it is positioned in the throttle shaft at a point after the incoming airstream has picked up fuel and has become a vaporized fuel mixture. The throttle plate is controlled by the throttle lever, or trigger, and controls the operating speed of the engine. When the throttle plate is fully opened, it allows the maximum amount of vaporized fuel to enter the crankcase. If it were closed completely, it would completely cut off the fuel supply, and the engine would stop. When the engine is running at idle, the throttle is open just enough to allow the proper amount of fuel vapor to enter the engine and cause it to idle. It is held partly open by the throttle, or idle speed, screw.

That's how fuel is vaporized in the carburetor and introduced into the crankcase. A small amount of dirt in the air horn, fuel jet, fuel line, or venturi will impair engine performance. The amount of fuel and air traveling through the carburetor is determined by screw adjustments found on the carburetor. If these adjustments are not precisely correct, the engine either will not run properly or will not run at all. Also, it is easy to damage these parts by tightening the screws excessively. This not only damages the screws but also the rather delicate metal holes in which they are seated. In the case of such damage, a carburetor replacement is often necessary.

The Fuel Filter

Both air and fuel must be pure and clean before they enter the carburetor. The fuel line extending from the fuel pump or carburetor into the fuel tank is weighted and loose on one end. That way, it always rests at the bottom of the fuel tank, regardless of the position of the tank or engine. The weighted end of this fuel pickup line also contains a fuel filter in a filter housing. This filter is designed to remove water, dirt, and debris from the fuel before it travels to the carburetor. When the fuel filter becomes clogged, it will not allow a full supply of fuel to pass through. Most often, the filter can be cleaned by washing it in clean gasoline and squeezing it dry. But periodically, the fuel filter must be replaced, as with all things.

The Air Filter

The air horn of the carburetor is completely covered by another filter, the air filter. This filter is even more susceptible to dirt than the fuel filter because it is exposed to the air and, thus, to much dirt and dust. The air filter must be cleaned very frequently— at least once for each eight hours of service. Many of today's air filters are called "permanent," but Parp says nothing's permanent, and certainly not air filters. It's a good idea to replace permanent air filters yearly or more often, depending on the amount and kind of work done by the engine.

Parp notes that a dirty air or fuel filter may do worse than stall the engine. If grit or dirt is carried into the crankcase with the vaporized fuel, it can score the cylinder walls, wear out the piston rings, and damage the bearings. Any of these occurrences can be very serious and can necessitate a complete overhaul—or, possibly, result in a ruined engine. That's why frequent cleaning of air and fuel filters is such an important part of daily maintenance.

Reed Valves

Although many engines are designed so that the piston is the only door between the carburetor and the crankcase, and its movement alone allows the fresh fuel/air mixture to enter, other engines are designed with a small piece of spring steel called a reed valve. Access to the reed valve is usually achieved by removing the carburetor and reed valve housing, or assembly. Most manufacturers specify a reed valve gap of .010 inch. When a reed valve is fatigued, this gap will exceed the specification, and the engine will not operate properly. The reed valve

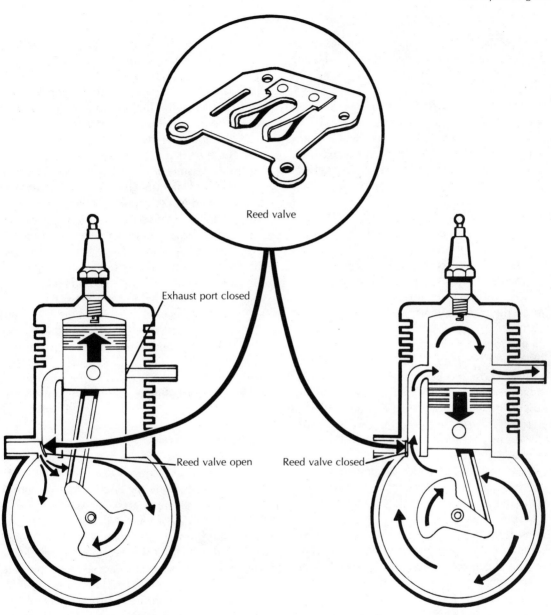

Reed valve

Exhaust port closed

Reed valve open

Reed valve closed

Intake and Compression

Power and Exhaust

Illus. 1—4—Phases of a Typical Reed-Valve-Ported, Two-Cycle Engine

In this type of two-cycle engine, the reed valve opens and closes the carburetor inlet port instead of the piston. Otherwise, it operates the same way as any two-cycle engine.

must then be replaced. Many mechanics make a habit of checking or replacing the reed valve any time the carburetor is removed from the engine.

Piston-ported systems are by far the most common fuel inlet designs used in modern two-cycle engines. There are other designs, such as rotary valve engines, but they are being used less frequently every year and are unlikely to come under the wrench of the home mechanic.

The Fuel Pump

As mentioned earlier, the initial force that draws fuel into the engine is the low pressure created in the crankcase by the upward movement of the piston. As the piston moves up and down according to engine speed, however, it causes fluctuations in the pressure inside the crankcase.

In order to provide the proper amount of fuel to the carburetor at the correct pressure at all times, most two-cycle engines utilize a diaphragm-type fuel pump that is integral to the body of the carburetor. Most carburetors manufactured for use on two-cycle engines come with the fuel pump. Sometimes it's difficult to determine if it's the carburetor or the fuel pump that's failed. This makes it especially important to understand the function and operation of the typical diaphragm fuel pump.

The fluctuations in crankcase pressure resulting from the piston's movement cause the diaphragm of the fuel pump to open and close passages between the fuel supply and the carburetor. When low crankcase pressure (signaling a need for more fuel) pulls the diaphragm in, the inlet valve is opened, and fuel flows into the fuel chamber of the fuel pump. This same pressure pulls on the outlet valve to the carburetor to keep it closed. When higher pressure in the crankcase pushes the diaphragm out, the inlet valve is forced to close, and the pressure in the fuel chamber pushes the outlet valve open. The necessary fuel is then pumped to the carburetor.

All of this pumping and pushing occurs in direct relationship to the high or low pressures present in the crankcase. Thus, if there is no leak in the system, the variations in crankcase pressure cause the fuel pump to deliver fuel in accordance with the engine's speed and, therefore, its requirements.

But there's a catch. At low engine speeds, the low pressure in the crankcase is not strong enough to pull air through the air horn fast enough to do a good job of vaporizing the fuel droplets at the venturi. Conversely, at high speeds, the air flowing in the venturi becomes stretched and thin—but the fuel doesn't stretch accordingly. Thus, the engine requires a richer mixture of fuel and air at both idle speeds and high speeds. That's why small-engine carburetors have high-speed and low-speed mixture control jets, and screws that adjust needles affecting these jets.

The high-speed screw controls a jet located in the venturi at the point of lowest pressure. The low-speed screw controls three jets located in the air horn below the venturi, near the throttle valve.

Carburetor Service

Most modern two-cycle engines utilize carburetors made by special carburetor manufacturers rather than by the engine manufacturers. The two chief suppliers of small-engine carburetors are Walbro and Tillotson. These companies and others also manufacture carburetor rebuilding kits to fit their various models. With these kits, even an inexperienced mechanic can, with care and attention, rebuild—actually, refurbish—a tired carburetor. These kits typically include new high- and low-speed adjustment needles, fresh seals and plugs, intake and impulse fittings, and diaphragms and screens. Parp says there is nothing to stop the average tool owner from doing a good job of rebuilding a quality small-engine carburetor. Usually, this is the practical solution to a carburetor failure. Attempting to isolate and repair a single carburetor

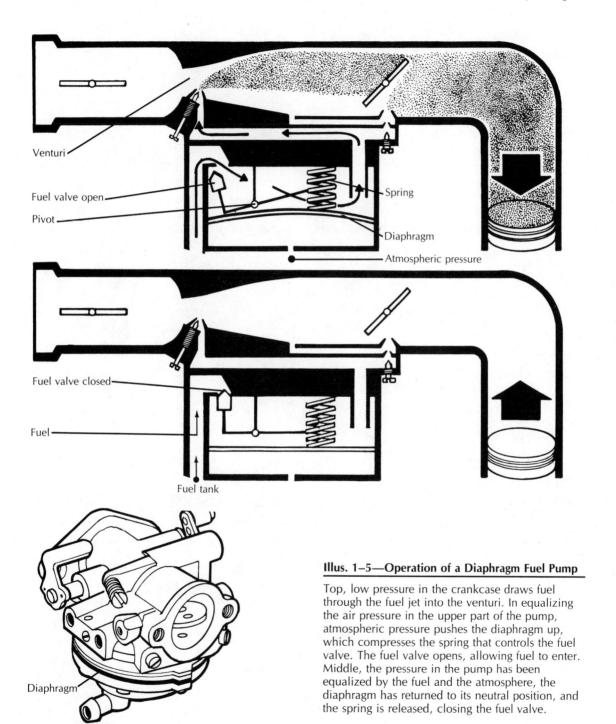

Venturi

Fuel valve open

Pivot

Spring

Diaphragm

Atmospheric pressure

Fuel valve closed

Fuel

Fuel tank

Diaphragm

Fuel pump attached beneath carburetor

Illus. 1–5—Operation of a Diaphragm Fuel Pump

Top, low pressure in the crankcase draws fuel through the fuel jet into the venturi. In equalizing the air pressure in the upper part of the pump, atmospheric pressure pushes the diaphragm up, which compresses the spring that controls the fuel valve. The fuel valve opens, allowing fuel to enter. Middle, the pressure in the pump has been equalized by the fuel and the atmosphere, the diaphragm has returned to its neutral position, and the spring is released, closing the fuel valve.

malfunction is very difficult. Besides, when one thing goes wrong in a carburetor, you can usually assume that the whole thing should be disassembled, cleaned, and rebuilt.

Even if you never rebuild a carburetor, it's a great help to understand the basic functions of the carburetor, fuel pump, and fuel tank. That way, you can isolate those problems that relate to the fuel system.

Two-Cycle Ignition Systems

Now that our fuel system has created a vaporized fuel/air mixture in the combustion chamber, we need a way to set fire to it. This igniting of the mixture is managed by creating an electrical spark through the use of one type or another of an electromagnetic induction system.

Electromagnetic systems rely upon fundamental characteristics of electricity and magnetism to generate an ignition spark. You may remember performing an electromagnetic experiment in an early science class. In the typical experiment, if a wire is moved across the lines of a magnetic field, an electric current is induced in the wire. If the wire is part of a complete

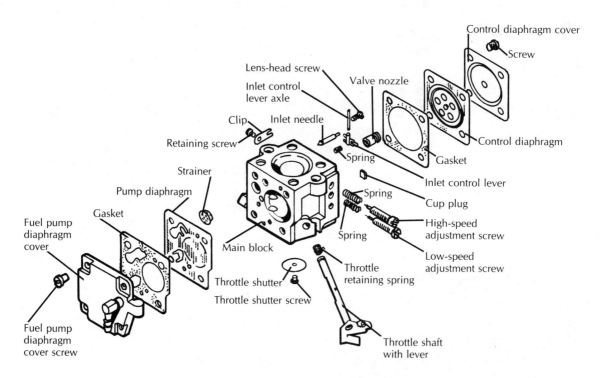

Illus. 1–6—A Typical Carburetor on Two-Cycle Engine Backyard Power Tools

A rebuilding kit for this Tillotson carburetor includes replacements for all parts except the main block and the two outside covers. In rebuilding a carburetor, all of the replacement parts may not be needed.

circuit, the electricity will light up a bulb or power some other device.

Another part of the relationship between electricity and magnetism is that whenever an electric current flows through a conductor (in this case, the wire), a magnetic field is brought into existence around the conductor. Also, if the conductor is a tightly wound coil of wires, the magnetic forces join to create one magnetic field that is much stronger than that surrounding a single wire. The number of turns in the wire determines the strength of the field.

The strength and direction of a magnetic field's force around a conductor is determined by the strength and direction of the electrical current in the conductor. If you change the current, you also change the magnetic field. If you stop the current completely, the magnetic field collapses. If you stop the current in a coil of wires, the magnetic forces collapse across the turns of the coil. This induces a new current.

Electricity only flows in a complete circuit, and a current always takes the path of least resistance to complete its circuit. Electricity is alive only when it can travel from one place to another, and back again by a different road. And, it always takes the easiest road.

All ignition systems are comprised of two electric circuits, a low-voltage primary circuit and a high-voltage secondary circuit, also called a high-tension circuit. The primary circuit itself does not produce a strong enough current to ignite a spark. Its function is to induce a high-voltage current in the secondary circuit to fire the spark plug.

Most ignition systems for four-cycle engines and automobiles induce current through electromagnetic induction only in the secondary circuit. The current for the primary circuit is supplied by a battery that causes either an alternator or generator to produce an electromagnetic current.

A battery used to induce current in a primary circuit is too heavy and too limited in use,

because it must be kept upright, to be of service in a two-cycle-engine power tool. Two-cycle engines employ magneto-ignition systems to electromagnetically induce current in both the primary and the secondary circuits. Magneto-ignition systems are lightweight, portable, and have a wide range of uses since they are independent of such power sources as batteries or house currents.

The Flywheel and the Magneto

The two major parts of a magneto-ignition system are the flywheel and the magneto coil component. The flywheel is a heavy, weighted wheel mounted on the crankshaft. As part of the drive system, its weight maintains momentum of the turning crankshaft to help keep the engine running smoothly. In the magneto-ignition system, the flywheel houses the magnets that, as they pass by, induce current in the magneto component. In most two-cycle engines the flywheel is first spun by the operator pulling on a starter rope. Also, the flywheel is fastened to the crankshaft by a pin called a half-moon key, or Woodruff, so as to maintain correct ignition timing.

The magneto component is in a fixed position behind the flywheel. (The word magneto is short for magneto-electric machine.) It is made of two coils, or windings, of tightly wound wire held together by a cylinder-shaped container. The inner winding, the primary coil, is made up of about 200 turns of thick, copper wire. The outer winding, the secondary coil, is made up of 10,000 or more turns of very thin wire. It is the action of the flywheel magnets passing by these coils that produces the electromagnetic induction that leads to an ignition spark. Three other parts play important roles, however.

Armature Core, Condenser, and Breaker Points Set

In order to produce a magnetic field around the primary circuit coil strong enough to induce a current in the coil, the magnetic forces from the flywheel magnets are concentrated around the magneto coil by a laminated core of soft, iron plates, called an armature core. Soft iron is such an excellent conductor that, although the magnets never touch it and come only as close as what is called the armature air gap, the armature core transfers sufficient magnetic force to assure the induction of the primary coil current.

The current induced in the primary coil forms a magnetic field around the secondary coil, which produces current in the secondary circuit. Since neither current is of sufficient electrical pressure, or voltage, to cause the plug to spark, current must be prevented from reaching the plug prematurely so that a short circuit is avoided. Therefore, a condenser intercepts the primary coil current and keeps it from short-circuiting to the spark plug.

Current with greater voltage is still needed to spark the plug. This is provided by an arrangement known as the breaker points set. The breaker points set is a connection in a circuit that, when open, breaks the circuit to interrupt the flow of current. When the breaker point set is closed, the current flows through the circuit. (A light switch is a common household circuit-breaker arrangement.)

The breaker points set is mounted near the crankshaft and is caused to open and close by an irregularity on the crankshaft. This irregularity is called a cam lobe. Only one point in the set is moved by the cam lobe on the crankshaft; the other is stationary. Each time the crankshaft turns, the cam lobe pushes the movable point away from the fixed one. At that instant, the points are open and the circuit is broken. When the cam lobe passes its point of contact with the movable point, a steel spring brings the points together again, and the circuit is once more complete.

When the cam lobe opens the points, the flow of current in the primary coil circuit is interrupted. Since the flow of current creates a strong electromagnetic field around the primary winding, the interruption causes this field to

Illus. 1–7—The Flywheel Magneto-Ignition System (Breaker Point System)

The magnets in the rotating flywheel pass the armature core and induce a current in the primary circuit. This current is prevented from short-circuiting by the condenser until the flywheel cam lobe breaks the current, which collapses a magnetic field upon the secondary circuit. The collapsed magnetic field induces a strong current which then causes the plug to spark as the flywheel cam lobe closes with the fixed point to complete the circuit.

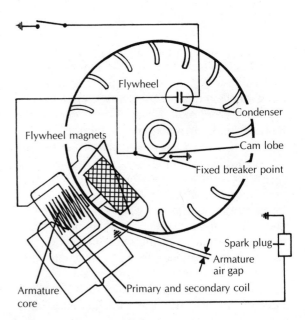

collapse across the secondary winding with its many turns of thin wire. This compresses the current and tremendously increases the voltage. The current always moves to the secondary winding when the primary circuit is interrupted because it seeks the path of least resistance and because the condenser prevents the current from leaping across the open breaker points.

This sequence causes the high-voltage current to travel along the secondary lead to the spark plug. Here there is no condenser, and the gap in the spark plug is very small. Since the spark plug is screwed into the cylinder head, the electrode connected to the spark plug threads forms an electrical ground. The current jumps the gap to complete its circuit and thus creates the spark.

As the spark plug fires, the condenser absorbs the flow of high-voltage current to keep it from arcing across the breaker points, preventing it from burning the contact points and short-circuiting the spark plug. The condenser also absorbs the slight current that the collapse of the magnetic field has induced in the primary circuit, which otherwise can short-circuit the spark plug, causing it to misfire.

The Complete System

When you pull the starter rope and spin the flywheel, the flywheel turns the crankshaft and moves the piston in the cylinder. The crankcase pressure changes caused by the moving piston activate the fuel system and bring a charge of vaporized fuel into the combustion chamber, where it is compressed by the piston. Now it needs only a spark to cause it to burn.

Spinning the flywheel with the starter rope also causes the flywheel magnets to pass near the armature core and the magneto coil. The armature transfers the concentrated magnetic forces to the magneto coil. The magneto coil converts the magnetism to electrical energy. When the cam lobe on the crankshaft, also turned by spinning the flywheel, moves past the mov-

able breaker point, the points close and the electricity flows through the points to ground, thus completing the circuit that fires the spark.

We now have fuel to burn, a place to burn it, and a spark to start the fire. As the spark ignites the compressed fuel vapor in the compression chamber, the fuel/air mixture burns, forcing the piston back down under power. As the piston moves, it uncovers the inlet port and allows a fresh charge of fuel vapor to be pushed into the combustion chamber by crankcase pressure, while the burned gases escape through the exhaust port. Simultaneously, the piston power is transferred to the connecting rod that turns the crankshaft. The crankshaft transfers rotating power to the work attachment, such as the blades of a rotary lawn mower.

So all in all, Parp says, your arm provides the primary energy in a magneto-ignition system—not scientifically, perhaps, but really. Because, when you pull the rope and spin the flywheel, you send the vaporized fuel into the combustion chamber, and you provide the energy that makes it possible for the magneto system to deliver the spark at the correct instant.

Breakerless Electronic Ignitions

Many of today's small-engine ignition systems do not use breaker points. Instead, they incorporate solid-state electronic, or breakerless, ignitions. Each system has distinct advantages.

The advantages of the standard breaker points system are: (1) its capability to be adjusted, replaced, or repaired by a home mechanic; (2) its relatively low cost, making it less expensive to purchase and replace, even if you have a mechanic do the work; and (3) its simple method for altering engine timing in unusual conditions, such as extremely high altitude.

The advantages of a breakerless electronic ignition are: (1) its lack of moving parts to wear down or go out of adjustment; (2) its relative insusceptibility to moisture and dirt because it is sealed in a single unit; (3) its engine's greater efficiency at all speeds; and (4) its small amounts of polluting emissions.

Most trouble with electronic ignitions stems from bad connections. Check for loose or broken wires around the sealed black box—after, of course, you've inspected the spark plug and high-voltage leads. Don't attempt to open up the black box that houses the electronic components; only specially trained mechanics should work on these systems. You can remove the unit and either take it to one of these specialists or just replace it with a new one.

Power Transference: The Clutch

With the notable exception of the simplest lawn mowers and a few other power tools, most small-engine-driven machines use a clutch to disconnect the engine from the work-performing parts. If this were not so, the chain of a chain saw would turn continuously whenever the engine was running, even at idle. This would be dangerous and would cause unnecessary wear on both the machine and the engine.

Manual Clutches

Many blowers, mowers, and other machines have a simple manual clutch. Although manual clutches come in a vast array of designs, they all work in much the same way—you move a lever or handle that engages the crankshaft and the working parts. Typical manual clutches and their related problems are covered in the chapters on specific tools. A close examination of any machine will usually tell you all you need to know about its particular clutch system.

Other small-engine-driven machines utilize a disk clutch system. The disk clutch works by engaging two friction surfaces. Some disk clutch mechanisms operate in an oil bath and are therefore called wet disk clutches. Others are, of course, dry. They both work in essentially the same manner. Two disks with friction surfaces are brought together to transmit power from the drive shaft to the load. This kind of clutch is usually engaged through a simple, operator-manipulated lever or linkage system.

Centrifugal Clutches

The centrifugal clutch is another system commonly found on small-engine-driven machines. It is almost as simple as a manual system and is less likely to fail. It does, however, have parts that require maintenance and occasional replacement.

With chain saws in particular, and with many other power tools, it's undesirable for the working parts to be moving all the time that the engine is running. Besides the safety factor, it is better for an engine to be engaged for work after it has reached operating speed.

Since an engine's crankshaft is a turning mechanism, it possesses centrifugal force. A centrifugal clutch consists of a drum casing with a hub that fits over the drive end of the crankshaft. The hub fits over a bearing assembly, and the crankshaft can turn in the hub without turning the drum.

Inside the drum, clutch shoes are attached by springs, and the entire assembly, called the friction assembly, is held to the crankshaft by retaining washers and a nut or a half-moon key or pin. When the crankshaft is turning slowly or not at all, the springs keep the clutch shoes from touching the inside walls of the clutch drum. Thus, as the engine idles, the drum stays still and the shoes turn within it.

As the engine accelerates, the crankshaft turns faster, and the centrifugal force on the clutch shoes increases. This force pushes the shoes outward, against the inside of the clutch drum. The clutch drum is attached in some way to the work-performing parts, and they turn as well.

Note that many small-engine-driven machines are designed to operate at or near maximum engine speed. At more moderate speeds, the clutch shoes may not press firmly against the walls of the clutch drum, and the resulting friction can cause the clutch shoes to wear excessively and quickly. Check the owner's manual for any specific tool to see if it is designed to operate at moderate speeds.

Clutch shoes, springs, and bearings are affected by moisture, grease, and normal wear. If they become wet or greasy, they should be cleaned. Eventually these parts must be replaced due to wear.

The Cooling System

Most backyard tools are powered by air-cooled engines, whether two- or four-cycle. Air-cooled engines are simpler and easier to maintain than other engines because they function without the need for radiators, hoses, water lines, or pumps. Also, it is easy to design an air-cooled engine capable of operating in any position. They are, of course, much lighter than liquid-cooled engines.

Nonetheless, all cooling systems require some maintenance. In an air-cooled system, a fan or blower mounted on the crankshaft blows air over the engine. The engine is usually covered, or partially covered, with metal shrouds that direct the air and help circulate it to all parts of the engine. In most two-cycle engines, the fan is an integral part of the flywheel.

Most small engines are also finned, especially at those parts that get the hottest. The fins help circulate the air. They also serve to present a greater surface area to the airflow. Note that any dirt or grease that is allowed to collect on

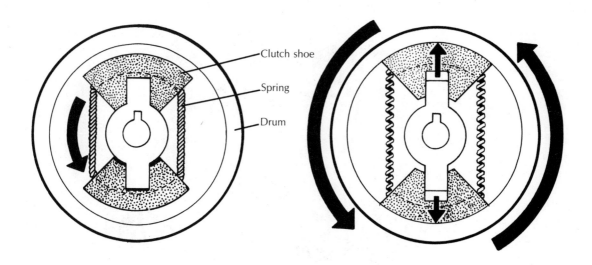

Clutch shoe

Spring

Drum

Illus. 1–8—Parts and Operation of a Centrifugal Clutch

As the engine idles, the clutch shoes rotate freely inside the drum. When engine speed increases, the crankshaft turns faster, and centrifugal force pushes the clutch shoes out against the inside of the clutch drum, thus engaging the drive shaft of the tool.

these cooling fins will greatly increase the operating temperature of the engine. Since the entire surface of any air-cooled mechanism is designed to help dissipate the heat generated by the engine, it is essential to keep the entire mechanism clean in order for the cooling system to operate effectively.

The functioning of the cooling system completes the groundwork for a good understanding of two-cycle-engine operation on backyard tools. Many of these systems are common to four-cycle engines, too, though the differences between the two power sources are great enough to war-

rant a complete chapter devoted to the four-cycle (Chapter Three). To make servicing your power tools as easy as possible, Parp has included complete engine trouble-shooting charts for both two-cycle and four-cycle engines in Appendix B. If you have an engine problem with one of your yard tools, you can determine whether it's a two-cycle engine or a four-cycle engine as described in the Appendix. Then you can go on to look for the symptom and the solution to the problem. You'll find out how to perform the repairs suggested in the solutions in the next three chapters.

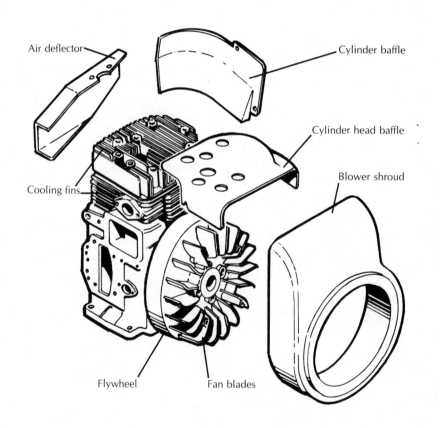

Illus. 1–9—Parts of a Typical Small-Engine Air Cooling System

CHAPTER TWO:
Two-Cycle
Engine Maintenance

Parp says good maintenance habits are the key to long-lasting engines and properly operating equipment. Parp's sketch of engine operation and theory, set forth in Chapter One, describes some of the things that can go wrong if maintenance is inadequate, and it hints at others. An overall understanding of how engines and tools work helps the owner to see what can go wrong and what can be done to prevent it.

That's what maintenance is—preventing trouble in expensive and often important equipment. When Parp's everyday comfort (and possibly his life) came to depend on an ancient chain saw during a snowbound and desolate winter high in the Sangre de Cristo Mountains, he stopped taking routine maintenance routinely. He had survived other tough wilderness winters without a chain saw. But this time he really wasn't prepared, having arrived in December, and he didn't want to have to survive on a day-to-day basis for months. So he babied that saw, and the difference his care made was astounding. The saw ran all winter without a failure on one old spark plug and no spare parts. Parp is convinced that if he had let that saw go dirty and untightened for a single day, it would have died. Instead, after the winter, he was able to give the saw to a woman with six kids. She also learned proper maintenance, and the saw is still cutting today, many spark plugs and sawchains later.

Good maintenance starts as soon as you receive a machine, whether it's new or used. You'll likely want to fuel it and start it up right now. Parp says to take ten minutes to read the owner's manual. If you've acquired a used machine without an owner's manual, try to obtain one through a dealer or direct from a manufacturer. If that fails, consult a mechanic for fuel and lubrication specifications. If that fails, use this book and your own best judgment. (If you've bought a chain saw, or intend to, Parp modestly recommends *Barnacle Parp's Chain Saw Guide*, Rodale Press, 1977.)

GENERAL MAINTENANCE

General maintenance includes keeping your power equipment clean, sharpened, and in good repair. It means reading your owner's manuals and following all manufacturer's maintenance and operating recommendations to the letter. Many people take such advice lightly and, as a result, make frequent trips to the dump. When a manufacturer recommends a specific oil, for instance, such advice is not simply self-serving, even if that manufacturer also distributes the recommended oil. This is more obviously true of such recommendations as sharpening techniques, fuel mixtures, specific spark plugs, and so on. True, substitutions are often possible, but they can also lead to unforeseen and unimagined difficulties. Today's best small engines and appliances are manufactured to close tolerances for top performance. To meet and stay within these tolerances, machines often require specific treatment.

Be sure to keep any information plates on the engine and in readable condition. It's a good idea to copy the information for separate filing in case the plate becomes damaged. These plates often contain critical information such as fuel requirements, engine model and type designations, the manufacturer's name, and so on. If you keep the engine long enough to gain value from its work, you'll eventually need this information when ordering parts or additional accessories.

Everyday maintenance should include a complete check and cleaning of all equipment used. Check for loose screws and other fasteners both before and after work. Check all controls and switches to be sure they are clean and tight. Mufflers, air filters, and fuel filters should be cleaned frequently. Work-performing attachment units should be cleaned, tightened, oiled, and, as applicable, sharpened. Sprockets and other grease points should be greased regularly, according to manufacturer's recommendations. Finally, everyday maintenance includes cleaning equipment body parts, shrouds, and the rest plus an occasional treatment with auto body wax.

Caution: Engine and body parts should be cleaned in a recommended mechanic's solvent. Never use gasoline for cleaning except when servicing the air filter or fuel filter. These parts should be washed outdoors in a small amount of gasoline and then either blown dry or allowed to air dry. Using solvent on air or fuel filters may contaminate the fuel lines, carburetor or the internal parts of the engine. Using gasoline to clean other parts results in many serious fires, explosions, injuries, and deaths every year.

You can arrange your own source of compressed air with an old tire (no leaks) and a hose designed to fill one tire from another. You can purchase the hose from an automotive supply shop.

Caution: Never use your mouth and lungs to blow anything clean that comes in contact with gasoline, since it can be injurious if inhaled or swallowed.

DO YOUR OWN TUNE-UPS

In Parp's opinion, a two-cycle tune-up consists of a complete maintenance procedure—the check and repair, as necessary, of all engine systems: fuel, ignition, and exhaust. If repairs of the crankshaft, piston, piston rings, or cylinder are added, Parp calls it an overhaul. Most backyard tool owners are understandably reluctant to perform a complete overhaul. Special tools and know-how are required, and a complete shop manual for the individual engine is essential. Yet, nearly anyone with modest ability and a modest tool collection can perform a tune-up on a simple two-cycle engine. Most often, the hardest part is removing the various sheet-metal shrouds, work attachments, and other gadgets to reach the engine itself.

Certainly, nothing is more conducive to a good understanding of mechanics than learning to do your own tune-ups. That understanding leads to increased respect for the efficiency and genius of today's ultralightweight power tools. This respect, in turn, leads to better, more conscientious maintenance procedures and, hence, to longer-lasting equipment, better performance, and greater pride of ownership. When you do your own tune-ups, you save a lot more than the difference between the cost of the parts and a professional mechanic's hourly rate.

Fuel and Oil

As we've seen, two-cycle engines are lubricated by oil that is mixed with the gasoline and placed in the fuel tank. As the engine operates, tiny droplets of oil are carried by the vaporized fuel into the crankcase. They cool and lubricate the crankshaft, bearings, connecting rod, piston, cylinder, and other engine parts that move or are affected by moving parts.

If oil is not mixed with fuel in a two-cycle engine, or is added in an insufficient quantity, the engine runs very hot, friction develops between moving parts, and great stress is brought upon the entire engine. Continued stress will soon result in total engine failure, and usually a completely ruined engine. Also note that many cheap two-cycle oils sold today become unstable and deteriorate rapidly. They may perform poorly and can cause carbon deposits, sludge, and varnish to accumulate in the engine.

If too much oil or the wrong type is added to the fuel, the oil will burn and leave gum or carbon deposits that will also have a disastrous effect on the engine. Most automobile engine oil, for example, includes viscosity-improving additives. When these oils are exposed to the high temperatures inside a two-cycle engine, they undergo a chemical change known as polymerization—that is, they turn into something a lot like glue. All two-cycle engine manufacturer warranties carry a clause that voids the warranty if multi-viscosity lubricants or automobile additives are added to the fuel. All warranty station mechanics are trained to look for indications of this error, and the evidence is always obvious and conclusive.

Fuel used in two-cycle engines must be clean, fresh, leaded, regular-grade gasoline. High-octane fuels are blended to burn more completely than are regular-grade fuels. In order to achieve additional combustion, unburned portions of the fuel reach a point of self-ignition in the compression chamber. In other words, there are two ignitions for each charge of vaporized fuel. Since the two ignitions do not occur at the same time, the second has a hammering effect on the piston. This occurrence, together with the much higher temperature caused by the double ignition, causes rapid engine damage in a two-cycle engine.

Always carefully and thoroughly mix in the recommended amount of two-cycle engine oil with your regular gasoline, preferably the oil distributed or recommended by the manufacturer of the engine. Mix fuel with oil in a separate container, not in your engine's fuel tank. Fill the container halfway with gas, then add the specified amount of recommended oil. Fill the rest of the container with gas, shake well to mix, and then fill your engine's tank.

If you have an owner's manual or other reliable source of correct information, use it to determine the proper fuel/oil mixture for your particular engine. If you have purchased a used machine for which you have no owner's manual, by all means determine the correct fuel/oil mixture before you proceed. Check with a dealer who sells that brand and type of machine, or contact the manufacturer. If you write to the manufacturer, be sure to specify the type and model number of the engine in question. Even among engines from a single manufacturer, the lubrication requirements often vary considerably due to the type of bearings and other factors. If all else fails, consult an expert small-engine mechanic. Do not attempt to guess at any two-cycle engine's lubrication requirements — you could ruin your tool.

Fuel Storage and Handling

Always store fuel and fuel mixtures in clearly labeled, red safety cans, never in glass or plastic jars. The cans must be equipped with a good ventilation system and must be stored away from any source of heat or open flame—preferably in an open, well-ventilated shed outdoors that's a safe distance from any dwelling or garage. Never carry a fuel can in the passenger area of an automobile or in the cab of a pickup truck. Whenever you refuel a machine, move either the fuel or the machine at least 50 feet away before starting the engine. If at all possible, move the machine away from the fueling point. This is especially necessary with earth augers, brush-cutters, chain saws, and similar equipment. Fuel spilled from these machines into brush, grass, or pine needles immediately emits dangerous fumes that are easily ignited by hot exhaust or newly started power tools.

Carburetor Adjustments

If you use a small engine at all, you already know that you must frequently adjust the carburetor. Carburetors need adjusting whenever you make a change in, or renew, the work-performing parts; whenever a carburetor undergoes a change due to wear, humidity, fuel variations, weather, or improper use; and, finally, whenever the engine runs slow, runs fast, or otherwise does not perform as it should for whatever reason.

Most two-cycle engines are equipped with carburetors that allow three basic adjustments. These adjustments are usually made with screws that are easy to find by removing the engine's carburetor cover. Adjustments are made by turning these screws cautiously in small increments. The screws are labeled almost universally as below:

"I," or "T," is the idle, or throttle, speed adjustment screw.

"L" is the low-speed mixture needle adjustment screw.

"H" is the high-speed mixture needle adjustment screw. (This screw may not exist on certain machines, which indicates the high-speed mixture is not owner-adjustable.)

The "I," or "T," screw is usually a large, prominent screw and is often accessible without removing the carburetor cover. This screw is actually not an internal carburetor adjustment screw; it does not affect the fuel mixture. However, it is a screw you will adjust quite often, because it alters the speed at which the engine idles by moving the throttle plate so that it does not completely close off the fuel/air supply.

The "L," or low-speed mixture needle, affects the richness of the fuel/air mixture while the engine is running at idle or at very low speeds. It is also called the idle mixture screw.

The "H," or high-speed mixture needle, affects the mixture of fuel and air at higher engine speeds.

Note that Parp calls both the "L" and the "H" screws *needles*. Both are finely pointed on

the ends that extend into the carburetor. These points and the matching seats are easily damaged. Never tighten any carburetor adjustment screw down. Always stop at what would be very lightly finger tight, even though you are using a screwdriver.

Carburetor adjustments vary considerably with engine and carburetor type. In addition, they are affected by operating altitude, type and use of equipment, and other factors. Parp will supply specifications for some individual backyard tools in subsequent chapters, but be sure to use the specifications listed in your owner's manual whenever possible. Use the manufacturer's specifications as a basis for making any further adjustments necessitated by altitude, atmospheric conditions, or other factors. Below is the proper sequence of steps in carburetor adjustment, but, in general, remember to make all needle adjustments in small increments and with caution. Never force the needle to the bottom.

1. Remove and thoroughly clean the air filter. It can be rinsed in a small amount of clean gasoline and then blown dry with compressed air. Reinstall the air filter.

2. Locate the idle, or throttle, speed screw. If it is not clearly labeled with an "I" or a "T," you usually can identify it by its larger size and by its proximity to the throttle shaft or connected linkage. To find this area, move the throttle lever, or trigger, and watch for moving linkage. This will lead you to the throttle shaft.

3. Locate one or two mixture adjustment screws. Most often, these are labeled "L" and "H." If they are not labeled, you can identify a mixture screw by the spring that helps hold it in adjustment. The thin screw is the low-speed adjustment, and the thick screw is the high-speed adjustment.

4. Use a small screwdriver to turn each mixture screw clockwise just until it seats in gently. Do not tighten or force these screws.

5. Turn each mixture screw counterclockwise one full turn if you are in a location at or near sea level. At altitudes higher than 5,000 feet above sea level, turn each screw counterclockwise ¾ turn. If you have an owner's manual or another source of information, follow the manufacturer's specifications for initial settings.

6. Turn the throttle speed screw counterclockwise until it is touching its point of pressure. Then turn it clockwise one full turn.

7. Close the choke, or move the choke lever to ON or START position. Pull the starter rope. When the engine fires, push the choke to OFF or OPEN position. Now start the engine, and try to keep it running long enough to warm up. If it stalls, turn the throttle speed screw clockwise ¼ turn. Keep trying until the engine is warm and will idle, however roughly.

8. After checking to assure a clean air filter, and with the engine warm and idling, preferably with no work load on the engine, turn the low-speed mixture adjustment screw to obtain a smooth, fast idle. You may have to turn it either clockwise or counterclockwise, depending on factors such as altitude, atmospheric conditions, or even the age of the machine. Either way, turn it in small increments. If the fastest idle speed seems too fast, turn the throttle speed screw counterclockwise to obtain a normal idle.

9. Rev the engine to high speed for a few seconds. Listen carefully, and do not hold the engine at high speed for more than ten seconds. If the engine sounds hesi-

tant, get your screwdriver ready, and rev it up again. With the engine running full speed, quickly but carefully turn the high-speed screw counterclockwise until it runs smoothly. Let off the throttle to cool the engine. Then turn the high-speed screw counterclockwise another 1/32 turn. (Parp says turn it just a tad.)

This procedure should result in a correct carburetor adjustment under most conditions unless something else is wrong. For instance, worn carburetor rings would mean that a more radical adjustment would be necessary in order to start the engine.

Carburetor Maintenance

The carburetor is the only part of an engine that is designed to let in the outside world. Parp has previously described the importance of the carburetor's air filter in keeping dirt out of the heart of the engine. Unfortunately, dirt can get past even the cleanest air filter.

It pays to clean the outside of the carburetor every time the air filter is removed. To prevent debris from falling in, get in the habit of closing the choke. Never blow debris into the air horn or choke area.

Use an old toothbrush dipped in solvent to wipe away the dust, dirt, and grease that collect on the outside of the carburetor and can sneak past the air filter to the crankcase. When cleaning the carburetor, take care not to disturb the settings of the mixture adjustment screws. When a carburetor fails or becomes clogged, or when parts such as mixture screw springs become fatigued, buy a carburetor kit from the same manufacturer and rebuild the carburetor.

Be sure to clean the air filter at least once for each eight hours of work. If you work less than eight hours, clean the air filter before putting the machine to rest. If you work in unusually dusty or dirty conditions, it may be necessary to clean the air filter every hour or so. This is

21

often the case with chain saws, earth augers, and similar equipment.

To clean a permanent-type air filter, first shake or knock it gently to remove loose dirt. Then clean it in a small amount of clean gasoline, and blow it dry with compressed air. Blow the air in the opposite direction to that which the air flows during operation.

Fuel Filter and Fuel Lines

Since most two-cycle fuel filters are weighted and designed to ride at the very bottom of the fuel tank, they are likely to pick up any dirt or water that enters the tank. Fuel filters should be removed, washed in gasoline, and squeezed dry once for each 20–40 hours of work, or as necessary. Conditions that would necessitate more frequent cleaning of fuel filters include working in high humidity or after any moisture gets into the fuel tank for any reason; extremely dirty or dusty surroundings; if stale fuel is used; or if the engine is not running smoothly for any unknown cause.

Use a piece of wire with a hook bent into one end to fish the fuel pick-up line out of the

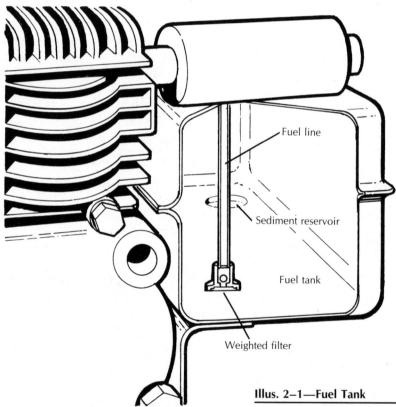

Fuel line

Sediment reservoir

Fuel tank

Weighted filter

Illus. 2–1—Fuel Tank

The weighted filter at the end of the fuel line leading to the engine keeps the fuel line at the bottom of the tank in order to maintain fuel flow until the tank is completely empty.

fuel tank. The weighted filter housing is usually bell shaped and contains the filter element.

To clean a screen-type fuel filter with compressed air, blow the air in the direction opposite to that of the fuel travel.

Fuel lines must be in perfect condition, and all connections must be tight. Loose fuel lines can leak, which, of course, can be a severe fire hazard if fuel spills on hot engine parts. Also, loose fuel connections can cause air to enter the fuel system, resulting in a loss of power or a stalled engine. Pinched fuel lines can affect the fuel/air balance in the carburetor and can cause carburetion problems that may mislead you into rebuilding or replacing a carburetor unnecessarily. Inspect fuel lines frequently, and tighten or replace them or their fittings at the first sign of trouble or fatigue.

Fuel Tank

Stale fuel is hazardous to an engine's health. As fuel becomes stale, the volatile portions evaporate and leave a varnishlike residue. This is especially true of premixed two-cycle fuel that contains two-cycle engine oil. Never store a machine for a long period of time without emptying the fuel tank and following Parp's tips for long-term storage at the end of this chapter.

If you use a machine infrequently and forget or neglect to empty the fuel tank, it's good insurance to drain and wash the fuel tank with clean gasoline before starting the engine. This is particularly true if the season has changed since you last started the engine. Winter fuels and summer fuels are different blends.

Manual Starter

Most backyard tools powered by two-cycle engines incorporate simple manual starters of the rope-pull variety. Parp says these starters are superior to electric starters in these tools because they are lighter, easier to maintain and repair, and far more reliable. Supposedly, some people are intimidated by manual starters, so one manufacturer or another is always coming out with electric-start chain saws, lawn mowers, and whatnot. Parp suspects that one electric-start machine is enough to send most people off in search of something with a rope on it. Electric starters may have a place on large machines but they do not belong on most backyard tools. They're simply too much trouble. They add weight to an engine, are more susceptible to breakdowns, and require extra maintenance for the battery that serves as their power source.

Manual starters can be some trouble. The cords wear out, stretch, or break, and the springs can be a real pain to replace. Yet, once you've worked with a manual starter, you'll see how simple they really are. They're merely tedious to repair, the rare times they need it.

Starter cords are not clotheslines cut to a certain length. They are specially constructed cords of superior material. Always use replacement cords sold or recommended by the original manufacturer, or buy a starter cord from a mechanic who stocks good quality cord of exactly the same size and strength. To maintain a starter rope in good condition, keep it clean and free of grease and oil. Do not attempt to patch a starter cord with a knot. It won't work, and it may damage the pulley, or rotar.

Replacing the Starter Cord

Some rope starters are situated behind the flywheel. If your engine has this arrangement and you are mechanically timid (for example, you feel you're not up to doing your own tune-ups), you'd best see a mechanic. Replacing the rope is a cinch, but removing and replacing a flywheel is often difficult, and you may end up with a damaged half-moon key or, worse, a broken flywheel vane. Either of those problems will send you to the mechanic anyway and will result in a much larger repair bill, so you might as well have it done properly in the first place. The cost of this job should be low.

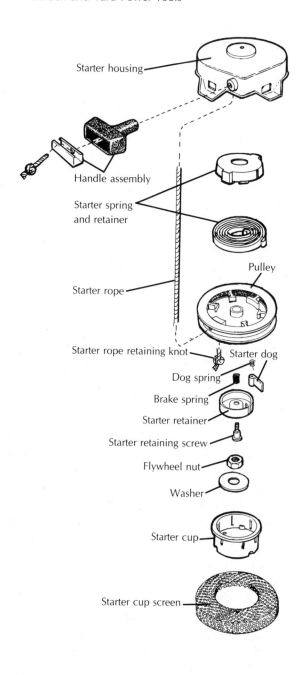

Starter housing

Handle assembly

Starter spring
and retainer

Starter rope

Pulley

Starter rope retaining knot

Starter dog

Dog spring

Brake spring

Starter retainer

Starter retaining screw

Flywheel nut

Washer

Starter cup

Starter cup screen

Illus. 2–2—Parts of a Typical Rope-Pull Starter

Most rope starters, however, are mounted in a top or side cover plate, directly above the flywheel. To replace the cord, remove the cover to expose the starter mechanism. If you must remove the fuel tank, as on certain machines, gently disconnect the fuel line, and set the tank a safe distance away. Be sure your ignition switch is OFF.

As you look at the starter mechanism, you'll see that the rope is attached to a pulley or rotar. In the center of the pulley is the starter axle. The pulley is usually attached to the axle with a clip. Take careful note of the entire arrangement of your starter, including the manner and device of attaching the rope to the pulley. You might be wise to draw a picture or take a snapshot of the assembly if you don't have a manual with good illustrations. Be sure to install the new cord and all other parts according to the original design. The retaining knot in the cord, for example, should be identical to the original in type, size, and length.

Caution: A starter, or rewind, spring is under considerable pressure; it can seriously injure you or an observer. Do not allow the spring to unwind freely, and do not simply pull or pry it loose. Note that the spring is not slack even if it seemed to unwind when the rope broke and the rope came completely off the pulley. If you do not have to remove the spring in your particular starter and if the spring is not damaged, by all means let it alone. If you must remove the spring, release as much tension as possible before disassembling the starter. Do this by removing any remaining rope from the pulley with a screwdriver or a needle-nose pliers.

To remove the pulley from the mechanism, remove the clip while holding the pulley down. Then carefully lift the pulley ½ inch or less from its position. Reach under with a screwdriver, and push the spring down firmly while you pull the pulley off its axle. Now thread in a new rope, securing it with a knot identical to the original. Wind most of the rope onto the pulley, and replace the pulley in its original position. Then turn the pulley until it engages the starter spring, and lock it back in place with a new clip.

Replacing the Rewind Spring

To replace a rewind spring on most manual starters, remove the rope and pulley as described under Replacing the Starter Cord. Be sure to keep your head away from the spring. Then point the spring in a safe direction and dislodge it, if necessary, with a sharp blow to the back of the housing. Use a wooden mallet or a hammer with a soft head to hit the housing.

Most replacement springs for manual starters now come with convenient safety restraints. The restraint consists of a wire loop or clip that is automatically removed as the spring is pressed into place. Do not remove such a restraint before positioning the spring.

When the spring is in place, reassemble the rope pulley and retaining clip. Oil the spring lightly with AFT-type oil. (AFT signifies that this single-viscosity oil meets engineer-specified standards of durability.) Then, reset the spring tension so that the rope pulls properly.

To reset the proper tension, wind the rope onto the pulley, and put the pulley in place. Pull the starter handle enough to put stress on the spring. While maintaining tension on the handle, loop the rope around the pulley inside the housing, using a screwdriver to lever it if necessary. Wind the rope twice around the pretensioned pulley. The tension is correct if the pulley still has about ½ turn left after the rope is pulled all the way out.

Spark Plug

Most power tool users recognize that the spark plug is an essential item and must be kept in good condition in order to supply the spark necessary to fire the engine. Always begin any engine ignition system maintenance and service with the spark plug. If the spark plug is burned, worn, cracked, wet, fouled, broken, or the wrong type, the engine will run poorly or not at all. Whenever your engine won't start or runs poorly, and you're sure enough fuel is being supplied and the switch is ON, there's a good chance that the spark plug is malfunctioning.

It is impossible to check a spark plug without removing it from the engine. To remove the spark plug, use a good-quality ratchet-handle wrench with a deep-well socket of exactly the right size to ensure a good fit. Many backyard tools come with a simple tool kit that usually contains a combination tool sometimes called a "squrench." That's a good name for it. These tools are at least better than the cheap spark plug wrenches with rod handles. It is easy to damage a spark plug with a cheap wrench or with one that does not fit correctly. It's also easy to damage your hand.

To test a spark plug, first turn your ignition switch to OFF, and then disconnect the cable. You may have to work at the rubber insulating cap to work it free; do this gently to avoid tearing the rubber. Pull the cable off with a firm finger grip or with pliers. Pull it off by the rubber boot, not by the wire itself. Then try to loosen the plug by applying firm, steady pressure with the wrench. If it is frozen or seems to resist reasonable force, apply penetrating oil around the edge of the hole. Let it soak in, then use the wrench again. Don't snap at it or jerk on the wrench.

In a spark plug test, you want to determine if a spark is being created. First, examine the plug. If there is obvious damage or wear, simply replace the plug according to the instructions that follow. If there is considerable fouling, check Table 2–1, the Spark Plug Troubleshooting Chart, to determine the probable cause. If the plug looks good and is reasonably new, proceed with the test.

Reconnect the insulating spark plug cable to the spark plug. Turn the ignition switch to ON. While holding an insulated part of the plug, put the threaded part against engine ground or against bare metal somewhere on the engine.

Pull the starter cord and observe the spark. It should jump the gap between the electrodes and should be reasonably bright. If you have any doubt, replace the plug. Otherwise, you may decide simply to clean and regap it. To clean, carefully scrape deposits from the electrodes with a sharp blade. To regap, use a round wire feeler gauge, and set the gap to the original specifications.

The specified spark plug gap for most two-cycle engines is .020 inch or .025 inch. Many four-cycle engines, especially the very common Briggs & Stratton products, use a gap of .030 inch. Make electrode gap adjustments with care. Increase the gap by prying up the side electrode, or ground electrode, with a thin screwdriver braced against the side of the plug. Decrease the gap by tapping gently on the electrode with a pocketknife handle or light hammer. Do not put any pressure on the center electrode, and do not use this as a ply base when increasing the gap.

To replace the plug, simply set the gap, as described above, and install the plug. Reinstall the spark plug cable and boot. Always use the spark plug recommended by the manufacturer, or, second best, a suitable substitute. By the way, don't believe all plug substitution charts. In all cases, use a quality brand-name spark plug recommended for your engine model.

Good spark plugs are very well made and often last for an incredibly long time. They are also very inexpensive, especially if you're talking about a single-cylinder engine. Just remember that not all spark plug problems are easy to detect. A film of oil can short the insulator, and a hairline crack in the plug can be quite invisible. When in doubt, replace the plug.

Table 2-1: Spark Plug Troubleshooting Chart

Use this table to determine the probable cause of different kinds of spark plug fouling.

Appearance of Electrode Deposits	Indications
Dark gray to dark brown—not thick or excessively flaky	Normal engine operation— plugs darker than four-cycle plugs because of oil in fuel mixture.
Black, thick, and oily	Too much oil in fuel mixture, or wrong type of oil.
Black, thick, and sooty	Exhaust problem, possibly caused by a dirty muffler, dirty or clogged exhaust ports, or excessive carbon buildup.
Thick, flaky—like graphite	Engine running rich. Incorrect carburetor adjustment. Dirty air filter. Choke may be sticking.
Very light tan, almost white color; flaky, as if fuel not burned completely	Engine running lean. Possible carburetor problem or air leak.
Light deposits, electrodes burned, blistered, or melted	Engine running hot. Incorrect timing, wrong spark plug, dirty or clogged cooling system, missing air baffle, exhaust system clogged, or broken flywheel.
Ashy, yellow deposits bridging ports of the plug	Caused by using improper oil with viscosity improvers or additives. Unfortunately, engine is ruined, and warranty is suspended.

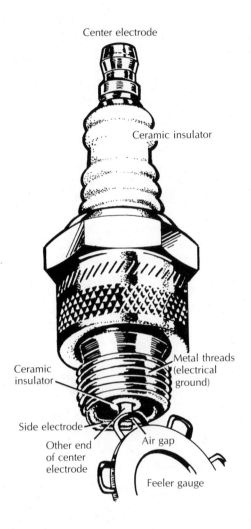

Center electrode

Ceramic insulator

Ceramic insulator

Metal threads (electrical ground)

Side electrode

Other end of center electrode

Air gap

Feeler gauge

Illus. 2–3—Setting a Spark Plug Gap

First measure the gap with the correct size of feeler gauge. Then carefully adjust the gap with a thin screwdriver.

Spark Plug Cable

If you performed the preceding spark plug test and saw no spark at all, it's likely that you have a problem in either the spark plug, the spark plug cable, or the magneto coil. To find out the exact source of the problem, disconnect the cable and remove the spark plug. Insert a metal rod or screw into the spark plug boot to connect with the spring or contact inside. Hold this together with your fingers protected by the insulation. Hold the makeshift contact near bare engine metal with an air gap of about ¼ inch. Turn the ignition switch ON, and pull the starter cord. You should see a strong spark. If you get a spark without the plug but not with it, either your spark plug is bad or you're not getting a good connection. If you get no spark either way, the current is not reaching the spark plug contact. In that case, check the spark plug cable for obvious shorts, oil contamination, or breakage. If possible, replace the cable and test again. If your cable is an integral part of the magneto system, the entire system will have to be replaced. If the cable is separate and you replace it, and you still get no spark, your problem is most likely in the magneto, discussed later on.

Ignition System

Ignition system maintenance consists partly of the procedure often called a tune-up. A real tune-up, however, especially in a two-cycle engine, consists of servicing all of the engine's systems—fuel, ignition, and mechanical. It is a good idea to service all of these systems whenever ignition service becomes necessary, but for the sake of clarity, Parp will treat ignition service separately.

Routine Maintenance

Routine maintenance of ignition systems includes spark plug and ignition cable service as well as general cleaning. It's important to remove dirt, sawdust, and grease from the flywheel air-intake area to prevent contamination of ignition parts housed in or near the flywheel. Of course, all oil and grease must be regularly removed from all wires, cables, and other ignition parts. Frayed wires and defective switches should be repaired or replaced immediately. Tighten all connections frequently.

Servicing Magneto Components

Professional mechanics consider breaker points replacement and similar jobs as routine ignition service, but for many home mechanics these are far from routine. In order to service the breaker points and condenser as well as check the magneto for continuity, it is usually necessary to remove the flywheel. In most two-cycle engines, the breaker plate is mounted on the crankshaft behind the flywheel. The nut holding the flywheel to the crankshaft must, of course, be a very strong fastener. This obstacle is the most difficult one you'll encounter in ignition service and is enough to stop most people from doing a complete tune-up. But, if you are equipped with this warning and the proper tools, and if you remember that the half-moon key is easily damaged through incorrect flywheel removal, you should have no trouble. Removing the flywheel is discussed farther on.

Most small-engine equipment dealers carry ignition tune-up kits to fit the power tools they sell. The first step in an ignition tune-up is to acquire one of these kits. Be sure that it is the kit designed for your particular engine and that it is distributed by the original manufacturer. These kits cost a fraction of what you would spend for an ignition tune-up performed by a professional mechanic. Nevertheless, many tool owners are wise to have this work done by a servicing dealer. Only you can decide whether you should do it yourself or take it to a mechanic.

Complete ignition service consists of the following: a thorough cleaning of the assembly; a check for damaged, worn, or frayed wires or parts; a renewal of nonpermanent ignition parts; and a check of all adjustments and required gaps. The adjustments include the spark plug gap, armature air gap, magneto edge gap, and ignition timing. The parts that must be replaced are the breaker points, the condenser, and the spark plug. You may also need to replace the magneto coil, the primary and secondary leads, the flywheel half-moon key, and any damaged or oil-soaked wires or connections.

If you do all these jobs *plus* clean or rebuild and adjust the carburetor, remove carbon from exhaust ports, clean the muffler, clean the cooling fins and shrouds, lubricate all moving parts, tighten all fasteners, clean or replace the air cleaner and fuel filter, renew the reed valve (if applicable), and service the work-performing attachment, you can call it a tune-up—if your engine's internal parts are in good condition. You can't tune an engine that has worn piston rings, sloppy bearings, a damaged piston, or a scored cylinder. If your engine has any of these serious problems, a tune-up won't help. A mechanic with the proper testing equipment can tell you if you have any of these problems.

Engine manufacturers supply authorized repair stations with specialized tools and instruments. Many of these tools and instruments are related to ignition service. At the very least, they include flywheel removal equipment and ignition timing devices. For the most part, we can substitute for these specialized tools, especially when dealing with the simpler two-cycle engines.

Parp assumes you have already checked, cleaned, regapped, or replaced your spark plug. Now you want to replace your break points and condenser and check all ignition adjustments. The following general instructions will apply to most standard two-cycle engines but not, of course, to all. If your engine doesn't seem to go along with Parp's suggestions, you'll have to accept this as a general procedure and simply keep your eyes open for whatever is necessary in your case. If you get into real trouble, package it all up and see a mechanic. In general, you should be able to complete the job without a hitch. (Tune-up tips and specifications for many backyard tools appear throughout this book. See Index for your specific machine.)

Disassembly

First, find the starter housing. That's where the starter rope winds up. The flywheel is under the starter housing. The parts you have to remove to reach the flywheel vary considerably from tool to tool, but they always include the starter housing, the starter unit, and any sheet metal covers or shrouds. You will not need to disassemble the starter unless you are also doing starter repairs. With many machines, you 'll have to remove the fuel tank and disconnect the fuel line to get at the points.

In any case, start by exposing the flywheel. If your object is simply to adjust the breaker points, you should now determine if you can do that without removing the flywheel. That is, if the breaker points are in a housing separate from the flywheel, which is often the case, skip to Breaker Points Adjustment further on in this chapter.

Removing the Flywheel

Many crankshafts are tapered on the flywheel end. This means that the flywheel is pressed onto the taper with considerable force. Also, the flywheel nut, or retainer, is extremely tough to remove.

Whenever the flywheel turns, the crankshaft also turns. When the crankshaft turns, it moves the piston up and down.

To protect the piston and limit its travel, remove the spark plug, and turn the flywheel so that the piston is down. Then fill the cylinder above the piston with a clean, medium-weight rope or cord. Some manufacturers sell a special plastic cylinder plug to do the same job. If you have one of these, first move the piston all the way down. Then screw in the cylinder plug, and turn the flywheel until the piston rests against the plug.

Most shop mechanics use an air impact wrench to remove the flywheel nut. This tool exerts so much force and shock that the flywheel

literally does not have time to turn. The nut just comes loose. Some engine manufacturers sell special flywheel holders to prevent the flywheel from turning while the nut is being loosened. If you have one of these tools made especially for your engine, by all means use it. But do not attempt to use a holder made for a different engine, and do not attempt to use a screwdriver. Flywheels are very easily broken and are quite expensive. If you break just one fin, you'll have to replace the entire flywheel.

Next to an electric or pneumatic impact wrench, the best tool for removing the flywheel nut and other difficult fasteners is a hand, or manual, impact wrench. This is a tool Parp has found to be very valuable in many situations. Since it does not depend on electricity or compressed air, it is well suited to backwoods living. It's close to essential for anyone who works on small engines, and has many other uses as well, especially in automotive mechanics. It consists of a driver and a fitting similar to the drive end of a socket wrench handle. Most impact drivers come with a set of bits that includes slot- and Phillips-type screwdrivers and socket wrenches that fit the driver. The drive ends come in $\frac{1}{4}$-inch, $\frac{3}{8}$-inch, or $\frac{1}{2}$-inch sizes, so you can buy a set to match your main socket wrench set. The most universal is the $\frac{3}{8}$-inch size. If you buy one, be sure to get a reversible impact driver of good quality—a reliable, brand-name tool. Cheap ones can't take it, and good ones, as always, are a bargain.

When you hit the head of the impact tool with your hammer, the drive mechanism turns the socket just a little. The shock of the hammer blow is concentrated in this slight turn and will loosen almost any stubborn fastener, including a flywheel nut.

The piston is protected from the shock by a rope stuffed into the cylinder, and we have the flywheel held firmly with a flywheel holder. You can now use an impact tool to loosen the

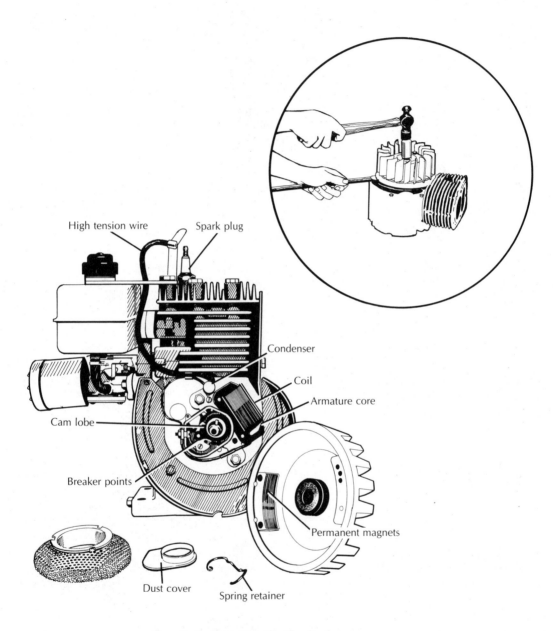

Illus. 2–4—Removing the Flywheel

An impact, or knock-off, tool makes removal easier. Once the flywheel is off the engine, the major parts of the magneto-ignition system can be inspected.

flywheel nut or, as a last resort, you can use a long breaker bar and socket and hit the bar with a hammer. Another substitute for the flywheel holder is blocking the flywheel with pieces of wood. It's better, though, to go to the slight trouble and expense of procuring a flywheel holder from a small-engine parts dealer.

Bang—the flywheel nut is loosened, and the worst part of the ignition service procedure is past.

Before you remove the flywheel, check it for grime. Use a pair of locking pliers to hold the crankshaft still, being careful not to damage the crankshaft or threads. Try to turn the flywheel either way. If it moves at all while the crankshaft is held still, the half-moon key is probably damaged or worn and must be replaced. Put it on your shopping list for the trip you'll take to the parts supplier later.

Now remove the flywheel. Another special tool, a flywheel puller, will come in handy. This tool screws onto the crankshaft and is then either tightened or hit in order to force the flywheel up and off its pressed fitting on the taper. Some flywheels, notably those on chain saws and similar machines, can be pried up safely with two screwdrivers. Still, it's best to determine the manufacturer's recommendations, if possible, and then follow them closely.

Once the flywheel is off, you can examine it for cracks and other damage such as a large chip on one side or a broken fin. If you see any serious problems, add a flywheel to your parts shopping list.

Breaker Points Adjustment

Chances are, the points assembly is now visible. It may be contained in a plastic case; if so, remove the cover. Inside the protective box, you'll see the points, condenser, and breaker plate. Unlike an automobile, there is no distributor because, of course, there's only one spark plug.

As Parp described earlier, the points are opened and closed by the cam lobe on the crankshaft. The critical breaker points gap occurs when the lobe has the points open as far as possible. If the gap is too small, the current may cross over, and the circuit interruption that caused the spark will not occur. If the gap is too large, the points will open too soon and close too late, resulting in a weak spark and incorrect ignition timing.

Before we adjust the breaker points gap, Parp should mention that some engines have the breaker points assembly housed in the flywheel itself. If this is the case with your engine, you're apt to find two rubber or plastic seals set into the flywheel, fastened with countersunk screws. Loosen these screws just two turns, and pry out the seals with a small screwdriver. Now your breaker points and condenser are exposed, too, and we're all in the same place.

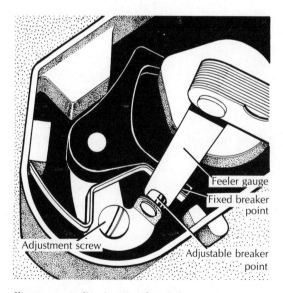

Illus. 2–5—Adjusting Breaker Points Gap

Turn the adjustment screw until the adjustable breaker point touches the correct size of feeler gauge.

Use a set of feeler gauges to determine when the points are open as far as they go. Turn the crankshaft clockwise until the points open. Find the gauge that fits between the points with light contact. Now turn the crankshaft a slight fraction further, and see if the next size gauge will fit between the points. Follow this procedure until you have to use a smaller gauge to fit the gap. Then go back up to the point at which the largest gauge fit. This is where the point gap is at a maximum. This gap is the one you need to measure and adjust.

If the points won't open no matter how much you turn the crankshaft, the problem may not be worn breaker points. Maybe a screw has come out or broken (usually the screw that's supposed to hold the fixed point), or perhaps the movable point's fiber block is worn down. Or, in some engines, the plunger between the crankshaft and points assembly could be worn or broken. Few two-cycle engines feature this configuration, but some imported machines use a plunger system, as do all Briggs & Stratton four-cycle engines. In the average two-cycle engine, the problem is nearly always the screw for the fixed point. Whatever the problem, it must be isolated and corrected before the points can be adjusted or replaced.

Before deciding to replace the points, examine the contact. If they are clean, shiny, unpitted, and unburned, chances are that you can simply set them to the specified gap. If they are burned, pitted, or bent, they should be replaced. If you're snowbound somewhere west of Jackson Hole and can't get parts, you may be able to get by with filing the points and setting the gap. Use as fine a file as you can find, preferably an ultrafine nail file. The file on a Victorinox Swiss Army knife does very well and is one reason Parp has carried one for 20 years.

In order to adjust the breaker points gap, you need to know the manufacturer's specification. In most cases, the recommended gap is .020 inch, and this will often do in an emergency. McCulloch chain saws use a gap of .018 inch. Most Homelite products use a gap of .015 inch, sometimes .016 inch. Stihl engines commonly use a .014- to .016-inch breaker points gap. To determine the best gap for your engine, consult your manual, a local mechanic, a parts dealer, your manufacturer, or his local distributor.

To set the gap, move the breaker points to their maximum open position, as described above. *Always set the gap by moving only the fixed point.* Leave the movable point in the open position. To move the fixed point, discover what fastens it to the breaker plate. Normally, it is simply a lockscrew and a slot. When you loosen the screw, you can move the assembly in the slot. Some ignitions utilize an adjusting mechanism. It should be easy to spot.

Mostly, you'll just loosen the fixed point fastener and then carefully move the fixed point away from or toward the movable point in order to increase or decrease the gap. Use a flat feeler gauge to determine when the gap is correct. Insert the gauge straight in, not at an angle, or canted. The gap is correct when the right-size feeler gauge just barely touches both points. Tighten the screw and it's done. Do not overtighten; the threads damage easily.

Replacing Breaker Points Assembly and Condenser

Parp assumes that you've gone through the steps above and have concluded that you should renew the breaker points. Whenever you replace the points assembly in any small engine, also renew the condenser. If the points have burned, the condenser is also suspect.

If you have removed your flywheel and exposed the breaker points assembly and condenser, you can probably see what you have to do to remove them. Be sure to do no more. You don't want to remove the breaker plate unless absolutely necessary. If you're unsure of what you're doing, draw a picture or take an instant photograph of the entire assembly. Label the wires, or code them with bits of colored tape. There are only a few wires, but you don't want to confuse them. Then loosen the screws, and remove them as necessary. Take care not to drop them into the engine. Also, remember that that flywheel sitting there has magnets in it; if you lose a screw, look there first.

Remove the old breaker points assembly and condenser, and install the new parts. Try to use any new parts that may have come with your tune-up kit. This may include screws, wires, connectors, or fasteners. Renew as much as possible and, of course, clean as you go with a fresh, lint-free cloth. Be sure the new points are properly aligned and will make good contact. If necessary, bend the fixed point until the points face each other squarely. You can't bend the movable point because it moves when you try to bend it.

When the points and condenser are installed and you're certain all wires are properly reconnected, loosen the screw holding the fixed point and set the proper breaker gap, as described earlier in the chapter.

Ignition Timing

It is not unusual for ignition timing in a two-cycle, magneto-system engine to remain stable through years of use. Only three things can adversely affect it: if you set the breaker points gap incorrectly or the gap is disturbed through some accident such as a loose screw, timing will change; if the breaker plate or housing becomes loose, timing will change; and if the magneto coil comes loose, is incorrectly installed, or somehow changes in relation to the flywheel magnets, timing will change. Otherwise, it should remain stable.

Most two-cycle engines are timed so that ignition (the spark) occurs slightly before the piston reaches the uppermost limit of its travel. The point at which the piston is at the uppermost limit of its travel is called Top-Dead-Center, or

TDC. If, as usual, the spark is supposed to occur at a certain time before the piston is TDC, the proper timing of the ignition is specified as a certain distance Before-Top-Dead-Center, or BTDC. If the spark is supposed to occur after the piston reaches TDC, it is specified as a certain distance After-Top-Dead-Center, or ATDC. Again, most two-cycle engines are timed to fire a certain distance BTDC.

Some mechanics time small engines only by the formerly traditional method of measuring the distance of the piston from TDC and setting the maximum opening of the points to coincide. This procedure sounds easy and precise, but it is not.

Most modern two-cycle engine manufacturers supply an easy mark for setting the proper ignition timing. Some place a timing mark on the flywheel, which is then aligned with another predetermined point, either another mark or the leading edge of the magneto coil. Some manufacturers place timing marks on the coil and the breaker housing. Even if your manufacturer specifies ignition as .090-inch BTDC, they may also have supplied handier ignition marks. If you have only the distance BTDC, or whatever distance you are given, you will have to use a mechanic's calipers or ruler to measure the correct position for the piston, and then set the breaker points accordingly.

If you have an engine with timing marks inscribed on the flywheel, you can probably check the timing as you reinstall the flywheel. Insert the thinnest feeler gauge you have, or a piece of paper or cellophane, between the open breaker points. Turn the crankshaft so the points close down on the gauge. Now, turn the crankshaft until you can just barely remove the gauge. At this point, the points have just opened. Insert the half-moon key in the crankcase, and align the flywheel to fasten onto it. The flywheel timing mark should align with another timing mark or indicator. Most likely, the second mark is on the coil itself. If not, see if the flywheel mark is aligned with one edge of the coil or armature. If so, this is the corresponding mark. You may have to loosen the coil to adjust it.

If you think your engine's timing is off and there are no timing marks on the flywheel, you'll have to proceed with the old ruler method. Before you start, however, be sure you determine the exact timing for your engine relative to TDC. If you don't have this information, things can only get worse.

To set the timing with a ruler according to TDC, remove the cylinder head, and turn the crank until the piston is the correct distance from TDC. Use a mechanic's or machinist's ruler to measure the distance. Loosen the retaining screws or bolts on the breaker plate or housing, and turn it until the points are just beginning to open. Then tighten the bolts, renew the cylinder head gasket, replace the cylinder head, and reassemble the ignition system.

Magneto Edge Gap

Do not change the magneto edge gap unless absolutely necessary. This gap has a wide tolerance and may often be anywhere between .14 inch and .30 inch. That's a huge tolerance. The gap is measured between the trailing edge of the north pole of the magnet and the inner edge of the left leg of the armature when they are closest.

Inspection

Examine the armature and magneto coil laminations and wiring. To some extent, you can patch frayed insulation with electrical tape. If the laminations are damaged, however, replacement is the only remedy.

Also, turn the reinstalled flywheel to be sure it does not touch the coil or armature at any point. If the flywheel touches any part, it or the part it's touching must be tightened. If that doesn't correct the problem, the part is damaged and must be replaced.

Armature Air Gap

To check the armature air gap, measure the distance between the pole shoes of the armature and the flywheel. This gap is more critical than the magneto edge gap, as it determines how close the magnets pass to the armature. To adjust to manufacturer's specifications, loosen the armature screws in the slotted holes, and gradually move the armature to the correct gap. Check the armature ground lead to be sure it is properly connected.

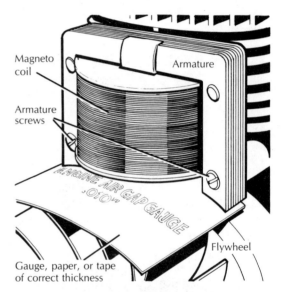

Illus. 2–6—Adjusting Armature Air Gap

Insert the correct size of feeler gauge, paper, or tape between the armature core and the flywheel. Loosen the armature screws, and slide the armature up or down for the correct gap. Retighten the screws.

Exhaust System Maintenance

A discussion of exhaust system maintenance at this point should not be taken as an indication that Parp thinks it any less important than fuel or ignition system maintenance. What goes in must come out, in mechanics just as in biology.

When you feed fuel to an engine, part of that fuel is transformed into chemical energy, and then into mechanical energy. In other words, much of the fuel is "used up" in the process of running the engine and doing work. But nothing on earth is 100 percent efficient. There are waste products that, in the mechanics of an engine, are the burned and unburned fuel particles known as exhaust. Exhaust consists of gases, liquids, and solids. All three must be expelled from the engine, or it will clog up and cease to operate, just as a living organism would if it did not expel its wastes.

The gases are the most obvious waste products in exhaust. When you operate an engine, you see, smell, and hear these gases leaving through the muffler. The liquid waste is much less obvious because it represents a small percentage of the exhaust and because you usually can't see or hear it. The solid waste, or carbon, is the most insidious because it is not expelled as easily by the engine. It tends to settle and collect throughout the exhaust system, especially in exhaust ports, exhaust passages, and the muffler. Clearly, an engine that is operated for a long period will collect carbon deposits sufficient to impair or prevent engine operation. The solid carbon wastes eventually block the escape of the fluid wastes. Exhaust system maintenance prevents this problem from becoming serious, at least until the engine has worked long enough to require a complete overhaul, including carbon removal from the cylinder, piston, and internal engine areas.

Two-cycle engine exhaust is normally dark in color because of the lubricating oil in the fuel mixture. Two-cycle engines normally make a fair amount of noise because, inherently, they are relatively inefficient fuel users. Yet, the engine should sound steady, making a regular popping sound that is especially noticeable near the exhaust or muffler area. All modern two-cycle engines are equipped with mufflers to deaden the sound, thereby helping to protect the users'

hearing. Additionally, many small machines have some kind of spark-arrester system. This equipment helps to prevent the machine from setting itself on fire and, equally important, protects the environment from sparks that fly from the exhausts of two-cycle engines. The spark-arrester system is especially important for chain saws and other machines used in woods or open fields.

The spark arrester, muffler, and exhaust area must be cleaned frequently to prevent the carbon buildup that, left alone, would eventually choke off the engine. **Caution:** Never use gasoline, kerosene, or turpentine to clean exhaust system parts. Always use an approved, nonflammable mechanic's cleaning solvent.

You should perform a complete exterior cleaning of the exhaust system at least once for each 20 hours of engine operation. Engine exhaust ports should be cleaned at the same time, or, if that is inconvenient, at least once for each 40 hours of work. Of course, worn, corroded, or damaged muffler or exhaust system parts should be repaired or replaced immediately.

To clean exterior parts, remove the screws that secure the muffler, or exhaust area cover, and the spark arrester. Soak all metal parts in a solvent, and then remove any remaining carbon with a wooden scraper. At the same time, use a stiff toothbrush and solvent to clean as much of the rest of the exhaust system as you can reach. If you can get into the exhaust ports easily, clean them, too. If not, go to the trouble of exposing and cleaning the exhaust ports about every other time you clean the muffler.

Before cleaning the exhaust ports, turn the ignition to OFF, and pull the starter cord slowly while observing the piston through the ports. Move the piston until it completely covers the ports from the inside; this will block debris from falling into the engine. Start cleaning the exhaust ports with a toothbrush and a moderate amount of solvent. Be very careful not to damage the piston or piston rings. Allow the solvent to work for a few minutes, then brush it off. Complete

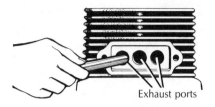

Exhaust ports

Illus. 2–7—Cleaning the Exhaust Ports

Clean exhaust ports of carbon with a soft, nonabrasive object, such as a wooden rod. Be sure the piston covers the ports to keep debris from falling into the cylinder.

the cleaning by removing any remaining carbon with a small wooden scraper. Do not use a metal scraper; it will damage the ports and the piston. Use the toothbrush to remove any debris, then wipe the entire area with a clean, lint-free cloth.

Pre-Storage Maintenance Procedures

Any time a small engine is left idle for 24 hours or more, it should be prepared for storage. Short-term storage is for 30 days or less, while long-term storage is for more than 30 days. Proper pre-storage maintenance helps to protect the machine from rust, corrosion, and harmful fuel settling or evaporation, as well as hard starting and engine strain after the storage period.

Short-Term Storage

Even if a machine is going to be idle for only a day or so, it's best to prepare the engine for short-term storage. For one thing, you may not get back to the machine as soon as you expect. For another, short-term storage maintenance leaves the machine in good condition and ready to work. You can pick it up in two or three days with full confidence.

If the machine is to be stored for fewer than 30 days, first follow the complete cleaning and maintenance procedures outlined in previous

sections of this chapter. Clean the air and fuel filters, the exhaust system and muffler, the cooling shrouds and cylinder fins, and the outside of the starter and ignition areas. Thoroughly clean and lubricate the work-performing attachments, and sharpen the blades or teeth. Be sure to grease sprockets and the like with the grease recommended by the manufacturer. If the machine has a battery starter, be sure the battery is fully charged and that all contacts, ports, and cables are clean and dry.

Fill the fuel tank with fresh, clean gasoline properly mixed with the recommended two-cycle engine lubricant. If the work-performing attachment has its own oil tank, as in chain saws and similar equipment, fill it with the recommended lubricant; it keeps your machine ready to start. Be sure all tank caps, body screws, and other fasteners are in place and properly tightened.

Finally, store the machine in a dry place, off the ground or cement floor. If the roof leaks, as Parp's old tool room does, cover the machine with a sheet of plastic, but don't wrap it around the machine as this may cause condensation, rust, and corrosion.

Something feels very good when things are put away right and waiting for the next work session. Maybe it's just that Parp is glad not to have a handle in his hand.

Long-Term Storage

Whenever you store a two-cycle machine for 30 days or more, the fuel tank must be drained. This prevents fuel evaporation and the resulting varnish and residue that collect in the tank, fuel lines, and carburetor.

To drain the tank completely, first empty out any remaining fuel. Then start the engine, and let it run at idle until all the fuel is burned. Do not use so-called fuel stabilizers during long-term storage. The claims that they prevent fuel from evaporating and from leaving a varnishlike residue are not borne out in truth.

When the fuel is completely used up, remove the spark plug and turn the crankshaft (by pulling the starter cord) until the piston is above the exhaust port. Then pour two teaspoons of the recommended two-cycle engine oil through the spark plug hole into the cylinder. Pull the starter cord slowly several times to distribute the oil evenly throughout the engine. Clean and check the spark plug, and inspect the spark plug gasket. Then reinstall and tighten the spark plug correctly.

Now, follow the same cleaning and maintenance procedures recommended under Short-Term Storage, except remove all shrouds and body covers in order to better clean underneath them. Be especially thorough in cleaning cylinder fins, cooling ports, ignition cables, and so on. Also provide any long-term storage maintenance recommended for specific work-performing attachments. In the case of chain saws, for example, remove the bar and chain, and place the cleaned, sharpened chain in a bath of chain oil.

If the machine includes a belt drive, loosen and clean the belt. If there is a chain drive, clean the chain and oil it lightly. Be sure all grease fittings and lubrication points are properly cleaned and lubricated. If you discover any missing or broken parts or fasteners, order them immediately so you can complete the repairs while the machine is in storage.

If the machine must be stored outside, try to set it on a platform or on concrete blocks. In that case, wrap the entire machine in plastic, and tie it firmly in place.

Ending Storage

To take a two-cycle machine out of storage, remove the spark plug, and turn the engine so the hole is down. Briskly pull the starter rope to clear excess oil from the cylinder. Clean and gap the spark plug, and fill the fuel tank with fresh fuel mixture. Then, follow the standard starting procedure.

Now's the time that Parp should patch that leaking tool room roof. But the rainbows are kicking in Brown Lakes, and all too soon the ice will weaken and the season will end. Parp's going to fish some trout. Maybe Ish's jeep will start.

CHAPTER THREE:
Four-Cycle Engines

The four-cycle engine is the type of engine most commonly used throughout the world—in automobiles, generators, shredders, and other larger applications. You will not find four-cylinder engines on many of the smaller backyard tools, however, for two reasons: they are much heavier than their two-cycle counterparts, and they must remain in a relatively stable position during operation. Thus, they are not as well suited for use on chain saws, trimmers, and other lightweight tools that must be capable of operating in virtually any position. On the other hand, they are used to power some backyard tools, such as pumps, generators, snow blowers, tractors, and some lawn mowers, so it is useful to know how they work and how to keep them working.

Except for basic internal combustion theory, a chain saw engine bears little resemblance to the average American-made automobile engine. The automobile engine has 4–8 cylinders, a distributor, a battery and alternator electrical system and starting system, a liquid cooling system, an elaborate oil distribution system, various emission control devices, and all kinds of gadgetry. A chain saw has none of that.

Neither do most snow blowers, lawn mowers, or tractors, many of which do rely upon four-cycle engines. Whether they use a four-cycle or a two-cycle engine, almost all backyard tools are driven by single-cylinder, air-cooled, manual-start, magneto-ignition system engines.

This means that most backyard tools share the same cooling system, ignition system, and starting system previously described in Chapter One. So, for descriptions of the cooling, igni-tion, and starting systems most often used in four-cycle, engine-powered backyard tools, read the appropriate sections of Chapter One on two-cycle systems, if you haven't already done so.

Parp also suggests that anyone unfamiliar with basic internal combustion theory should read up on the subject in Chapter One. Familiarity with two-cycle operation will be a great help in any attempt to understand, operate, or maintain four-cycle engines. There are, however, many principles and devices used in the various systems of a four-cycle engine that are peculiar to those engines. Parp will now provide a description of the most important and most common of these peculiarities.

Four-cycle engines differ from two-cycle engines in several ways. Superficially, they are usually heavier and larger. Part of the additional size and weight is attributed to the oil reserve or mechanisms. Two-cycle engines are lubricated by a special oil that is mixed right in with the engine's fuel supply. Four-cycle engines are lubricated by oil that is splashed or pumped from a reserve pool or separate oil tank onto the engine's moving parts during operation.

As explained in Chapter One, a two-cycle engine completes all necessary phases in two strokes of the piston, one up and one down. A four-cycle engine requires four strokes of the piston to complete its cycle. The strokes are named (1) the intake stroke, (2) the compression stroke, (3) the power stroke, and (4) the exhaust stroke. These engine strokes represent the four operations necessary to keep an engine running: intake of fuel, compression of fuel, ignition of fuel, and expulsion of unburned waste products.

GENERAL FOUR-CYCLE ENGINE THEORY

For now we'll ignore the problem of starting the engine and assume that it is operating. We know that as the engine operates, the piston travels up and down in the cylinder. This vertical motion is transformed by the connecting rod and crank into the rotary motion that turns the crankshaft and thus performs the work at hand. The vertical motion of the piston is caused by the sudden burning of fuel during the power stroke. During the other, nonpower strokes of the engine, the piston and crankshaft are kept in motion by the momentum of counterbalanced crankshaft weights and the spinning flywheel. During the nonpower strokes of the engine, the rotary motion of the crankshaft is transferred to the connecting rod and piston, where it becomes vertical motion. This reverses the power transference that occurs during the power stroke.

In a four-cycle engine, a crankshaft gear is attached to the crankshaft and turns with it. As it turns, it engages another gear, the camshaft gear, on another shaft, the camshaft. The camshaft gear has twice as many teeth as the crankshaft gear. This results in a gear ratio of 2:1 and allows the crankshaft to make two complete revolutions for each turn of the camshaft. Machined into the camshaft are cam lobes, or eccentrics, that act to raise and lower valves by pushing valve rods in the engine. As the camshaft turns, the high point of one lobe pushes up one valve. Meanwhile, the other lobe is turned away so that a valve spring pushes a valve down. These operations are precisely timed to meet the engine's operating requirements. One valve allows the engine to take in fuel—it's called the intake valve. The other valve, the exhaust valve, allows the engine to expel exhaust.

Thus, in an operating four-cycle engine, as the piston travels up and down in the cylinder, the crankshaft turns and engages the camshaft, which in turn opens and closes the appropriate valve at the right time. Two complete turns of the crankshaft are necessary to complete all phases of engine operation. This represents four piston strokes, two up and two down—hence, a four-cycle engine. Now, let's go through each stroke in more detail.

Intake Stroke

In Chapter One, Parp described how a piston moving in a cylinder creates pressure changes in the cylinder and crankcase. This same situation occurs in four-cycle engines. At the beginning of the intake stroke, the piston is moving downward in the cylinder. At the same time, the camshaft is turning so that a cam lobe has pushed up on the intake valve to open a passage for the fuel/air mixture.

Since the piston is moving downward, a low-pressure area is created in the combustion chamber so that the fuel/air mixture is sucked into the cylinder. Since the exhaust valve is closed and since the pressure in the carburetor and intake manifold is higher than the pressure in the combustion chamber, a fresh charge of vaporized fuel/air mixture is drawn into the cylinder. As the piston reaches the bottom of its intake stroke, the cam lobe holding the intake valve open turns down, and the valve spring closes the valve.

Compression Stroke

After the downward, intake stroke, the piston starts to move upward in the cylinder. The camshaft continues to turn so that neither of its lobes is pushing up on the valve, and both intake and exhaust valves are closed. The piston rings prevent the fuel/air mixture from escaping the combustion chamber. The piston greatly compresses the trapped fuel/air mixture and preheats it to prepare it for ignition.

Power Stroke

Just before the piston reaches the top of the compression stroke, the timed spark occurs in the spark plug. This spark causes the compressed, and preheated, vaporized fuel/air mixture to burn very rapidly, thus greatly expanding it. The force of these burning, expanding gases pushes the piston downward in the cylinder, driving the connecting rod against the crankpin, which produces the rotary motion of the crankshaft. Note that the power transmitted is sufficient to turn the crankshaft and thus spin the flywheel and counterbalanced crankshaft weights to keep the engine running, while also leaving enough extra power to be able to operate the work-performing attachment.

Exhaust Stroke

The only necessary function remaining is to expel the waste products of the burned fuel/air mixture. After the power stroke, the momentum of the flywheel and crankshaft sends the piston upward once more. Just before the piston starts upward on the exhaust stroke, the camshaft turns so that one of its lobes begins to push up on the exhaust valve. As the exhaust valve opens, the ascending piston literally pushes the exhaust gases out through the open exhaust valve, and then through the exhaust system and muffler into the atmosphere. When the piston reaches the top of the exhaust stroke, the exhaust valve closes and the piston begins its next downward, intake stroke to begin a new cycle of strokes. This process will continue until the engine runs out of fuel, is shut off, or experiences a mechanical failure.

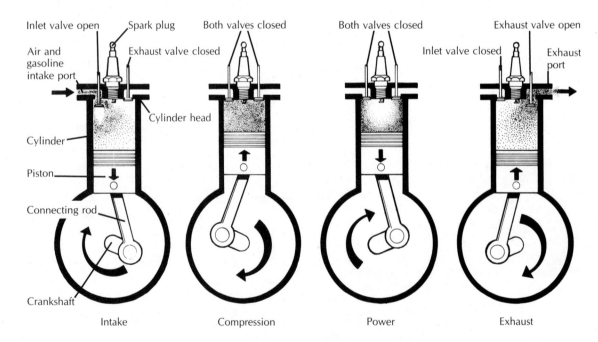

Illus. 3–1—Phases of a Typical Four-Cycle Engine

Though the functions of a four-cycle engine are essentially the same as in two-cycle engines, the piston in a four-cycle engine must perform four strokes to complete the operation.

FOUR-CYCLE LUBRICATION

One thing that can cause an early mechanical failure in any engine is improper or inadequate lubrication. As we've seen, there are more moving parts in a four-cycle engine than there are in a two-cycle engine. Therefore, there are more parts in a four-cycle engine that can break if they don't receive adequate lubrication. Parp says that's the most common cause of four-cycle engine problems.

Four-cycle engines are lubricated by oil that is held in a reserve, or pool. The oil can be splashed onto the engine's moving parts, pumped by a pressure system, or distributed by a combination of both methods.

Splash Lubrication Systems

Most air-cooled, single-cylinder, four-cycle engines are lubricated by a splash system. This system uses either a special dipper or spoon that is actually an extension of the connecting rod below the crankshaft, or a slinger, which is a geared mechanism driven by the camshaft gear. Both devices simply splash oil upward from the crankcase onto the crankshaft, connecting rod, piston, and other moving parts. The gear-driven slinger system is more common on vertical crankshaft engines, whereas the dipper system is more common on horizontal crankshaft engines. Both systems require a relatively stable engine-operating position and, of course, an adequate oil supply easily reached by the dipper or slinger.

Oil Pressure Lubrication Systems

In four-cycle engine applications where weight is not a significant factor and where the engine's operating position is relatively unstable, as in tractors and similar machines, lubrication is often performed by a pressure or oil pump system. There are several types of oil pressure lubrication mechanisms, but all are quite simple.

The gear pump is probably the most common type of oil pump found on backyard tools. It consists of two simple gears that turn in opposite directions inside a close-fitting housing. The oil comes in one side, fills the housing, and is carried around in the gaps between the gear teeth until it is forced through the outlet port on the other side as the gears turn. A simple ball-on-a-spring pressure relief valve is usually built

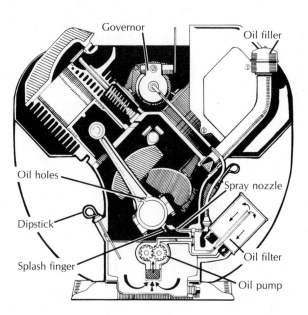

Governor
Oil filler
Oil holes
Dipstick
Splash finger
Spray nozzle
Oil filter
Oil pump

Illus. 3–2—Lubrication Systems for Four-Cycle Engines

This engine shows both methods of supplying lubrication to four-cycle engines—the splash system and the oil pump. The action of the splash finger creates an oil mist that works its way into oil holes and other engine parts. The gear pump directs oil to more remote parts of the engine.

into the pump housing to prevent the buildup of extreme pressure when the oil is thick and cold. This relief valve is the part most likely to fail in this kind of pump. Little else can go wrong unless the housing wears or cracks, an inlet or outlet fitting fails, or, very rarely, the gears wear and become loose in the housing. However, any pump can be stopped by dirt or debris that clogs passages or fittings.

Another common type of oil pump used in backyard tools is the plunger type. This kind of pump is usually driven by a lobe, or eccentric, on the camshaft similar to the lobes that operate the intake and exhaust valves. As the camshaft turns, the lobe moves a plunger in a cylinder. The plunger closes off the oil inlet port and forces the oil, under pressure, out of the outlet port. As the plunger returns to its original position, a ball check valve in the outlet port blocks the oil from coming back into the pump cylinder. At the same time, the inlet port is uncovered, and the low pressure in the pump cylinder pulls a fresh change of oil into the pump. The plunger may also be a part of the lobe itself, which is cast around the crankshaft, off center.

Whatever the pump design, an oil pressure system pumps oil through an outlet and into oil passages that carry the oil to the various bearings and other moving parts of the engine. Again, this type of system can be stopped by dirt or debris that clogs the passages.

Note: All four-cycle lubrication systems are designed to return circulated oil back to the reservoir in the bottom of the crankcase.

FOUR-CYCLE FUEL SYSTEMS

Most of the basic principles Parp outlined in his description of two-cycle fuel systems in Chapter One also apply to four-cycle engines. With backyard tools, four-cycle engines are used more than two-cycle engines and four-cycle engines come in a much wider variety of designs and power ranges. Since most four-cycle en-

gines are larger and heavier than two-cycle engines, they are often used for work in which the engine itself is not moved frequently. Also, since four-cycle engine positions must be relatively stable because of four-cycle lubrication systems, a simple gravity-fed fuel system is commonly used. A gravity-fed fuel system requires that the fuel tank be mounted higher than the carburetor. This is often the arrangement used for generator engines and other stationary engines with similar functions.

Also, since size, weight, and mobility often are not significant factors in four-cycle engine applications, many components such as fuel pumps, fuel tanks, air cleaners, carburetors, ignition system parts, starting mechanisms, and so on can be of any size and design. This allows manufacturers to design or select components that will fit best a particular engine's use. It also means that the home mechanic is likely to encounter a great variety of designs; certain basics, however, apply in most cases.

Components of Four-Cycle Fuel Systems

Most four-cycle fuel systems include the following components:

1. A relatively large fuel tank above the carburetor. The fuel tank includes a fuel tank breather cap and a fuel filter or screen.
2. A fuel shut-off valve located on the fuel line just below the fuel tank.
3. A large, in-line fuel filter, often with a glass bowl or trap designed to separate water, dirt, and debris from fuel before it reaches the carburetor.
4. A large, self-contained fuel pump, usually housed and positioned separately from the carburetor.
5. A carburetor. (See Chapter One for basic carburetor theory and operation.) Again, four-cycle engines utilize a wider vari-

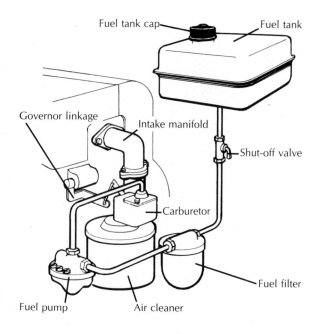

Fuel tank cap — Fuel tank

Governor linkage

Intake manifold

Shut-off valve

Carburetor

Fuel filter

Fuel pump   Air cleaner

Illus. 3–3—A Four-Cycle Fuel System

ety of carburetor designs than do two-cycle engines, and the carburetors are often larger and more complex. Some designs utilize an automatic choke.

6. A governor with governor linkage. The governor controls engine speed by opening or closing the throttle port of the carburetor.

7. An intake manifold. In a single-cylinder, four-cycle engine, this is a simple passageway from the carburetor to the intake valve port.

8. An air cleaning system.

The Fuel Tank

Most modern four-cycle engines for backyard tools use a rectangular fuel tank that holds a quart or more. Although some engines are designed to be connected to a separate fuel source, most have a tank that is either strapped

to a mounting platform near the top of the engine or built onto the engine mounts.

Many four-cycle fuel tanks do not include a fuel filter such as those built into the pick-up line of a two-cycle system. Instead, a simple filter screen covers the tank outlet, and a separate, heavy-duty fuel filter is installed in the fuel line between the fuel tank and the carburetor. An in-tank fuel filter screen must be removed and cleaned periodically.

Four-cycle engines that must operate at various angles are sometimes designed with two separate fuel outlets. Also, most four-cycle fuel tanks feature some kind of drain system—most often, a simple screw plug in the bottom of the tank. **Caution:** Never open a fuel drain plug while the engine is operating or is still hot. Always move the engine away from any flame or heat source before opening the drain plug.

The Shut-Off Valve

A fuel shut-off valve is often necessary on four-cycle engines and is always a convenient device. The shut-off valve is located in the fuel line below the fuel tank. It consists of a simple plug that is moved by a screw attached to an exterior handle. When you turn the handle, the screw moves the plug in to block the passage of fuel.

Many four-cycle applications include provisions for two different types of fuel from two different fuel tanks. An engine may be designed to operate on either kerosene or gasoline fuel, and a tank may be provided for each. In such a case, a shut-off valve for each tank is clearly necessary. A shut-off valve is also necessary in kerosene fuel systems, because the fuel must be shut off while the engine is being started on gasoline.

The Fuel Filter

Fuel filters used on four-cycle engines are more likely to resemble the typical automobile fuel filter than the typical two-cycle fuel filter.

Disposable, in-line fuel filters are being used more every year, but they are still less common than the larger, longer-lasting, bowl-type fuel filters. The bowl-type filter uses gravity to separate heavier contaminants such as water, dirt, and debris from the fuel. The fuel enters an inlet, passes through a screen that removes dirt and debris, enters a low-setting bowl where water and other contaminants are separated, then moves up through a passage to the outlet. To clean this type of filter, remove the bowl and screen. Wash both in clean gasoline—never in solvent—and wipe the bowl dry with a clean, lint-free cloth. Blow the screen dry with compressed air in the direction opposite to that of the fuel flow. Bowl-type filters rarely need to be replaced unless the bowl cracks. The screen may eventually need to be replaced if it's punctured or if it corrodes.

The Fuel Pump

Four-cycle engines sometimes use a diaphragm-type fuel pump like those commonly used on two-cycle engines, described in Chapter One (see Illus. 1–5, page 9). These may be integral with the carburetor design or may be quite separate.

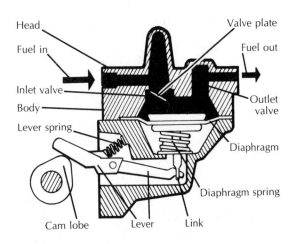

Illus. 3–4—Lever-Type Fuel Pump

More often, a lever-type mechanical fuel pump is used on four-cycle engines. A lever-type fuel pump is driven by a cam lobe, or eccentric, similar to that which moves the valves and oil pump. As the camshaft turns, the lever is pushed up by the cam lobe or is held down by a spring. The other end of the lever operates a linkage system that moves a diaphragm similar to that used in a simple diaphragm fuel pump. When the lever is pushed up by the cam lobe, it pulls the diaphragm down. This results in a low-pressure area above the diaphragm that allows fuel to enter the fuel chamber. At this time, the inlet valve is open, and the outlet valve is held closed by the pressure in the outlet line. By the time the cam lobe has turned away, allowing the spring to push the lever down, the fuel chamber is full. The force of the spring moves the linkage and the diaphragm upward. The resulting fuel pressure closes the inlet valve and opens the outlet valve so that the fuel is forced out under pressure. This sequence of events happens so rapidly that there is a steady, pressurized fuel flow from the outlet.

Note that a common failure in this type of fuel pump occurs when the lever spring becomes fatigued or broken. Other parts may also fail and may occasionally need to be renewed, such as a leak in the diaphragm.

The Carburetor

Parp has outlined basic carburetor principles in Chapter One. That chapter also includes a drawing of a Tillotson carburetor, representative of the type found on many modern small engines, both four-cycle and two-cycle (see Illus. 1–6, page 10). Yet, there are many other carburetor designs, and the types used on four-cycle engines are more likely to vary widely according to engine design and application. Again, since size and weight are often not significant factors, carburetors for four-cycle engines will often be much larger and heavier than those used on two-cycle engines. Whatever the design, the function of the carburetor is always the same. It draws fuel into the air passage at the venturi in order to vaporize the fuel, mix it with air, and meter the proper fuel/air mixture to the cylinder.

The three chief carburetor designs for four-cycle engines are the updraft type, the downdraft type, and the sidedraft type. In an updraft carburetor, the airflow enters the bottom of the carburetor, and the vaporized fuel/air mixture leaves through the top. A downdraft carburetor is, of course, just the opposite. A sidedraft carburetor draws air from one side and delivers the vaporized fuel/air mixture from the other side.

Float-Type Carburetors

Unlike two-cycle engines, many four-cycle engines utilize a float-type carburetor. The float keeps the fuel in the carburetor at a constant level.

A float-type carburetor contains a fuel float chamber near the fuel inlet. Inside the chamber, a hinged float mechanism moves up and down with the fuel level. As it travels, it moves a needle valve, which protrudes into the fuel inlet opening. As the fuel level drops, the descending float retracts the needle from the inlet to allow more fuel to flow past. When the fuel level is higher, the rising float pushes the needle further into the inlet to decrease the flow of fuel. The effect is a constant level of fuel at the juncture of the airstream, thus maintaining a constant fuel/air mixture.

Automatic Choke Carburetors

Automatic choke carburetors are rarely found on two-cycle engines, and almost never on two-cycle-powered backyard tools. But they are quite common on four-cycle engines, and many backyard tool owners often find that they must service these mechanisms. Note that manual chokes used on four-cycle engines are basically the same as the manual choke described in Chapter One—that is, the choke regulates the airflow in the carburetor by determining the size of the air passage with the choke plate.

Most automatic chokes are activated by heat, usually from the exhaust manifold, or by an electrical device connected to the starting circuit. A few automatic chokes are operated by the vacuum produced by the downstroke of the piston.

The first type uses a heat-sensitive spring that closes the choke when the engine is cold. As the engine warms up, the heat straightens the spring, which opens the choke.

The electrically activated automatic choke also uses a heat-sensitive spring, but the heat is supplied by electricity from the starting circuit. In this case, the heat from the starting circuit causes the spring to close the choke. When the engine is running, there is no voltage in the starting circuit, so the cold spring holds the choke open.

In the vacuum-operated automatic choke, a diaphragm under the carburetor is connected to the choke plate. When the engine is not running and no vacuum is being created, a spring pushes the diaphragm up to hold the choke

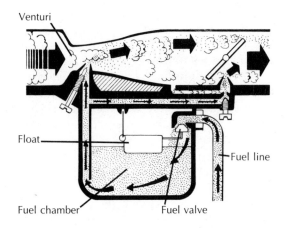

Venturi

Float

Fuel line

Fuel chamber

Fuel valve

Illus. 3–5—Float-Type Carburetor

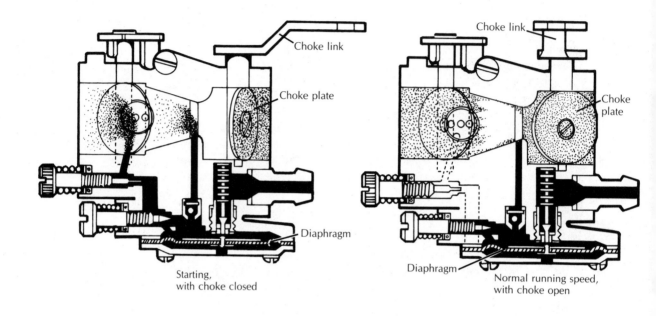

Starting,
with choke closed

Normal running speed,
with choke open

Illus. 3–6—Automatic Choke Carburetor

closed. When the engine starts, the engine vacuum pulls the diaphragm down, against the force of the spring, and opens the choke.

The Chokeless Carburetor

Some four-cycle engines operate with a float-type carburetor that actually has no choke at all. This kind of carburetor has a special chamber, the well, for extra fuel that is used only during the starting and cold running phases. The well automatically fills with fuel each time the engine is turned off. When the engine is turned over, low pressure across the main nozzle causes the fuel to rise from the well. This supplies the rich mixture needed for starting the cold engine. As long as the engine is running, the well cannot refill.

The Governor

Governors are quite common on four-cycle backyard power tool engines, very rare on two-cycle engines. A governor protects the engine by limiting its speed. There are hundreds of governor designs, and although they appear quite simple, governors are extremely delicate, and most home mechanics should avoid tampering with them. However, this book will be used by many people who have no access to a mechanic and who may really need to repair or adjust a governor. Accordingly, Parp will cover both the mechanics and, later, the servicing of typical governor mechanisms.

In all cases, the governor is activated as the engine approaches a dangerously high operating speed. Sometimes the governor is activated

46

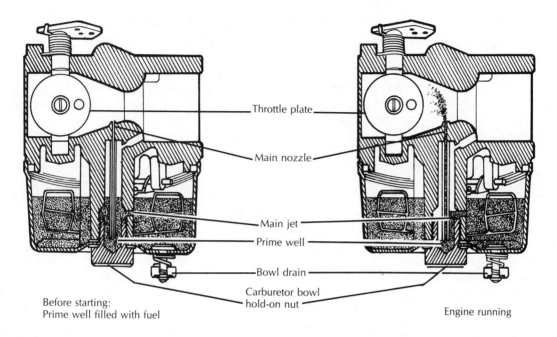

Before starting:
Prime well filled with fuel

Throttle plate

Main nozzle

Main jet

Prime well

Bowl drain

Carburetor bowl
hold-on nut

Engine running

Illus. 3–7—Chokeless Carburetor

by a mechanism attached to the crankshaft, or a separate shaft. Sometimes the governor is activated by the breeze from the flywheel. In all cases, the activated governor decreases engine speed by partially closing the throttle, thereby limiting the amount of vaporized fuel entering the cylinder. Since this operation usually depends on a sensing device that must in some way be tuned to the speed of the engine, it follows that certain parts of a governor mechanism are quite delicate and can be distorted easily beyond proper operating tolerances.

Mechanical Governors

A mechanical governor is driven by centrifugal force supplied either by the crankshaft or the flywheel, or by a separate rotating shaft driven by the crankshaft. If you examine the external parts of an engine that uses a mechanical governor, you will not see the driving mechanisms. They are contained inside the engine.

All governors tend to hold the throttle wide open. In a typical system, one end of the governor lever is attached by linkage to one end of the carburetor throttle lever. When the governor lever is up, it pushes the throttle lever in such a way that the throttle plate is held open. When the governor lever is down, it pulls the carburetor lever and turns the throttle plate to a partially closed position.

The other end of the governor level is attached to a counterweighted mechanism that, in turn, is attached to the drive shaft or flywheel, either directly or indirectly. This mechanism is designed to be affected by the centrifugal force created when it is turned by the crankshaft. When the engine is not running and the crankshaft is not turning, centripetal force or springs hold in the weighted mechanism. This allows the associated end of the governor lever to rest down, thus pulling up the other end and holding the throttle plate open. When the engine starts and approaches a predetermined speed, the weights are thrown outward by centrifugal force. This pushes up that end of the governor lever and pulls down the other, which in turn pulls the carburetor lever down to close the throttle plate partially.

All of this happens so fast that the effect is that of a steady engine speed. When the load on the engine changes one way or the other, the change in engine speed causes a corresponding change in the performance of the governor in order to maintain proper engine speed limits.

The governed speed can be adjusted by changing the governor spring tension via a screw mechanism attached to the linkage that secures the governor spring.

Air-Vane Governor

An air-vane governor does the same work that the mechanical governor does, but it is activated by airflow from the blower or flywheel. The increasing airflow of the speeding engine blows against a winglike device called the air vane. At a predetermined engine speed, the air-

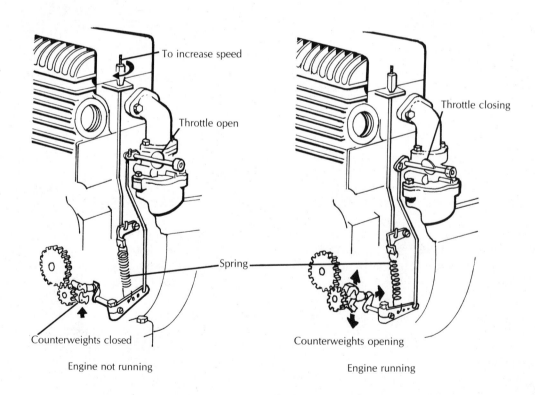

To increase speed

Throttle open

Spring

Counterweights closed

Engine not running

Throttle closing

Counterweights opening

Engine running

Illus. 3—8—Mechanical Governor

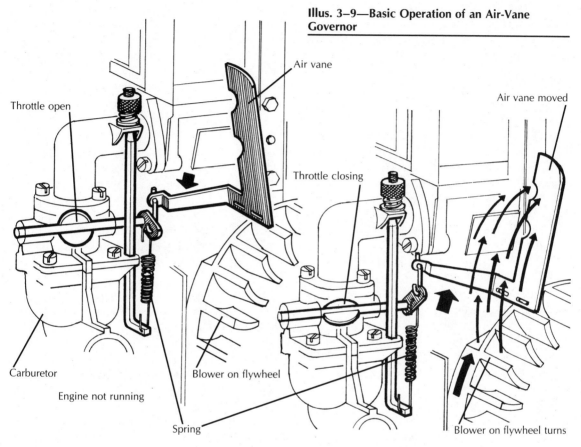

Illus. 3–9—Basic Operation of an Air-Vane Governor

Air vane

Air vane moved

Throttle open

Throttle closing

Carburetor

Blower on flywheel

Engine not running

Spring

Blower on flywheel turns

Engine running

flow is sufficient to push the air vane to one side, thus partially closing the throttle plate. When the engine operates at lower speeds, or when a load is placed on the engine, a governor spring overcomes the force of the airflow against the air vane, and the throttle opens somewhat to increase the fuel supply.

You should avoid attempting to adjust any governor unless it becomes absolutely necessary. If you do adjust a governor, be sure to do it in small increments, preferably to match the

engine manufacturer's rpm specifications. If that is not possible, adjust the governor spring so that the engine does not sound strained. Then reduce the governed speed 100 rpm by turning the governor spring adjustment screw one full turn counterclockwise.

Do not attempt to overcome engine sluggishness by adjusting the governor to a faster engine speed. **Note:** A governor spring must be replaced when it becomes damaged or fatigued through long use.

The Intake Manifold

Found only on four-cycle engines, the intake manifold is something like a hallway through which the vaporized fuel/air mixture passes after it leaves the carburetor and before it enters the intake valve port. In a single-cylinder engine, the intake manifold is a simple casting with two openings, one for the intake port, the other for the carburetor. In multi-cylinder engines, the intake manifold contains an opening for each cylinder, plus the opening that accepts the fuel vapors from the carburetor. The intake manifold must fit perfectly and must not leak. Cracked manifolds should not be repaired, because an uneven internal manifold surface adversely affects fuel flow. Replace them instead.

The Air Cleaner

Like most other components, air cleaners used on four-cycle engines tend to be larger and more complex than those used on two-cycle engines. Most two-cycle air cleaners are really filters fitted over the carburetor's air intake opening. Although they perform the same function, air cleaners on four-cycle engines can appear to be quite complex and can employ any one of a wide variety of cleaning or filter elements, among which are oil baths, polyurethane foams, and specially constructed paper filters. The air cleaner is another reason four-cycle engines look different when compared to two-cycle engines. The scavenger mechanic frequently will encounter older two-cycle engines with outmoded air cleaners and other components more likely to be found on today's four-cycle power plants. A glance at a pre–World War II chain saw will convince you that, in this case, progress has been good.

The Screen, or Flocked, Filter

There are seven basic types of air cleaners used on most modern four-cycle engines. The first and simplest is the screen-filter, or flocked-filter, type, which is identical to the air filters found on most two-cycle-powered backyard tools. This simple cleaner is occasionally used on four-cycle engines where weight or compactness is something of a factor. This is often the case with lightweight, four-cycle-powered lawn mowers and similar equipment. Many of these filters are considered permanent, although Parp says they cannot be cleaned and reused forever and should be replaced yearly in most cases, and sometimes more often. As mentioned in Chapter One, these filters must be thoroughly cleaned at least once for each eight hours of engine use. To clean, remove the filter from the engine, and wash it well in clean gasoline. The tougher screen types may be scrubbed with a toothbrush. Then blow or shake the element dry, with the airflow going in the direction opposite to that of operating airflow. Re-oil the filter if the engine manual calls for it.

The Paper Element Air Cleaner

Many four-cycle engines employ a pleated paper air cleaner housed in a fairly large metal or plastic cup, secured with a wing nut and bolt. Behind the base of the housing is a gasket that prevents uncleaned air from reaching the carburetor. These paper elements are fragile, but they are among the most effective designs available. They must be replaced when dirty. The gasket must be replaced at the first sign of drying, fatigue, or damage.

The Oil Bath Cleaner

Perhaps the most common air cleaning system used on older, large four-cycle engines in stationary applications, the oil bath cleaner is cleanable and an effective cleaner. In this system, the airflow enters through the lip around the edge of the cleaner top and is reversed, directed across the surface of an oil pool, in which it slings heavy contaminants. Sometimes the airflow also passes through an additional filter screen that is saturated with oil. Although an oil bath cleaner will continue to clean effectively for a

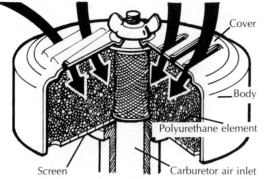

Cover

Body

Polyurethane element

Screen

Carburetor air inlet

Oiled Foam Plastic Cleaner

Illus. 3–10—Four Types of Air Cleaners Found on Four-Cycle Engines

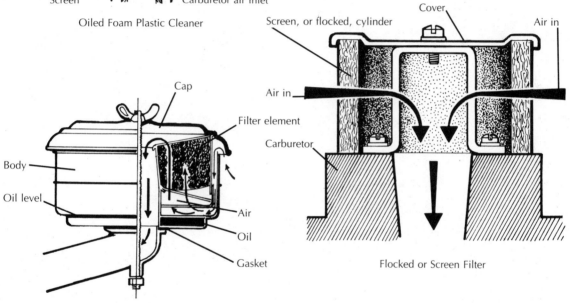

Screen, or flocked, cylinder

Cover

Air in

Air in

Carburetor

Flocked or Screen Filter

Cap

Filter element

Body

Oil level

Air

Oil

Gasket

Oil Bath Cleaner

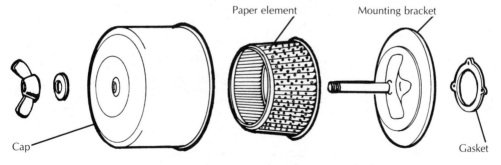

Paper element

Mounting bracket

Cap

Gasket

Paper Element Air Cleaner

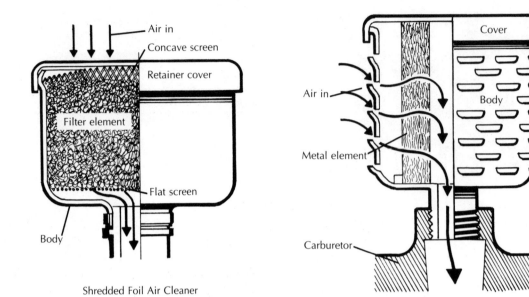

Shredded Foil Air Cleaner

Metal Cartridge Air Cleaner

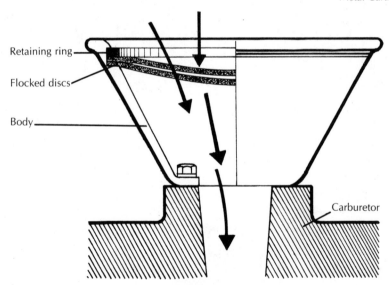

Ram Scoop Air Cleaner

**Illus. 3–11—Three Other Types of Air Cleaners
Found on Four-Cycle Engines**

long period of service, the system must occasionally be disassembled, thoroughly washed in a solvent, dried, and reassembled with a fresh supply of clean oil, preferably the type recommended by the manufacturer.

When working on an oil bath cleaner, take great care not to spill oil into the carburetor. Also, if you notice excessive gunk in the system or a greaselike smudging in the carburetor, perform your cleaning maintenance more often, and be sure to clean the carburetor air intake area.

The Oiled Foam Plastic Cleaner

This system provides a way to gain the superior serviceability of an oil system in a less stable engine application. In this system, the air comes through vents in the top of the cleaner and flows through a polyurethane sponge that is nearly saturated with oil. Again, these units are effective through many washings and re-oilings but eventually the polyurethane element may need to be replaced, at which time the entire system should be cleaned and fresh oil added. Be sure the oil doesn't drip onto the engine, especially into the carburetor.

The Metal Cartridge Air Cleaner

A metal cartridge air cleaner employs a mass of metal screens that are combined to separate large particles of dirt and debris from the passing airflow. These screens give long though marginally effective service if they are frequently removed, and knocked or blown clean. Eventually, when the element becomes clogged, it will have to be replaced. Metal cartridge air cleaners are not ideal in areas of extremely high humidity or dirt, says Parp, because they tend to collect more moisture. They are easily replaced with oiled polyurethane foam and oil cleaners.

The Shredded Foil Air Cleaner

Some engines come with a foil cleaner. In most of these, a canister is filled with shredded strips of aluminum or other foil, held in a hous-

ing between two screens. These systems are difficult to clean effectively, are inefficient and should be replaced when dirty by another type of cleaner.

The Ram Scoop Air Cleaner

This very simple system is actually an elaboration on the first system, the simple screen- or flocked-filter cleaner. But in this case, two flocked-filter disks or mesh screen disks are held near the opening of a scoop-shaped housing designed to increase the velocity of the air entering the carburetor. Flocked filters in these systems can be blown clear for reuse to some extent, but they should not be washed and must be replaced frequently. Mesh screen disks can be washed and blown clean and reused indefinitely. Again, always blow air in the direction opposite to that of normal operating airflow.

FOUR-CYCLE STARTERS

Most four-cycle engines are started by a simple rope-pull, manual starter similar to those found on most two-cycle machinery. Like other components, however, four-cycle starters are often larger than the units on two-cycle engines. When weight and size are not significant factors, four-cycle starters can be heavier and better constructed than the smaller two-cycle models. (For a review of rope-pull, manual starters, see Chapter Two. For information about starters on specific machines, see Index.)

Although cord starters are used most frequently, other types of starters are also found on four-cycle engines. Among these are the manual crank starter and various electric starter designs.

The Manual Crank Starter

A manual crank starter is easily identified by the crank, usually a hinged model that folds compactly into the top of the starter housing. These starters are very much like rope-pull starters, but they're larger, heavier, and primarily for use on four-cycle machines such as lawn mowers and generators. To start the engine, you open the hinged handle and turn it to wind a starter spring. When the spring is wound, you refold the handle. Then you push either the handle itself or a separate release mechanism. This unhooks a starter dog to release the spring tension that turns the crankshaft.

Electric Starters

Electric starters are more common on four-cycle engines than on two-cycle engines, and Parp's derisive comments on two-cycle electric starters in Chapter Two do not apply here. Because weight is not a significant factor, reliable, heavy-duty, electric-start mechanisms can be used. These mechanisms are usually far superior to the rather flimsy electric-start systems incorporated in two-cycle machines.

Electric starters start an engine in exactly the same way manual starters do the job. When you pull the rope or release the crank on a manual starter, you spin the flywheel, which turns the crankshaft, which moves the piston up and down. In four-cycle engines, the same action also turns the camshaft to move the valves. An electric starter also spins the flywheel, with the same results, but does so with an electric starter motor that automatically disengages when the engine starts. As you can see, the starter rope, or crank, and manual starting mechanisms are simply replaced by a starter motor and, of course, a power source to supply the needed voltage. Usually the power source is a battery of some kind, which means that a system for recharging the battery must also be included. Otherwise, the battery would grow weaker each time the starter was used and would soon lose all of its power. If the power source is simply household current, then, of course, no recharging system is necessary. This is the case with many electric-start lawn mowers.

All electric starters work by converting electrical energy from the power source into mechanical energy that is supplied in such a way as to crank the engine. There are a great many different electric starter designs, none of which are intended to be accessible for repairs by the home mechanic. However, many starter motors are easily removed from the appliance so that often the home mechanic can reduce significantly a repair bill by delivering only the removed starter unit to the shop. Even normal maintenance is somewhat limited. About all you can and should do is check all adjustments and connections, and periodically clean all components. If the system includes a battery, you should frequently check the battery cables for damage or insulation weakness caused by spilled oil or grease. You should clean the battery terminals and cable connections with a wire brush and occasionally wash off the top of the battery with a solution of baking soda and water.

Many electric starter motors need periodic lubrication of the gear splines located behind the engaging gear. To do this, simply remove the fasteners holding the starter to the appliance, and pull it out. You'll be able easily to determine the correct remounting position after you've oiled the gears and gear splines.

The Charging System

Any machine equipped with a battery-powered electric-start system must include a charging circuit. The charging circuit supplies the power needed to meet immediate system requirements while simultaneously keeping the battery charged. One of the following components is used to power the charging circuit: a generator, a starting motor-generator, or a flywheel alternator.

The Generator

Generators are rarely found on newer equipment, having been replaced mostly by alternators. However, you may have purchased or intend to purchase a reliable, used power tool that may be equipped with a generator, so Parp will describe generators here.

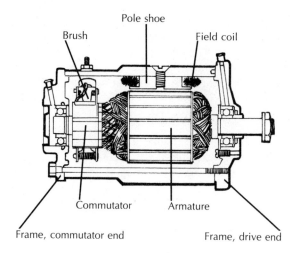

Brush   Pole shoe   Field coil

Commutator   Armature

Frame, commutator end   Frame, drive end

Illus. 3–12—Cross-Section of a Typical Motor-Generator

A generator is similar to the magneto coil described in Chapter One. A simple generator is used principally to keep the battery charged while the engine is running. It converts mechanical energy from the rotating crankshaft into electrical energy that is fed back to the battery at a precisely controlled level.

In a generator, a great many wire loops are wound around an armature made of soft iron. When the engine is operating, it spins the armature to produce voltage in the armature windings. The armature is also directly connected to other wire coils called field coils, which are wound around magnetic pole shoes. When the engine produces a voltage in the armature, part of the current flows through the field coils. This adds to the strength of the magnetic field and increases the current induced in the armature coils.

To supply power to the battery, a commutator is attached to one end of the armature. The commutator consists of several insulated metal segments, each of which is attached to a different loop in the armature coil. The current is picked up from the commutator segments by

special conductive brushes. These brushes are the only generator parts commonly replaced by the home mechanic. If other parts fail, it's best either to have the generator rebuilt by an expert or to buy a new or rebuilt generator.

The Starter-Generator

As the name signifies, a starter-generator performs two distinct functions. In the starting phase, it operates as an electric starter motor; in the charging circuit, it operates as a generator. As a starter, it converts electrical energy into the mechanical energy needed to turn the engine over. As a generator, it converts mechanical energy from the operating engine into electrical energy to keep the battery charged. Again, there is little that even the advanced home mechanic can do to revive these units. Gears and splines should be oiled periodically, and an adept home mechanic may be able to replace the brushes. Like all electric equipment, you should frequently check, clean, and tighten all connections. Other than these items, all repairs are best left to an expert, especially since a generator or starter can only be checked for proper performance with special instruments.

The Flywheel Alternator

A simple flywheel-alternator system can also be used to charge the battery. In this case, the power for immediate or accessory needs is supplied by the battery itself, and the flywheel-alternator system acts only to replenish the battery.

This system consists of a moving magnetic ring that has a permanent magnetic field, a stationary alternator, and a rectifier. The magnetic ring is attached to the flywheel and turns with it. It turns around the starter or alternator starter, which is attached to the engine in a permanent position. As the magnetic ring spins, it produces an alternating current in the alternator starter. This alternating current is then changed to direct current by the rectifier and fed to the battery.

FOUR-CYCLE EXHAUST SYSTEMS

The basics of exhaust systems and their maintenance described in Chapter Two generally apply to single-cylinder, four-cycle engines, although they rarely require cleaning because they don't become clogged with carbon (since oil is not mixed with the fuel). There are, however, added complications caused by the design and operation of these engines. Chiefly, these differences result from the use of multiple cylinders and valves. Just as a multi-cylinder, four-cycle engine needs an intake manifold, it also needs an exhaust manifold. Also, because the crankcase of a four-cycle engine is sealed off from the cylinder, all four-cycle engines must employ a crankcase ventilation system.

The Exhaust Manifold

This simple device is designed very much like the intake manifold discussed earlier. It is a simple passageway between the exhaust port and the muffler. Like the intake manifold, the exhaust manifold must be sealed gas-tight to

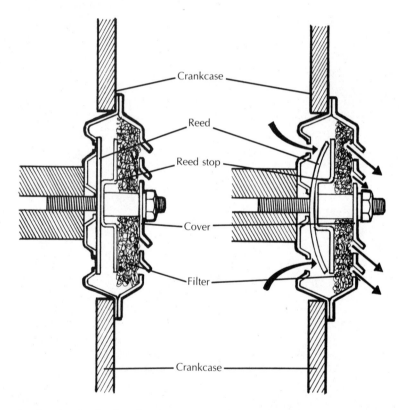

Breather Reed Valve Closed   Breather Reed Valve Open

Illus. 3–13—Reed-Type Check Valve Crankcase Breather

prevent leaks, and it must be smooth in order to prevent turbulence in the exhaust flow. Turbulent exhaust flow can cause pressure to back up toward the exhaust valve and cylinder and thereby decrease the engine's efficiency. A cracked or damaged exhaust manifold must be repaired or replaced immediately.

The Crankcase Breather

Because combustion gases blow past the piston and enter the crankcase, which also contains the oil reservoir in a four-cycle engine, the crankcase needs a ventilation system. Ventilation is provided by a simple device known as a crankcase breather.

The most common crankcase breather is a reed-type check valve that is installed in the crankcase wall and vented to the atmosphere. It allows air to flow in one direction, out of the crankcase. When the piston descends and increases the pressure in the crankcase, the reed of the check valve opens to release some pressure. Most crankcase breathers also include some kind of filter to keep dust and grit out of the crankcase.

Any crankcase breather system should be periodically cleaned and checked for wear or damage. Some include filter elements that must be examined regularly and replaced when they are damaged or worn.

MAINTAINING FOUR-CYCLE ENGINES

Most of the maintenance precautions and procedures described in Chapter Two also apply to four-cycle engines, so Parp will avoid repeating them here. There are, however, some differences. Many of these have been covered in the preceding pages, in conjunction with paragraphs describing various four-cycle components. There are a few others to be treated here.

Fuel

Four-cycle-powered machinery may sometimes use fuels other than regular-grade, leaded gasoline. Certain applications make it desirable to use kerosene as the chief fuel, and some engines can use either. In this case, a dual-tank system is used, because kerosene is not volatile enough to start an engine. So, gasoline in one tank is used to start the engine and warm it up while kerosene, kept in a second tank, is used as the main operating fuel.

One problem that often results in this combination is that the gasoline is used so little that it frequently goes stale before a tankful is used up. This can result in various starting and operating difficulties. If you own a dual-tank machine, Parp suggests you keep records of when you fuel your tanks. If you find that 90 days have passed, or that the season has changed since you last filled your gasoline-starting-system tank, you should drain and clean the gasoline fuel system, and refill it with fresh fuel.

Note: Since oil is not mixed with fuel in four-cycle engines, some people think the fuel can be stored indefinitely. It's true that you'll not have quite the difficulty with old gasoline as with old two-cycle mix, but the volatile portions of the fuel will still evaporate at the same rate and will leave a residue that can make it hard to start your engine, or can cause gum deposits to collect in your carburetor and fuel system. If in doubt, dump out the old fuel. Always use fresh, clean, regular-grade, leaded gasoline unless an alternative fuel is recommended by the manufacturer.

Lubrication

The single most common cause of four-cycle engine failure is improper or inadequate lubrication. It is also the cause of the most serious and expensive failures. Parp cannot overstress the importance of following the manufacturer's exact recommendations for type and quantity of engine oil as well as any other lubrication steps that are required.

Before starting any four-cycle engine, anytime, *always* check the oil. Once the engine's running, it may be too late and, in any case, it's impossible to get an accurate visual or dipstick reading after an engine has run for a few minutes. Obviously, one cannot check the oil on an engine that is running.

Always use the recommended oil, and fill the crankcase to the indicator mark, or to the level mark on the dipstick. Pour the oil in slowly, and check the crankcase often enough to be sure you aren't overfilling. In a four-cycle engine, adding too much oil is just as bad as not having enough. If the crankcase is overfilled, some of the oil can be burned with the gasoline, causing acute buildup of carbon, which can clog and damage the valves.

Change your oil at least as often as recommended by the manufacturer.

Crankcase Breather

Some crankcase breathers contain only a filter element. The filter should be removed periodically, washed in solvent, air dried, and reinserted. If the filter is torn or damaged, replace it with a new one as recommended by the manufacturer.

Reed check valves should be examined for damage frequently and should be replaced at the first sign of malfunction. When you reassemble a breather system, be sure to install the valve in the original position and direction. It's a good idea to draw a picture when you remove the breather assembly. Also, be sure to install the assembly in a way that does not allow the filter to interfere with the action of the reed check valve.

Governor and Governor Linkage

You should routinely inspect any governor assembly and its linkage. Be sure all screws and other fasteners are tightened securely and that

nothing has shaken off. If a governor spring becomes deformed during carburetor service or other service, be sure to replace it immediately. If a governor-equipped engine suddenly seems to be running too fast, check the governor for proper operation at once. If you don't have the proper equipment to adjust the governor to the correct engine rpm, take it to a mechanic. The cost of repairing the governor does not compare to the cost of replacing the engine.

Battery

Most starting problems on electric-start machines are caused by battery problems. Batteries on four-cycle machines take a lot of abuse, especially on machines that are left outside all of the time. Make battery inspection a part of your routine maintenance check.

First, look the battery over carefully. Be sure it isn't cracked or leaking. A cracked battery must be replaced. **Caution:** When inspecting or servicing any battery, do not smoke, and do not do anything that may cause sparks to fly. Batteries produce hydrogen gas, which can explode. When servicing a battery, first disconnect the ground lead. That's the one that goes to the engine, not to the starter motor. Whenever working with a battery, wear protective goggles, keep your head well away from the battery, and work in a well-ventilated area.

Be sure there is no acid or corrosion anywhere on the battery. This can be removed with a stiff brush and a thin solution of baking soda and water. Take care not to get any of this solution inside the battery—this could cause it to boil over, which can cause serious burns, aside from possibly ruining the battery.

Remove the battery caps (except on sealed batteries), and check the battery fluid level. Keep the fluid at the indicated level in each cell, with distilled or soft water.

If you use a battery charger, be sure to set the selector at the proper mark for either 12 or 6 volts. Charge the battery slowly, and definitely avoid overcharging, which can cause the battery to explode. Even if you aren't injured in the explosion, your engine will be.

When your battery is charged and all connections are clean, coat the parts and connectors with Vaseline or grease to retard corrosion.

Valves and Valve Seats

The two valves of the average four-cycle engine take a terrific beating as they move up and down. So do the valve springs and the carefully machined seats that the valves fit into when at rest. Even the most casual home mechanic can improve engine efficiency and prolong usefulness by periodically checking the valves and cleaning the area of the valve seats.

To reach the valves, remove the cylinder head and gasket. Be sure to keep track of where the bolts or other fasteners go. Draw a picture of the assembly, and put everything back exactly as you found it. Always replace the old gasket with a new one.

With the cylinder head removed, you can see the valves and valve seats. If the engine has performed considerable service, you may decide to do a complete valve job (see Chapter Four). Usually, you'll simply want to check and clean the valves. If carbon deposits are heavy or hard, use a bristle brush and solvent to clean the valves. If you cannot remove the carbon, you'll have to replace the valve. If the valves are warped, cracked, or excessively burned, you need to do the complete job. If you need to replace an exhaust valve, Parp says you should use a Stellite valve. Stellite is a hard material that resists corrosion.

If the valves look to be in good shape, simply clean the valve faces and seats with a clean, lint-free cloth moistened with solvent. Do not use gasoline. You should expect the exhaust valve to look worse than the intake valve, and it will need more cleaning. Exhaust valves are more apt to become stuck, too.

After long storage, the valves sometimes stick in their guides and prevent the engine from running. If a valve is stuck, apply penetrating oil, and work it loose by twisting it or tapping it with a plastic hammer.

Tappets, which are usually set screws, limit the travel of the valves, and the clearance or distance between them must be specific. To check the valve-to-tappet clearance, first determine the manufacturer's specifications. Some engines must be checked when hot, some when cold. Check the valve-to-tappet clearance with a flat feeler gauge of the size recommended by the manufacturer. The gap should just hold the gauge, though it should slide in the gap with some drag. The gap is usually changed by an adjusting screw, which should be apparent. If you do not find an adjusting screw, it's a nonadjustable model, and you should not try to adjust the clearance by any other means. Stop right where you are, and reassemble the engine. Don't forget to install a new cylinder head gasket and tighten all bolts to the manufacturer's torque specifications, if indicated.

Other Maintenance

For other maintenance procedures, see Chapter Two for general engine maintenance. Also check the Index or specific chapter of this book for your particular machine. In addition, be sure to check your owner's manual for the manufacturer's recommended maintenance procedures.

PREPARATION FOR STORAGE

See Chapter Two for general storage procedures, both short-term and long-term. Below are some special tips for four-cycle engines.

Short-Term Storage

Most four-cycle-powered machinery includes a fuel shut-off valve and a carburetor drain plug. When you store the machine longer than overnight, close the fuel shut-off valve, and open the carburetor drain plug to clear the carburetor. Then fill the fuel tank with fresh fuel, and follow the short-term storage procedure outlined in Chapter Two.

Long-Term Storage

To drain the fuel system of a four-cycle engine, first close the fuel shut-off valve, and open the fuel-tank drain to empty the tank. Then reopen the shut-off valve, and start the engine. Let it run until all the fuel is used. To prepare the cylinder for long-term storage, remove the spark plug, and pour in two tablespoons of the same type of oil recommended for the crankcase. Then reinstall the spark plug, and turn the engine over slowly to allow the oil to cover the cylinder. (Parp says don't try to pick the engine up; that won't work.)

If the engine is equipped with a governor, check the linkage to be sure it's operating properly and isn't rubbing or distorted in any way. Oil the linkage with a few drops of light oil, such as sewing machine oil or gun oil. (Never use honing oil or 3-in-1 oil, which will gum up.)

If the engine includes a belt drive, slacken the belt tension to avoid needless wear and stretching. If there's a chain drive, apply a light oil to the entire chain after removing any rust or mud. Be sure to lubricate all grease fittings and other recommended lubrication areas.

If the engine has a bowl-type fuel filter, remove and clean the bowl, then reinstall it.

Perform all other storage maintenance procedures recommended by the manufacturer and outlined in Chapter Two. Also, service the battery as described earlier in this chapter.

Ending Storage

To end storage, first check the oil, and add some if necessary. Then fill the fuel tank with fresh fuel, and open the shutoff valve. Remove and clean the air filter or air cleaner system. Check the battery, and service as necessary. Take a close look at the entire machine, and check carefully for any loose fasteners or damaged parts. On lawn mowers and similar machines, be sure the blade is tight on the crankshaft.

Finally, check your notes to be sure you've performed all intended or necessary repairs or adjustments. Then follow the procedures recommended in Chapter Two for ending storage.

Coyote days of March. Ice too soft, all the seasons closed, town folks getting restless, desperate skunks dare our shed where the freezer hollowly sucks power, the woods socked in. Nothing for it but the work at hand as the sun slowly swings our way again. By Chapter Six, the meadows may be crossable, if this snow ever stops. Still, those dried weeds by the creek are stark and beautiful, and lucky Parp can see the living places on the hill, sheltered by rocks and roots, where the small things scamper sideways in the dusk.

CHAPTER FOUR:

Be Your Own Mechanic

Parp hopes the preceding three chapters will help the casual or beginner home mechanic to understand the basic operations and systems of the small engines most commonly used to power backyard tools. Such an understanding, combined with careful maintenance procedures, will prevent many needless mechanical failures and can save hundreds of dollar in repair costs, even if you have no intention of doing any serious repair work yourself.

Any machine will fail eventually, even if you are conscientiously methodical in caring for your equipment. When failure occurs, you must decide if you want to repair the machine yourself, take it to a professional mechanic, or determine its biodegradability. (If you bury it completely in ground that stays wet most of the year, it will eventually disappear—though it could take a long, long time, says Parp.)

If your machine is still under a warranty, do not attempt any repairs yourself. Take it straight to a factory-authorized warranty repair station. If there's no warranty but you're unsure of yourself, take the machine to a professional mechanic.

If, however, you wish to become your own mechanic, or have no choice in the matter, this chapter will help you perform many engine repairs—some easy, some difficult. Parp stresses that here he deals with engine problems. If your problem is in the work attachment, please check the Index for your specific machine.

IDENTIFY THE PROBLEM

A seasoned and professional small-engine mechanic sometimes seems to proceed more on intuition than on any logical system of deduction. But it only seems that way. The mechanic may touch the machine, become distant and rather blank, then fool with this and fool with that. Then, suddenly, she or he may begin removing nuts and screws, apparently sure of the problem and confident in her or his ability. It's an illusion. The mechanic has eliminated many unlikely problems and, before your eyes, has done the minimal troubleshooting necessary to identify the problem. Without the basis of experience and knowledge comparable to that of a professional mechanic, we must be much more methodical.

Successful engine repair work depends on a careful, logical, and methodical approach from the beginning. The beginning is always the same: identify the problem.

Parp assumes you have left the field because your machine quit working and your initial efforts to improve its performance there have failed, or because the performance or lack of performance of your machine is sufficiently drastic to cause you to abandon resuscitation attempts. Now you have your machine in your work area, or have removed the engine to your workbench. In all cases, the following steps apply:

1. Prepare a work area with adequate lighting.

2. Check for any safety hazards.
3. Disconnect the battery or power source.
4. Clean the machine or engine, and drain the fuel system.
5. Follow troubleshooting procedures to determine the problem. (See Appendix B for a complete set of troubleshooting charts.)
6. With the problem strongly suspected or positively identified, gather and arrange all tools necessary for the repair.
7. Disassemble the machine or engine to whatever extent is necessary. Lay out the parts in the order in which they are removed. Make assembly drawings whenever possible. Make a list of all damaged, worn, or lost parts.
8. Clean all parts, whether you intend to replace them or not. Use a recommended solvent on all but fuel system parts. Take fuel system parts outside, and wash them in a small amount of gasoline, then blow them dry with compressed air. Dispose of the gas after you are finished using it.
9. Procure or make all parts necessary for the repair, plus any other parts or assemblies you think should be replaced. Replace all removed gaskets and seals with new ones.
10. Substitute the correct new parts for the old.
11. Reassemble.
12. Test and adjust.

In all engine repair work, you should perform or account for each step in this procedure. A few words about steps 1 and 2. Be sure your workbench or work area is clean and free of any dangerous distractions, such as unneeded tools, parts of other engines, oil spills, or liquids that might tip over. Arrange your lighting close to your work, but not in your way. Bare light bulbs can cause painful burns that may cause further injury by breaking when you move suddenly. Be sure nothing is underfoot.

Be sure no fuel is spilled. If your engine has a leaking fuel tank or line, immediately take the machine outside. Do not attempt to solder or repair a cracked fuel tank; always replace it. A disconnected battery should be removed from the machine, as should any sharp, rotating, or otherwise dangerous accessories. All of these precautions should become second nature, but never should they be taken for granted.

In your troubleshooting, you will often discover more than one problem. Try to isolate each problem and treat it separately, but bear in mind that one problem can cause another, either directly or indirectly. A bent crankshaft may result in a damaged half-moon key. In this case, repair the crankshaft first, then replace the half-moon key. Now Parp will describe recommended repair procedure outlines for some common engine failures. We'll begin with superficial repairs and end with a complete engine overhaul. Please bear in mind that these procedures have been generalized to apply to most small engines. Your engine may differ in some details, but the basic procedures should apply in most cases.

FUEL SYSTEM REPAIRS

In servicing small-engine fuel systems, remember that no manufacturer supplies unnecessary parts. It is quite possible for an inexperienced mechanic to make extensive fuel system repairs, even though you do not fully understand the function of each part. In truth, few professional mechanics fully understand the function of each part in a typical fuel system. But never assume that a part or line is unnecessary simply because you can't see what it does. A fuel system depends on high- and low-pressure fluctuations, partial vacuums, and gravity. All of these are invisible in an engine that is not operating. If you discover a tube, line, link, or fastener that is damaged, replace it as nearly as possible with an identical new part. Do not discard any part before replacing it and completing the repair.

Fuel Line Replacement

No fuel line will last as long as a good engine. Fuel lines often fail after 100 hours of use and once they fail, they should not be repaired except in an emergency. They should be replaced.

Fuel lines must be replaced with identical parts. The flow and pressure allowed in the new lines must be the same as in the old lines. There are two ways to do this. Either you can purchase the exact replacement fuel line parts sold or recommended by the manufacturer, or you can stock a supply of various fuel line sizes. If you are an occasional mechanic and own only one or two small-engine machines, the first is probably your best option. If you are a serious mechanic, are considering offering small-engine mechanical services to others, own many small-engine machines, or live far from a parts supply house, you should invest in your own supply of fuel lines of various sizes and types. In that case, you'll also need a good assortment of springs, clips, and other fasteners used in fuel systems. These can be purchased at any complete parts supply house or through mail-order services (see Appendix C for some mail-order sources).

Fuel lines are usually easy to remove and replace. Most often, they slip onto a metal fuel fitting designed to resist leaks, and are fastened on with a simple clip. To replace a line, unfasten the clips, and pull the line loose. Then press the new lines into place, and fasten with new clips. Avoid reusing old clips that have been on old fuel lines. If the lines were old enough to fail, the clips might soon follow.

Fuel lines may be manufactured of plastic, neoprene, aluminum, copper, or steel tubing.

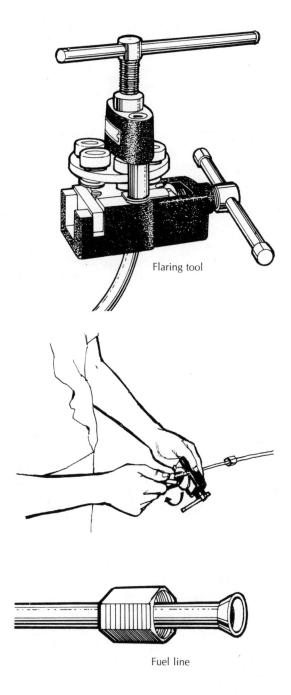

Flaring tool

Fuel line

Illus. 4–1—Flaring the End of a New Fuel Line

Most plastic and neoprene fuel lines are fastened with simple clips or clamps, as described above. Metal fuel lines are usually fastened with a threaded metal fitting, and the lines can be flared or unflared. If the fastener has a double nut (one nut that tightens down on another), always loosen the outside nut first when removing, and always tighten the inside nut first when replacing. Take care not to overtighten; the threads of soft metal fittings are easily stripped.

If the connection includes a metal fuel line flared at one end, you will need a flaring tool when replacing the line in order to duplicate the original flare. To flare a metal line, first slip the fastening nut or nuts over the line. Then flare the line to match the original flare and the flare seat of the nut as closely as possible. Use an automotive flaring tool or a small-engine flaring tool rather than a plumber's flaring tool. When you are sure the flare fits properly, simply tighten down the nut or nuts that connect the line (see Illus. 4–1).

Whenever you replace fuel lines, especially plastic or neoprene lines, be sure to check the vacuum line or lines, if any (from carburetor to crankcase or from crankcase to automatic choke), as they will probably need to be replaced also.

Replacing the in-tank fuel pick-up line on small engines can be tricky. There are many different designs and methods of installation. Most often, the line is fed from the direction of the carburetor into the fuel tank, and the weighted fuel filter and housing are added after the line is installed. If possible, check your owner's manual for details. Many manufacturers supply special instructions for installing the fuel pick-up line.

Some companies supply and specify a specially designed fuel pick-up line. These often have one end shaped to meet the filter housing and the other shaped to the carburetor or fuel pump inlet. Just be sure to note the configuration and proper installation of the original line as you remove it, and replace it the same way.

Fuel Pump Repair

As explained earlier, many small engines utilize a diaphragm fuel pump that usually is integral with the carburetor. This type of fuel pump is usually serviced or renewed with the carburetor, but it can be treated separately.

A diaphragm fuel pump normally is located under a side plate on the carburetor. You reach the diaphragm by removing the small screws, usually four of them, that hold the side plate to the body of the carburetor. To check the diaphragm, remove the screws and pull off the side plate. Then carefully pull the diaphragm away from the mounting studs. If you see obvious cracks or damage, or if the mounting holes are distorted, the diaphragm must be replaced. If you don't see obvious damage, hold the diaphragm

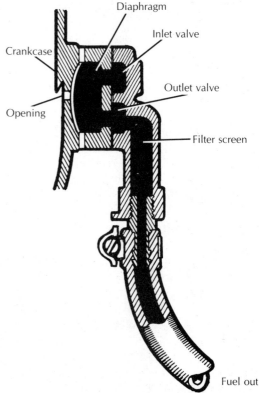

Illus. 4–2—Diaphragm-Type Fuel Pump

up to a bright light to check for tiny holes or cracks. Check the diaphragm for any kind of stretching or deformation.

Replacing the diaphragm is usually straightforward, as all manufacturers insure that the diaphragm fits over the mounting studs in one way only. Just be sure not to squeeze or stretch the diaphragm between the mounting studs. Carefully slip the diaphragm over all studs equally. The fit should be tight and exact. If it is not, you have the wrong diaphragm. Always renew any gaskets that are removed during carburetor or fuel pump service.

Obviously, a cracked side plate or a damaged mounting stud will prevent proper operation of the diaphragm. In this case, either the defective part or the entire carburetor must be replaced.

Unless your diaphragm fuel pump was defective when purchased, a failed fuel pump diaphragm usually indicates the need for a complete carburetor overhaul; in any case, it's a good idea.

A lever-type fuel pump is more complex and incorporates more moving parts that can break or wear. To check a mounted, lever-type fuel pump, pull off the fuel output line going to the carburetor. Then crank the engine. If fuel flows from the outlet, the pump is operating. If not, remove the pump from the engine. Check the diaphragm, lever, lever spring, and linkage. Except for a clogged valve, these are the most likely culprits. Replace any damaged or distorted parts, and be sure to reinstall the pump so that the cam lobe, or eccentric, properly engages the pump lever.

Carburetor Overhaul

As Parp says, you really don't have to fully understand a carburetor in order to overhaul it, provided you can obtain the proper overhaul and gasket kits, usually sold by the original carburetor manufacturer. These kits supply all the parts you'll need unless your carburetor body is damaged. In that case, buy a new carburetor, and install it with new gaskets.

It's important to clean the area around the carburetor before removing it from the machine. Otherwise, damaging dirt and debris can get into the engine.

Removing the carburetor rarely presents special difficulties. It is normally secured with 2 or 4 long bolts that simply unscrew with the proper wrench or screwdriver. Any brackets or other assemblies that might block access to some of the mounting screws or bolts must, of course, be removed first. In doing this, do not disassemble more than necessary. A careful study of your particular design will show you how to proceed.

When performing any carburetor service, use proper tools at all times. Do not use slip-joint pliers or wrong-size screwdrivers. A ¼-inch drive socket set is necessary in order to remove bolts and nuts safely without damaging the carburetor or parts. Before removing anything, be sure to memorize the original linkage and spring connections. A sketch is a big help. Note the exact connection of the governor spring, if applicable; installing the spring in the wrong hole will cause trouble. Work slowly and carefully, taking great care not to overtighten any nuts or adjustment screws. If you must leave a disassembled carburetor on your bench, cover it with a clean carton or otherwise protect it from dust and dirt.

When you've removed the carburetor, clean it and check carefully for cracks, dents, missing screws, and warped side plates. If the exterior seems sound, dismantle the carburetor methodically. If a diaphragm fuel pump is attached, start there. Remove the screws that hold the side plate over the fuel pump. Then remove the gasket and diaphragm, and place them in order on your bench. These soft parts will be discarded and replaced with new parts, but you'll want to arrange them in order as an aid to your memory during reassembly.

Now turn the carburetor over, and remove the top plate or metering diaphragm cover. Remove the diaphragm and gasket and set them down in the order removed. Now you can reach the parts under the gasket. These may include the valve nozzle, inlet needle, inlet control lever, retaining screws, and springs. Lay out each of these parts in order. Then unscrew both the high- and low-speed adjustment screws, and remove them with their springs.

Now examine the carburetor body carefully. Remove any remaining soft parts. Then submerge it in solvent, and let it soak for at least 30 minutes. While it's soaking, lay out your new parts from your overhaul kit. Place each new part beside the old part, and look for any discrepancies. When you're sure you've got the arrangement right, set the old parts aside. Do not discard them until the job is done.

When the carburetor body has soaked clean, remove it from the solvent, and brush it gently with your mechanic's toothbrush, then blow it dry with compressed air. Do not use any hard tools to clean jets or ports.

If your carburetor is a float type, check the float pin and needle valve for wear or damage. You may have to purchase these parts separately, as they do not always come in overhaul kits. If the float leaks or is distorted, it will have to be replaced. Do not attempt to repair a damaged, leaky, or fuel-soaked float.

Many manufacturers provide overhaul kits that are designed to renew several different carburetor models. In this case, you're apt to find extra parts or duplicates of parts in different sizes. Be sure to compare the new parts with the old parts in great detail to be sure you're using the correct replacement.

Table 4–1: Carburetor Troubleshooting Chart

Symptom	Possible Cause(s)
1. Engine runs rich, won't hold adjustment.	a. Hole in pump diaphragm. b. High lever setting.
2. Engine idles too fast or unevenly.	a. Adjust idle speed. b. Throttle plate damaged or incorrectly installed. c. Defective carburetor gasket.
3. Engine lacks power, runs very lean.	a. Dirty or damaged fuel-metering jet. b. Dirty idle or main system. c. Float set too low.
4. Engine won't hold adjustment, runs lean.	a. Damaged or deteriorating fuel-metering diaphragm. b. Damaged inlet connection gasket.
5. Fuel pump erratic or not functioning.	a. Damaged vacuum or impulse line. b. Impulse channel contaminated.
6. Carburetor floods constantly.	a. Loose or damaged welch plug. b. Damaged or dirty inlet needle. c. Float set too high.
7. Inadequate acceleration, engine runs lean.	a. Low lever settings. b. Damaged gaskets.

Now reassemble the carburetor in exactly the reverse order of disassembly. Pay attention to each part, and do not overtighten screws. To be sure you're renewing the part responsible for poor service, check Table 4–1, the Carburetor Troubleshooting Chart.

When the carburetor is reassembled, replace it on the engine using a new gasket. Check the throttle and choke linkages to be sure they're properly reconnected. Then proceed to adjust the carburetor for operation according to your owner's manual or Parp's instructions in Chapter Two. The engine should start right up.

Carburetor Float Adjustment

Many four-cycle engines used on relatively stable and level equipment incorporate a float mechanism in the carburetor to maintain the correct fuel level. Parp described a common float mechanism in Chapter Three. The procedure for overhauling a float-type carburetor is very similar to the procedure described above, and the overhaul kit supplied by the manufacturer includes detailed instructions for specific models.

If you are overhauling a float-type carburetor, you may need to replace a cracked, dented, or saturated float. In any case, you should check the adjustment of the float to be sure it is neither too high nor too low. If it is set too high, it will allow excessive fuel to flood the carburetor. If it is set too low, the engine will not receive adequate fuel and will stall easily. Also, the float hinge and hinge pin must work smoothly and easily. If these parts are damaged, they may catch or stick and prevent free movement of the float.

The float must ride perfectly level and must be set as close as possible to the manufacturer's specifications. With the float installed, turn the carburetor upside down so that gravity exerts an even force on the float. Measure the distance from the top of the edge of the float to the surface of the carburetor body, and set according to specifications. Measure all around the float to

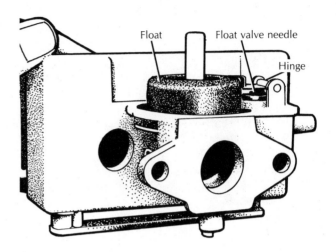

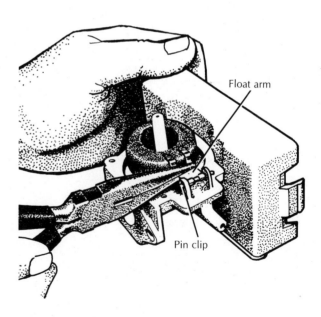

Illus. 4–3—Carburetor Float Adjustment

Measuring the position of the float on the carburetor (top), and using needle-nose pliers to adjust float position (bottom).

be sure it is level and, if necessary, remove the float and bend the float tab specified in the directions. Most rebuild kits include a float level gauge for this purpose. Do not press down on an installed float.

Whenever you adjust or replace a float, always check the inlet needle and valve, even if you are not performing a complete overhaul. The inlet needle is moved in and out by the movement of the float and rides, of course, in the inlet valve body. The needle must be clean and smooth. If it is gummed up or roughened by wear, it must be replaced. Likewise, check the valve body for wear; examine it carefully for a ridge or shoulder typically found after extensive service. If either the needle or the valve is damaged, replace both at the same time. Be sure to purchase the correct replacement parts. Compare the new and old parts for any discrepancies between them.

Automatic Choke Adjustment

After overhauling the carburetor, you should check the automatic choke, if there is one, and adjust as necessary. Make all automatic choke adjustments with the engine cold and the air filter removed.

If your choke is the most common type, mounted on the exhaust manifold, crank the engine slowly while changing the position of the choke lever until it is in the proper position. If the choke is set to allow too rich a fuel supply to the carburetor, the choke will close too far and open too slowly. If it is set to allow too lean a fuel supply, it will not close fully and will open too quickly. To change the setting, loosen the adjustment screw, and reposition the adjustment bracket. If the setting is too rich, move the bracket up; if it's too lean, move the bracket down. Take care not to overadjust. Then retighten the adjustment screw, and replace the air filter.

If your automatic choke is a combination electric-thermostatic choke, things get a little more complicated. Find the choke arm leading to the choke linkage. As you move this arm, a hole in the choke shaft will come into alignment with a slot nearby. Line up the hole and the slot, and insert a straight piece of metal rod so that the rod enters the small notch in the choke base inside the manifold. Then loosen the retaining bolt near the shaft, and move the choke arm until the choke valve is closed. Finally, tighten the retaining bolt, and remove the steel rod.

Electric Choke Adjustment

An electric choke mounted directly on the carburetor is very similar to the typical automobile choke. To adjust this type of choke, loosen the lockscrews at the side of the choke cover. To gain a richer fuel mixture, turn the *inside* section of the thermostat clockwise; to make a leaner mixture, turn it the other way. Retighten the lockscrews before testing, and readjust as necessary.

Briggs & Stratton Automatic Choke Carburetor Adjustments

The Briggs & Stratton automatic choke carburetors differ sufficiently from other carburetors to justify a separate set of adjustment instructions. These carburetors are commonly found on many kinds of backyard machinery, especially some older appliances, so Parp expects this information will be useful to many operators and owners of used equipment powered by Briggs engines.

To properly adjust Briggs carburetors, first start the engine and allow it to reach a normal operating temperature without overheating. If the engine will not start due to incorrect carburetor settings, close the needle valve by turning it clockwise just until it seats. Do not exert force. Then open the needle valve 1½ turns counterclockwise. Now proceed with the following instructions:

1. Set operating control so that engine runs at normal operating speed.
2. Turn needle valve clockwise until engine begins to slow from the lean fuel mixture.
3. Turn needle valve counterclockwise until the engine begins to choke from the fuel-rich mixture.
4. Turn needle valve clockwise again, and set midway between rich and lean. Then adjust slightly to the rich side.
5. Set operating control on SLOW. Set idle adjustment screw to a fast idle.
6. Check acceleration by moving control from SLOW to FAST. If the engine stalls or begins to stall, either increase the idle speed as necessary or turn the needle valve to allow a slightly richer mixture, or do both.
7. If engine floods, set control on STOP and crank engine several times; this will clear excess fuel. Now set control on FAST and start engine. If flooding continues, turn needle valve clockwise $1/8$ turn. If that's not enough, try another $1/8$ turn.

Note: Mowers powered by Briggs engines equipped with automatic chokes may require a leaner setting in order to avoid flooding during warm engine starts.

Briggs & Stratton Automatic Choke Repair

A typical Briggs & Stratton automatic choke is activated by the low pressure created during the intake stroke of the engine. This is the type of choke that also acts as an accelerator pump as engine speed decreases under a heavy load. To inspect the Briggs automatic choke for proper operation, remove the air cleaner and replace the mounting stud. With the engine cold, look into the carburetor to be sure the choke valve is fully closed. Then place the speed control in the STOP position, and crank the engine. The choke valve should open and close smoothly.

To reach the typical Briggs automatic choke mechanism for repairs, remove the carburetor and fuel tank from the engine, then remove the choke link cover and disconnect the choke shaft. Separate the carburetor from the top of the fuel tank, taking care not to damage the automatic choke diaphragm. If the diaphragm is not damaged or worn out, it can be reused.

The choke spring under the diaphragm must be the specified length. If possible, check the manufacturer's literature to determine the correct spring length. If you are unsure, or if the spring or diaphragm is damaged, replace both. The spring on a Briggs Pulsa-Jet carburetor should be $1\frac{1}{8}$ inches long. The Briggs Vacu-Jet spring specification is $\frac{15}{16}$ inch, and the model number 110900 spring should be $1\frac{5}{16}$ inches long. The acceptable tolerance is roughly plus $\frac{1}{16}$ inch. If a spring has stretched much more than this, it should be replaced along with the diaphragm. In a real emergency, you can sometimes get by with cutting out a portion of the spring. In that case, leave the spring approximately $\frac{1}{32}$ inch longer than specified.

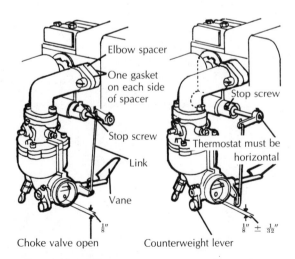

Choke valve open   Counterweight lever

Illus. 4–4—Briggs & Stratton Automatic Choke Arrangement

In the Briggs design the diaphragm seal between the carburetor and the tank top is critical. This seal depends on a machined surface on the tank top. To be sure this surface is perfectly flat, use a straightedge and a .002-inch feeler gauge. Hold the straightedge flat on the machined surface, and attempt to insert the feeler gauge. If the feeler gauge fits anywhere between the straightedge and the surface, the entire tank must be replaced. This is a fairly common condition on older appliances.

To replace the spring and diaphragm, first attach the spring to the diaphragm. Be careful not to damage or distort either part; both are quite delicate. Now place the diaphragm on the tank surface with the spring installed in the spring pocket. Next, place the carburetor on the dia-phragm, and get the mounting screws aligned and started. Close the choke valve, and hook the choke link into the choke shaft.

The Briggs diaphragm must be preloaded. To preload it, first tighten the carburetor mounting screws, being sure that the diaphragm remains aligned and the choke link is correctly hooked. Now open the choke plate fully, then return to a normal position. It should close completely. If not, the spring has probably come out of position, either relative to the diaphragm or to the spring pocket in the tank surface.

Governor Control Spring Replacement

This information also applies only to Briggs & Stratton engines, especially models numbered in the 92500 and 92900 series. Replacing the

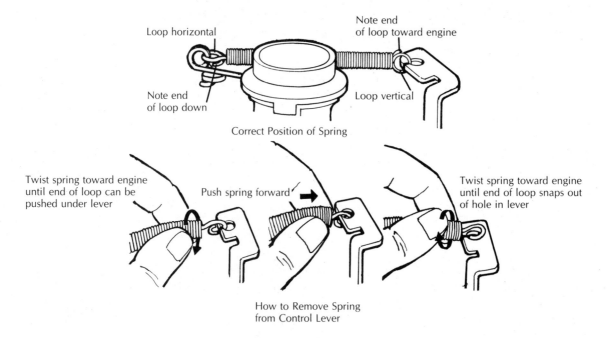

Loop horizontal

Note end
of loop toward engine

Note end
of loop down

Loop vertical

Correct Position of Spring

Twist spring toward engine
until end of loop can be
pushed under lever

Push spring forward

Twist spring toward engine
until end of loop snaps out
of hole in lever

How to Remove Spring
from Control Lever

**Illus. 4–5—Briggs & Stratton Governor
Control Spring**

The correct position of the spring (top), and
removing the spring from the control lever
(bottom).

governor control spring on these models is one of the most common jobs encountered by the owner of Briggs-powered equipment.

Before you remove the old spring, take careful note of its proper position and installation. One end of the spring is attached to a link with the spring loop horizontal and the end of the spring loop pointing down. The other end is attached to a lever with the spring loop straight up and down and the end of the spring loop pointing toward the engine.

To remove the spring, twist the lever end until you can push the point of the loop under the lever. With the loop pushed under the lever as far as possible, turn the spring in the direction of the engine until the loop pops up through the hole in the lever. Now lift the spring, and twist it counterclockwise until you can pull it loose from the link.

Now you can install the new spring. Attach the link end first, and hold the link still while you attach the loop. With the loop point to the left, insert it into the eyelet of the link. Then twist the spring clockwise until properly attached. Now carefully bring the other end of the spring toward the lever. Turn it roughly ¾ turn so that the loop point is up and aimed toward you with the loop horizontal. Push the loop over the lever, and insert the point into the hole. A clockwise twist of the spring will snap the loop into position. The lever end of the spring should now be vertical and the link end horizontal.

Air-Vane Governor Overhaul

The typical air-vane governor is mechanically the simplest governor in use. Unless the vane itself is broken (a very rare occurrence) the entire mechanism can be overhauled by replacing the spring and linkage. There are several variations, but there is always one link between the vane and the throttle control lever, and one spring between the governor adjustment mechanism and the air-vane link. Be sure to purchase identical replacement parts, and install them exactly as in the original. Unless you have altered the factory settings, the installation of a new link and spring set will restore the governor to the original specifications, and no further adjustment will be necessary.

IGNITION SYSTEM REPAIRS

For Parp's tips on general ignition maintenance, particularly those items regarding spark plugs, ignition cables, flywheel removal, and tune-up procedures, see Chapters Two and Three. These basic items should be part of your routine maintenance; Parp does not consider them to be repairs. Also, for ignition tips and specific remarks for the many machines discussed in subsequent chapters, see Index.

Ignition problems are often difficult to diagnose. One general rule applies to ignition parts that may not be functioning properly: when in doubt, replace. This may seem a wasteful approach, but most parts are relatively inexpensive, and replacing a suspect ignition cable may save many hours of machine downtime.

In most cases, ignition system repairs will go more smoothly if you remove the engine from the machine. There are certain obvious exceptions, however. Chain saws are best left in one piece, generally, except for removing the cutting attachment. Rotary mowers should be disassembled as little as possible. Since the ignition systems of rotary mowers are located on top of the machine, it is not necessary or advisable to remove the engine for most ignition repairs.

Incidentally, here's an important tip regarding most rotary mowers: the flywheels on these machines are far lighter than those on most other machines. Much of the inertia required to keep the engine operating is supplied by the mower blade. Consequently, these machines usually will not start, and certainly will not operate properly, unless the mower blade is securely mounted. Since this is the case, you must exercise extreme caution during service, especially when test starts, or cranks, are necessary. You also should know that turning or spinning the blade of a rotary mower turns the engine over and can cause unexpected ignition, a very hazardous situation. The basic rule on rotary mower repairs is to remove the spark plug wire before attempting anything else.

Emergency Flywheel Repair

You live 300 miles northwest of Nowhere, and you depend on your generator, pump, or chain saw for everyday comforts or necessities. The bush pilot brought in your mail yesterday, and the ignition parts you wisely ordered long in advance have finally arrived, so you are now tuning up your machine. But you just broke a flywheel fin while attempting to pry it off the crankshaft. You know that if you run the machine in this condition the engine will soon be destroyed by vibration. But you can't wait six months for a new flywheel. Your only hope is this: locate the flywheel fin *directly opposite* the one you just broke and attempt to break it off to match. Then write out your order for the new flywheel, and use the machine as little as possible. Also, order the proper tool or tools for removing the flywheel from that particular engine. A hand impact tool, described in Chapter Two, a closed-end shock nut, and various pullers and holders are well worth the homesteader's investment.

Emergency Magneto Repair

You're performing a tune-up on a much-needed piece of equipment and have noticed that the insulation on the magneto coil is damaged. If you wish to use the machine and cannot immediately obtain a replacement coil, you can carefully cover the bared wires with a thin layer of plastic electrical tape. Do not apply a thick layer, which might interfere with the function of the ignition. In a real emergency, separated

laminations can sometimes be glued together, but the only real remedy is replacement.

Briggs & Stratton Breaker Point Plunger and Bushing

Many owners of Briggs & Stratton four-cycle engines experience ignition failures caused by oil on the breaker points or plate. This is due to the plunger system peculiar to certain widely used Briggs engines. When the plunger hole becomes worn, crankcase oil leaks past the plunger and splashes onto the points assembly.

If you own one or more Briggs engines and have to make repairs yourself, you should invest in the special tools Briggs supplies for the job. You'll need a plug gauge, Briggs part number 19055; a reamer, number 19056; a bushing driver, number 19057; and a finish reamer, number 19058.

To check the plunger hole for excessive wear, loosen the breaker points assembly screw just enough to shift the assembly out of the way. Then pull out the plunger and insert the flat end of the 19055 plug gauge. If you can slide it into the hole ¼ inch or more, you need to install a special bushing, or sleeve, to seal the oil leak.

While you have the plunger removed, you should also check it for wear. If it is .870 inch or less in length, you need to replace it as well. This is quite common in engines that have been in service for a considerable period of time. Purchase the repair bushing and replacement plunger at any Briggs parts supplier, along with the special tools listed above.

Installing the bushing itself is not difficult, but it does require removing the points assembly, armature, and crankshaft. With this disassembly completed, ream the plunger hole smooth with tool number 19056. Be sure the reamer is perfectly in line. A mistake made here is a disaster.

With the hole reamed, install the bushing (Briggs part number 23513) using the bushing

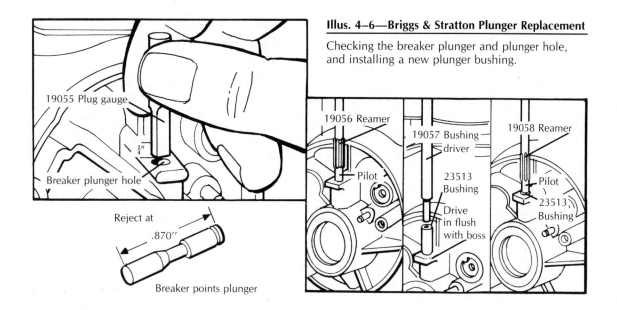

Illus. 4–6—Briggs & Stratton Plunger Replacement

Checking the breaker plunger and plunger hole, and installing a new plunger bushing.

driver, number 19057. Be sure to install the bushing fully so that it is perfectly flush across the top. Then use tool number 19058 to smooth out the inside of the bushing. Take great care to remove any chips, dirt, or debris. Now install the plunger with the groove facing up. There is only one correct installation. If the plunger is not arranged correctly, it will still allow oil to leak past and foul the breaker assembly.

Starter Belt Replacement

Many four-cycle engines with electric starter motors use a belt system similar to the fan belt in an automobile. These parts are susceptible to wear and to damage caused by dirt, oil, grease, salty air, and humidity. Check belts for damage after every 25 hours of use. It's best to replace these belts when wear or damage becomes evident. A weak belt may break just when you need it most, especially on a generator.

To expose the belt, first remove the shroud or guard covering the area. Then loosen the starter mounting bolts enough to push the starter toward the engine, and remove the slackened belt. Some systems, especially Briggs & Stratton, use two belts, and both belts must be removed and replaced at the same time, even if only one belt shows wear. Do not force the old belts off or the new belts on. Be sure to move the starter motor far enough toward the engine to loosen the belt or belts sufficiently.

Now simply install the new belt, which should be a replacement belt supplied by the original manufacturer. With the new belt or belts in place, pull the starter back to create adequate tension, but do not set it too tight. Briggs specifies a pressure of 30 pounds applied to the upper pulley, but you can translate that into ¼ inch of give, or slack, when you press down in the middle of the belt. Now tighten the mounting bolts, and replace the belt guard. Be sure all screws and bolts are tight, as the vibration in this area is enough to move a loose fastener.

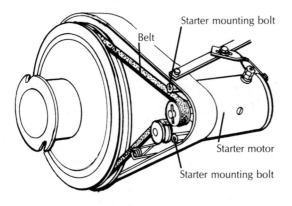

Illus. 4–7—Briggs & Stratton Starter Belt Replacement

Starter mounting bolt
Belt
Starter motor
Starter mounting bolt

Flywheel Ignition Ring Gear Replacement

Many four-cycle engines with electric gear starters use a ring gear that is attached to the flywheel. This gear is engaged by the starter motor to crank the engine. The ring gear is susceptible to wear and tear and is not difficult to replace.

In the original factory configuration, the ring gear is riveted to the flywheel. After ordering the replacement gear, check it for discrepancies against the original. The only significant difference should be the method of fastening. The replacement gear should be supplied with four flathead screws and locknuts.

To remove the old gear, use a ³/₁₆-inch bit to drill out the rivets. Be sure to drill into the exact center of each rivet. It helps to use a center punch to mark the center of the rivet. Be certain to remove any chips from the holes after drilling.

Now align the new gear with the drilled-out holes. Fasten it very securely with the screws and locknuts by tightening in sequence, gradually. Do not overtighten.

FUNDAMENTALS OF MAJOR REPAIRS

Most major repairs should be performed by an authorized mechanic.* There are three reasons for this: (1) the difficulty of these procedures; (2) the necessity for special tools; and (3) the danger involved. Whenever you perform major repairs, the danger of various kinds of accidents increases considerably. When you exert the kinds of pressure needed to loosen stubborn fasteners or reassemble difficult fits, a slip can easily result in a serious injury. Parp pleads for caution and hereby states that all safety considerations or precautions are well worth following.

Many tools used in engine overhaul procedures are dangerous in themselves. Aside from the clear dangers from screwdrivers and so forth, you will probably find it necessary to use some form of applied heat to loosen fasteners. Drill presses, arbor presses, and testing instruments present other dangers. Just proceed with caution, says Parp, and if a procedure is beyond your ability, don't attempt it. Even the most expensive small-engine shops are cheaper than hospital bills.

Be sure you are adequately tooled for any job you wish to tackle. Many expert mechanics make or modify their own tools, but generally this comes with fairly extensive experience. No one really needs a precision lapping tool, as Parp will soon reveal, but most other tools are invaluable for major engine repairs. Certainly a torque wrench is a must, as are the correct pullers, fitters, gauges, and wrenches for specific jobs. For many major jobs, you should have a heat tool, a micrometer, a cylinder hone, a piston ring compressor, and an arbor press. (Parp

*Note: Parp has not mentioned the exhaust system in this chapter. Basic exhaust system maintenance and service procedures are covered in Chapter Two. Other tips and procedures appear in subsequent chapters on specific types of machinery. Please check Index.

says not knowing the functions of these tools is another indication that you shouldn't be attempting major repairs.) When you find that you don't have the proper tools required for a certain job, don't proceed. Some books and some mechanics may suggest otherwise; some engines will end up in the parts barrel prematurely.

Before you begin any complex procedure, make every effort to diagnose the problem as closely as possible. Even with a complete troubleshooting chart and informed testing, it often pays to get a professional opinion. Many mechanics are willing to diagnose for a small fee. This can save much time and effort, especially if the pro finds a simple solution to what you thought was a major problem.

If you suspect that your engine has seized and requires a major overhaul, begin your troubleshooting with a simple crankshaft check. Perform this by removing the work attachment and attempting to turn the crankshaft by hand. If it fails to turn, check the flywheel for damage that may be restricting the crank. If you can turn the crankshaft, the engine has not seized, and you should begin your troubleshooting procedure by attempting to start the engine. If the crank does not turn, do not attempt to start or turn the engine over. Instead, proceed with a major overhaul, or pay a visit to your friendly junk dealer.

General Tips

Before taking anything apart, be sure that your problem is not simply a loose, incorrectly assembled, or out-of-adjustment work-performing attachment. If possible, remove the engine from the appliance for testing.

By all means, take a very close look before disassembling anything. Check for loose fasteners, a cracked or warped cylinder head, twisted covers that may interfere with the engine, contamination from spilled fuel, grease, oil or dirt, bent linkages, and other obvious and superficial

problems that can seem much more significant than they really are. Every mechanic has tales of unneeded overhauls.

Again, be sure the engine is as clean as you can get it before beginning any repairs. Clean the air cleaning system, the exterior of the carburetor, the fuel tank, shrouds, the spark plug, and ignition parts.

Warning: Disconnect the spark plug cable from the spark plug *before* beginning any repair work. When possible, leave the spark plug in place to keep dirt out of the cylinder. When necessary, be sure to reconnect the ignition cable before testing.

Many engine blocks are constructed of very soft metals, such as aluminum or magnesium. Even cast iron may be much softer than you might expect. Any threads or other fits are easily damaged, usually by overtightening or by a forceful slip while attempting to remove a part. Be careful during disassembly, and follow your manufacturer's torque specifications during reassembly whenever possible.

Heat Tools

Heat provided by a heat gun, a lamp, a crayon, or other tool is frequently required during major service. A judicious application of heat expands soft metal enough to be a great help in removing fasteners and certain fits called heat, or shrink, fits. Heat fits often require the expansion of an outer part in order to install an inner part. Parp uses an electric heat lamp (not for suntanning) that he finds indispensable for many procedures, from simple to elaborate. It cost $10 and is ten years old.

Types of Fits

Other fits are often made easier with heat even when it is not called for by the manufacturer. Push fits, slide fits, and press fits are often eased by heat. Be careful, of course, not to touch hot metal with your bare hands. Most slide fits work very easily without heat. A tap fit usually requires a soft hammer and no heat. Heat is often used to install bearings, pins, and other parts.

Replacing Gaskets

Unless it is specifically not recommended, plan to replace any gasket you remove during service. But, remember that no gasket can correct a part or fit that is defective because of wear, warping, dirt, or incorrect assembly. Any damaged surface must be repaired before installing a new gasket and reassembling the part. Likewise, pieces of old gasket, cement, or gasket sealer must be removed completely. This is a common service failure that often results in a severely damaged engine or, at best, one that doesn't operate perfectly.

Use a sealer or gasket compound only where it was used by the original manufacturer. When you use a sealer, use only a thin coat, applying it to both surfaces. Be sure you don't smear compound on other parts.

Replacing O-Rings

Neoprene O-rings are seals or collars that prevent fluid leaks, and they wear out. Except in a real backwoods emergency, always renew any O-rings you remove during service. These O-rings are very inexpensive and always outlast metal parts—unless they are removed. You can't remove an O-ring without distorting it beyond tolerance.

Parp says that all home mechanics who go further in their repairs than tune-ups need a complete supply of assorted O-rings. These assortments are inexpensive, come in their own neat file boxes, and are readily available at most parts dealers and mail-order houses. Always replace O-rings with the same size as the original. An O-ring tool is often helpful and occasionally required for installation.

Crankcase Seals

As with O-rings and gaskets, it is practically impossible to remove a seal without damaging it beyond tolerance. Crankcase seals prevent leaks, both as a sealant between the two halves of the case and also whenever a rotating part of the engine, such as the crankshaft, moves through a stationary part. Usually, this latter type of seal consists of a part called a wiper that fits into a sleeve. The seal sleeve fits tightly (a press fit, usually) into the stationary part and is sealed by the wiper. A spring device or fastener holds the wiper agains the rotating part. Be sure to use a seal identical to the original, unless otherwise specified by the manufacturer, and always install the seal in the original manner and direction. Many seals have subtle differences between one side and the other, and these differences usually determine the proper direction of installation. A seal-inserting tool is usually required, but a pipe or tube of the same

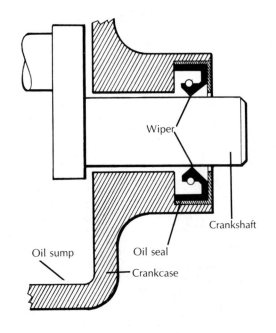

Illus. 4—8—Crankcase Seal Configuration

diameter, or sometimes a hockey puck, and a hammer for force can be substituted occasionally.

Damaged Threads

As Parp just said, it's easy to damage threads in soft metal parts and engines. Every mechanic encounters this problem, and the remedy is almost universal: use a Heli-Coil thread repair kit. These kits are available with full instructions at most parts supply houses. Parp says a Heli-Coil kit is the only really acceptable remedy for damaged threads in small engines.

Bearings

Principal bearings for reducing friction are found in the crankshaft, drive shaft, camshaft, starter mechanism, and clutch mounting. Most types of bearings used in small engines may be reused, provided they are not damaged or worn beyond tolerance. There are several types of bearings in common use, and a full description here would not be very useful. Many bearings are best removed by using heat to expand the surrounding metal. This is especially true of crankcase bearings.

If a bearing is distorted out of round, unevenly worn, or if its needles or balls are damaged or missing, it must be replaced. Some bearings are manufactured of absorbent materials designed to provide permanent lubrication. Check these bearings very carefully. Before installing or reinstalling, soak the bearing overnight in a fine oil. Check each bearing sleeve for oil holes, which must align with oil holes in the bearing journal. Be sure to replace any bearing with an identical new bearing, and in the original manner. Check bearings to be sure that they move freely after installation.

Renewing Valves

The job of renewing valves is one that stymies many home mechanics unnecessarily. On the other hand, it really is not a job for anyone who is completely inexperienced with mechan-

ical repairs. If, however, you routinely do your own small-engine repairs, you can certainly handle a valve job, provided you have the proper tools. In addition to the standard socket wrench sets, feeler gauges, and slot and Phillips screwdrivers, you should invest in a torque wrench, a valve-lapping tool, a special cutter for resurfacing the valve seats, and a valve spring compressor. A suction-cup toy arrow can be used for a lapping tool, but the proper tool is an inexpensive item. You'll also need some valve grinding compound and a wire brush, preferably one that fits your electric drill.

Chapter Three describes the function of the valves in a four-cycle engine. These valves, especially the exhaust valve, are susceptible to heat plus various pressures and contaminants, especially carbon from exhaust wastes. Normal wear can cause the valves and valve seats to leak, which results in a loss of compression of the fuel/air mixture in the cylinder and, thereby, causes poor performance.

As Parp frequently states, dirt is an engine's worst enemy. Carbon is just about the worst kind of dirt and can cause extensive damage unless it is removed in time. Excessive carbon deposits in the combustion chamber cause the engine to overheat and can eventually cause pinging in the incorrect ignition of the vaporized fuel. Pinging is very hard on the piston, connecting rod, and crankshaft, and it can cause early failure of these parts in addition to warping the cylinder head. Even a slight carbon problem can result in an overheated engine if pinging occurs or if the valves fail to seat properly.

We're actually going to cover two related jobs here. Since we must remove the cylinder head in order to reach the valves, we also can check it for warpage and replace the cylinder head gasket.

Cylinder Head and Gasket

There are three normal causes of compression loss in small engines. They are: (1) leaks at the cylinder head or gasket; (2) sticking or leaking valves; (3) worn piston rings. We will correct the first two problems during the valve job. If you also suspect your piston rings, you should perform a complete engine overhaul, or have one performed by a professional mechanic.

To remove the cylinder head, simply remove the fasteners that hold it. In many cases, a cylinder head is covered by a shield that also must be removed. Keep all cylinder fasteners in order, because they must be replaced exactly as they were removed. The bolts vary in length for good reason, and they are not interchangeable. If you are replacing the bolts, match the new to the old before reassembling.

With the fasteners removed, lift off the cylinder head. If it sticks, pull harder. Do not insert a screwdriver into the gasket, and do not pry off the cylinder head. If you do, damage will result.

Do not plan to reuse the cylinder head gasket. It must be renewed after being removed.

Now check the cylinder head for chips, cracks, or warpage. Use a true straightedge, laid across the flat surfaces of the head, and a .003-inch feeler gauge. If you can fit the gauge in anywhere between the straightedge and the flat surfaces of the head, the head should be machined flat. Most likely you'll take or send the head to a shop for this work, but since you've done the removal job, the machining itself won't cost much and won't take long. In an emergency, you can try replacing the gasket with two new gaskets, or even one old and one new. It may hold some compression for a while.

With the cylinder head removed, turn the crank until the piston reaches the bottom of its stroke. Check the cylinder for damage caused by dirt, carbon buildup due to long use, or other contaminants. This damage usually takes the form of vertical scratches or scores, a hard carbon ridge at the top of the cylinder, or both. Handling either of these conditions is definitely a professional shop job, and you'll have to decide whether you want to try to use the engine as is for a while

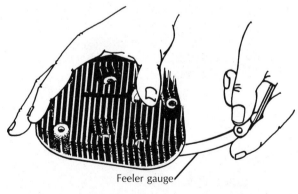

Illus. 4–9—Cylinder Head Configuration

After it is removed from the engine (left), the cylinder head should be tested to assure that it is perfectly flat (right).

Cylinder head

Gasket

Cylinder block

Cylinder

Crankcase

Feeler gauge

longer or incur the expense of either having the ridge reamed smooth or having the cylinder re-bored and an oversize piston installed to fit the new bore. (Many manufacturers do offer sleeves to fit the rebored cylinder so that you can use the originally specified size of piston. You will need to use a new piston with the new sleeve, though.)

If you are simply replacing the cylinder head gasket and will not proceed with the valve job described below, finish by scraping any carbon from the combustion chamber, clean everything carefully, and install the new head gasket and cylinder head shield, if supplied. Then proceed to reinstall the cylinder head according to the instructions under Cylinder Head Reassembly, found later in this chapter.

Valve Job

Many engines, including Briggs & Stratton engines, have a breather hose connected to the valve cover. To remove the valve cover, first disconnect the breather hose. Then remove the fasteners holding the valve cover. Briggs & Stratton models also use a breather disk valve, built into the valve cover. You should check this valve with a wire .040-inch spark plug gauge to be sure it is still functioning. Without applying force,

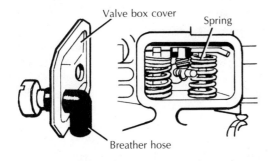

Illus. 4–10—Valve Job: Removing the Crankcase Breather Hose and Valve Box Cover

the gauge should not fit between the disk valve and the inside of the valve cover. If there is a gap of .040 inch or more, the cover and disk valve should be replaced. If possible, check your manufacturer's specifications.

Now you can see the valves and valve lifters. (To check the valve clearance, see Index.) If you're going to do the valve job, skip the clearance check for now, and proceed to remove the valve springs and retainers. Most small engines use a key-type retainer to hold the valve spring that can be removed without a compressor. To do so, insert a large screwdriver under the spring, and pry it up until you can turn the retainer with your other hand. When it is turned so that the valve stem is inside the largest part of the keyhole, withdraw the screwdriver, and the whole thing will come apart. Now just lift the valve out.

Other valve spring retaining devices generally require the use of a valve spring compressor, a relatively inexpensive tool that certainly will pay for itself, especially if you run several four-cycle engines. Check your parts supplier for the best tool for your engines. Also, although many retainers are easy to remove without a valve spring compressor, this tool makes reassembly much easier, and, in some cases, the home mechanic may find it close to impossible to reinstall valve assemblies without a compressor.

Use the valve spring compressor to compress each spring in turn. If the retainer is held by a simple pin, pull it straight out with a pair of pliers. If it's held by a two-part collar arrangement, insert a knife blade and pry the two halves apart—this will do no damage, and any unbroken retainer can be reused. New designs for both valve springs and retainers are predicted for the near future, and one aspect of these new designs is supposed to be ease of removal and service. If you encounter a new or unusual design, take time to examine it carefully, and draw any required diagrams before proceeding.

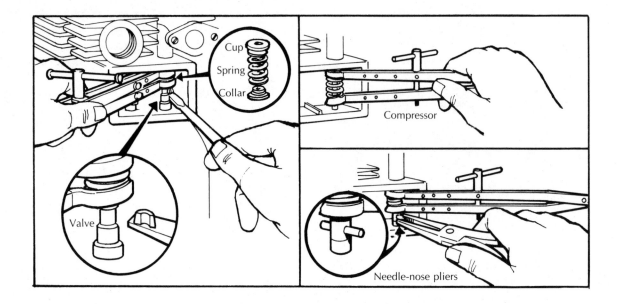

Illus. 4–11—Valve Job: Removing Valve Springs

A valve spring compressor makes spring removal easier.

Make certain any valve you remove goes back into the same hole it came out of unless you are installing a new valve. If you're working on a multi-cylinder engine, make a rack by punching holes in a strip of cardboard or boring holes in a strip of wood—an old yardstick makes a fine valve rack. Number the holes to correspond with the valves, and number each valve with chalk to avoid mix-ups.

Now, you have your valves, valve springs, and retainers laid out on your bench or in your valve rack. First, inspect each part for serious and obvious damage such as cracks, chips, or prior incorrect service. Valve springs should be straight. If they seem weak, replace them. If it's a used machine, be sure no one has previously ground the valve stems. If their stems have been ground, the valves should be replaced. If you discover this or any other significant damage, you'll have to install new valves. Dip all parts

in solvent to remove some of the grease and carbon. If a valve face is badly pockmarked, you can either replace it or have it resurfaced by a shop. If the edges of a valve or its contact area are chewed up, replace it. If in doubt, renew. Valves are not very expensive parts.

Now check the valve guides by inserting each valve. Hold the valve by the head with the stem inserted almost all the way. If you can move the valves from side to side more than a hair or two, the valve guides are worn, and you'll now need the services of a professional shop and special equipment to replace or recondition the guides.

Inspect the valve seats now. If they are in very bad shape, they should be replaced—another job for the shop, not for us.

Assuming your valves and valve seats are in reasonably good shape—perhaps badly carboned and slightly pockmarked, but with no severe damage to contact faces—you can now proceed to lap the valves and valve seats. Of course, this also must be done if you are installing new valves.

First, clean all parts as much as possible with solvent. Clean all exposed areas of the engine interior as well, including the piston head and upper cylinder. Don't use much solvent here, and don't do anything that may scratch or mar the cylinder. Remove carbon deposits from the piston with a flat scraping tool, but again be careful not to damage the surface itself. Clean the valves with a wire brush attached to your electric drill. If possible, check your manufacturer's specifications for the correct angle of valve faces and seats, and valve seat width. If your engine parts are far off the specifications, you'll need to have the job finished by a shop.

After all parts are cleaned and all springs and retainers are checked (and replaced if necessary), you're ready to restore the engine to service. Lapping valves involves a simple operation intended to mate the new, refinished, or cleaned valves perfectly to new or restored valve seats (that is, restored or replaced by your authorized mechanic or machine shop). This must be done to insure a completely gastight fit.

Use a fine lapping or grinding compound and a lapping tool. As Parp said earlier, you can use a suction-cup toy arrow. You'll have to turn it by hand, but the compound does most of the real work, so it doesn't make that much difference.

Spread a thin coat of the compound on the cleaned valve face, and place the valve in its proper valve guide without, of course, the spring and retainer. Some manufacturers supply a special lapping tool that fits into a slot in the valve itself. In the absence of this arrangement, attach the suction cup of your lapping tool to the top of the valve, and use this to turn the valve around in one direction and back again. Reposition the valve, and repeat several times. Do not exert much force; the compound will grind the seat

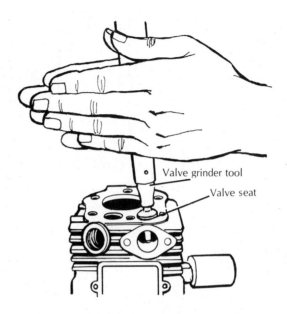

Valve grinder tool
Valve seat

Illus. 4–12—Lapping Valves

and face true in just a few minutes. Then remove the valve and use a rag dipped in a little solvent to wipe the compound and shavings off both the valve and the seat. Repeat with the second valve. Valves and seats should now mate perfectly.

Reassemble the valve springs, retainers, and valves just the way you removed them. You'll be glad, now, that you invested in the valve spring compressor, especially if you have no help. Be sure springs and retainers are fully installed and that everything is seated correctly. If you're not sure, start over until it's right.

Note that the intake valve is usually slightly larger than the exhaust valve and that the springs may differ as well. Be sure to install the correct spring with each valve and to install the correct valve in each guide.

If the retainer is held by a pin or a collar, place the valve spring and the retainer in your valve spring compressor, and compress until the spring is solid. Then set the spring and retainer into the valve chamber, and drop the valve into

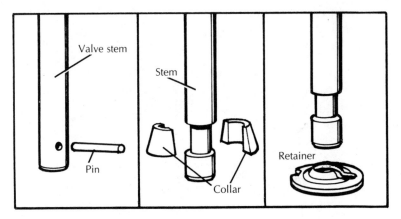

Illus. 4–13—Valve Spring Retainers

place with the stem through the retainer. Hold the valve down and the spring up while you replace the pin or insert the collar halves. Then lower the spring into place and remove the compressor.

If the retainer is the one-piece key type, place it with the spring into the valve chamber, and hold it with the large part of the hole toward the front of the chamber. Insert the compressed spring and its retainer into the valve chamber so that the valve, in place, will drop into the large hole. Now use the compressor to arrange the assembly so that the valve stem shoulder fits into the small area of the keyhole. Release the spring and withdraw the compressor.

Cylinder Head Reassembly

Now renew the cylinder head gasket and cylinder head shield, if used. Replace the cylinder head and bolts, being sure you have the right bolts in the right places. Use antiseize compound on the head, bolts, gaskets and mated surfaces to make future disassembly easier. **Note:** All manufacturers specify torque readings for cylinder head fasteners, as well as a correct sequence for tightening the bolts. If possible, use an accurate torque wrench and follow your

manufacturer's specifications for pressure and sequence. If this is not possible, first tighten the top and bottom bolts by hand, then the others. Then use a socket wrench and tighten each bolt alternately, starting with the top, followed by the bottom, then one on the right, one on the left, and so on. Your object is to tighten the head and compress the gasket evenly all around. Do not overtighten, but be sure all bolts are adequately secured to prevent loosening or a leak at the gasket. If you use a torque wrench but don't know the specifications, try 140 pounds per square inch (psi). If that seems inadequate, try 165 psi.

Checking Compression

Briggs & Stratton does not specify compression figures for its small engines. They say that accurate readings are achieved only with very specialized equipment and that the hand test for compression is an adequate indication. To perform this test on any engine, a Briggs & Stratton engine or otherwise, simply spin the flywheel by hand, counterclockwise against the compression stroke. If the flywheel rebounds sharply, the engine has sufficient compression. If there is little or no rebound, try spinning the flywheel several times in the opposite direction. If there still is no rebound, the engine has poor compression.

If you have a compression gauge and compression figures for your engine, test according to the instructions that come with the gauge. If compression has dropped much more than 10 percent, it's likely that your valves, cylinder, piston, rings, or gaskets are faulty.

Valve Seat Inserts

Some companies equip some engines with removable valve seats that can be replaced with inexpensive inserts. Briggs & Stratton's cast-iron cylinder engines are equipped with a removable seat on the exhaust side only. Many aluminum cylinder models have removable seats for both the exhaust and the intake valves.

Removing valve seats on engines so equipped involves using a seat-puller supplied by the original manufacturer. This tool usually has a shaped, screw-on nut that you insert below the valve seat. A bolt passes up through the seat into the puller body. As you tighten down on the bolt, the shaped nut pulls the valve seat up out of place. **Note:** You must use the correct puller for your brand of engine and the correctly shaped nut for the particular model.

With the old seat removed, you now need another special tool to drive in the new valve seat insert. Again, it must be the tool specified for your particular model of engine. This tool consists of a pilot and a driver.

To install the insert, place it so that the chamfered, or grooved, edge will go down into the cylinder. Then place the pilot of your driver into the valve guide, and use a machinist's hammer to tap the driver until the insert is in place. Any new insert must, of course, be lapped to the valve according to the preceding instructions.

Replacing the valve guides and seats is a good job to farm out to a machine shop. If the engine is worn enough to need a new valve seat

and the guides are also worn, chances are the whole engine has reached the point where it would be cheaper and better to replace it with a rebuilt or new assembly than to repair it. Certainly, buying the tools to do such a complete rebuilding job on one small engine would be uneconomical in both money and time. Besides, the chances of doing the job wrong the first time are excellent.

If you use an engine constantly and at a nearly constant speed with a constant load, you can expect the valves to wear rather quickly, and you'll find that they frequently need service. Under these circumstances, severe wear is likely to occur within 200 hours of use, instead of the usual 500 hours before an overhaul is necessary. To minimize this, you should consider installing long-wearing valves made of Stellite or a similar material. You can also use a special device that rotates the exhaust valve while the engine is operating. The device helps keep down carbon deposits. You can order valve rotators and Stellite exhaust valves for most four-cycle engines from a dealer, a manufacturer, a parts supplier, and sometimes even from a local mechanic.

ENGINE OVERHAUL

From here on, Parp assumes that the reader possesses the ability to disassemble and correctly reassemble an engine. Clearly, all of the problems of extensive service to all engines cannot be covered here. If you feel confident in such matters as engine seals, clips, and bearings, and have adequate tools, including an engine stand, piston pin driver, piston support, bearing driver, and piston ring compressor, you may decide to tackle a complete overhaul. If you're just learning, take a tip from Parp: procure one or more out-of-service engines at junk prices, and master all overhaul procedures before proceeding with an engine you care much about. Parp believes that almost anyone can learn to overhaul a small engine, but it does take work experience and, if available, tutoring. It certainly requires an investment in the proper tools, one which will pay off only if you use them more than once.

Engine Disassembly

The first step in a complete overhaul is to remove the engine from its mounts and disassemble the engine to whatever extent is necessary. Begin by removing any covers or shrouds. The vertical crankshaft engines on most rotary mowers are removed by simply taking off the blade and the bolts that hold the engine to the chassis. Then you can lift the engine straight up and out. Self-propelled models will include a belt or other drive mechanism that you must loosen in some obvious way.

Before proceeding with a four-cycle overhaul, drain the oil from the crankcase, and disconnect the ignition cable. Leave the spark plug in place. Next, remove the air cleaner to expose the carburetor, and disconnect the fuel line from the carburetor. If possible, fasten the end of the line with a clip, or take other steps to prevent fuel flow. Now remove the fuel tank by loosening its bolts. Some engine designs require that you loosen the fuel tank before you disconnect the fuel line; others do not. In either case, the next step is to remove the fuel tank, which will often involve removing some of the cylinder head bolts. Many engines have a ground lead connected to the fuel tank. Note its configuration, and disconnect it to remove the fuel tank.

Now find the engine's top cover—that's the metal cover over the flywheel side of the engine. Remove all retaining bolts, and pull the cover off to expose the flywheel and ignition system. If the engine is equipped with a mechanical governor, you must now disconnect the linkage between the governor and the carburetor. The linkage usually includes springs and clips or other fasteners. Examine your setup carefully, and make detailed drawings for reassembly.

Next, remove the cylinder head bolts, cylinder head, shield, and gasket. (For details, see Renewing Valves in this chapter.) Check the flywheel for grime, then remove it. If the engine is equipped with a starter clutch, remove it for disassembly and overhaul. Check the flywheel half-moon key, and examine the flywheel for damage. If needed or desired, you can now remove the points assembly and other ignition parts. Remove the carburetor, either from the engine or from the fuel tank, and set aside for overhaul. Also remove and disassemble the muffler, fuel pump, starter mechanism, and drive clutch assembly for overhaul.

To reach the crankshaft, remove the long bolts that fasten the engine halves together. Now disassemble the piston and connecting rod. Most designs utilize a connecting rod lock. To disconnect it, bend the tab of the lock with a screwdriver until you can reach the rod cap bolts with a wrench and thus remove the connecting rod cap. Mark the cap and the connecting rod so you can put them back together the same way they were originally.

Before proceeding with the disassembly, check the cylinder for a hard carbon ridge near the top. Remove this ridge by scraping, to prevent damaging the piston rings when you take out the piston. Now push the piston and connecting rod up through the cylinder.

To remove the piston from the connecting rod, first examine the method used to retain the piston pin. Most often, a G-shaped pin lock sits in a recess in the side of the piston. Remove this lock with needle-nose pliers. Plan to replace this retainer and the piston pin. If you find bearings in your piston, you may be able to reuse them, but if any rollers or needles are damaged, you'll have to replace the entire set. Whatever the pin and retainer arrangement, check it carefully for damage. If the engine has seen much service and you hope to extend it considerably, plan to renew all of these parts. If you're going to install a new, oversize piston in a rebored cylinder,

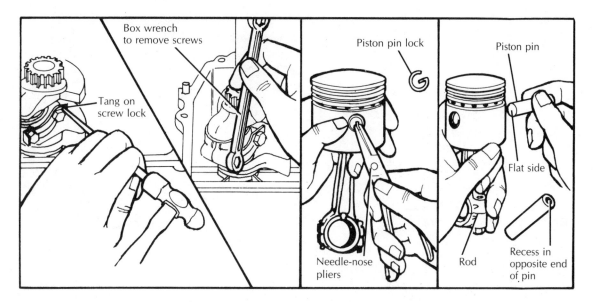

Illus. 4–14—Removing the Connecting Rod Cap and Disassembling the Piston and Rod

First, bend back the tab on the screw lock, then use a box wrench to remove the screws, then use a needle-nose pliers to the G-shaped pin that locks the rod retainer in place. Remove the retainer, and the rod will come loose.

renew all small moving parts on principle. This includes the piston pin, retainer, bearings, and fasteners. Replace or repair the connecting rod and drive shaft only as necessary.

Next, use a piston ring expander to remove the rings one at a time. Work carefully to avoid damage to the piston. If you are going to install a new piston and rings, this step is unnecessary. Start at the top of the piston with the first ring. With the ring expanded, hold the expander firmly and lift each ring over the ring lands, the ridges between the grooves that hold the rings.

With all rings removed, clean the piston thoroughly with a wire brush and solvent. Clean the entire piston. Be sure also to clean the ring grooves; this is best done with a broken piece of old ring. Be sure to handle rings carefully, old or new—their edges are sharp.

Incorrect installation of new rings and installation of rings other than those specified by the manufacturer are common errors. Be wary. Compare new rings with old, and be certain to install them exactly as the originals were installed by the manufacturer.

If you intend to reinstall your old piston, install a new ring in the top groove after it is completely cleaned. Check the piston by measuring the space between the ring and the side of the groove. Manufacturers specify varying tolerances for this gap. Briggs & Stratton specifies that if the gap is .007 inch or greater, the piston should be replaced. If possible, determine the gap tolerance specified by the manufacturer of your particular engine.

Parp assumes that the engine you're overhauling has done much work. If so, check the cylinder carefully to be sure it is not scored, excessively worn, or out of round. Use an inside micrometer to measure the cylinder at points ¾–1 inch from the top and at points the same

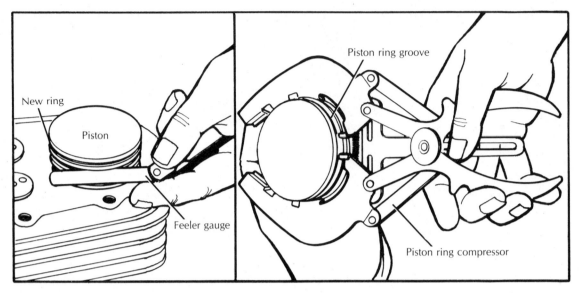

Illus. 4–15—Installing a New Piston Ring with a Piston Ring Compressor

distance from the bottom. Also measure at the center of the cylinder. Close the micrometer so that it won't scratch the inside of the cylinder. Open it at various points in the cylinder to the correct specifications. (Here, you will need to know your manufacturer's cylinder specifications and tolerances for wear.) The micrometer should touch both sides of the cylinder at the correct measurement. If it does not, the cylinder is out of round; that is, the wear on it exceeds the specified tolerances, and you must either install a cylinder sleeve or liner, or have the cylinder rebored. Only a few engines will accept a cylinder liner. Others must be rebored, a job definitely not for the home shop.

If the cylinder is damaged, take the engine to a professional small-engine shop and have the cylinder rebored. Purchase an oversize piston *and* oversize rings. Do not install original rings on an oversize piston. Check your manufacturer's parts list to determine the sizes of

rings and pistons available for your engine. The shop can do this, of course, and will rebore the cylinder accordingly. Do all cylinder repair work before installing new rings.

You may decide to reuse both the rings and the piston if they are undamaged and if the cylinder does not need to be rebored. Inspect the rings. If you see no obvious damage, check each ring for size. With rings and cylinder perfectly clean, insert the old rings one at a time into the cylinder, about 1 inch down. Use a feeler gauge to check the gap between the two ends of each ring. Determine the ring gap limit specified by your manufacturer; this varies greatly from engine to engine and even from ring type to ring type, so Parp can't offer an alternative to the manufacturer's specifications. Usually, though, the gap in compression rings should be less than .035 inch, and the oil ring gap should not exceed .045 inch. These figures represent the maximum gap allowed in many aluminum cylinder engines. Older, cast-iron models often require gaps .005 inch smaller. If one ring is clearly damaged or expanded beyond tolerance, replace the entire set. Never replace a single ring from a ring set.

Inspect the connecting rod, bearings, and journals for damage or wear. Replace the new parts as necessary. If the rod itself looks suspicious, take no chances. Replace it. If a journal is damaged or worn, have a machine shop check the journal, and then replace the rod. Check the rod for drilled lubrication passages and be sure they are clean.

If the engine has given considerable service, renew the piston pin and retainer on principle.

To remove the crankshaft, first clean the area and remove any burrs or rust from the drive end of the shaft. Remove the crankcase cover, if you haven't already done so, by tapping it with a soft mallet. Align the crankshaft and cam gear timing indicators, if present, and pull off the cam gear. Some designs require that you remove the cam gear with the shaft, but that will be obvious. On some engines with cast-iron cylinders, you must turn the crankshaft until the noticeable crankpin points toward the rear of the engine. Then pull it out, twisting as necessary.

If the engine has a cast-iron cylinder and ball bearings at the drive end of the shaft, use a different procedure. Remove the top cover, flywheel, and magneto assembly. Use a rod and hammer to drive the cam gear shaft out, then push the cam gear itself forward into the obvious recess toward the front of the engine. Then simply pull the drive shaft out *from the ignition side.* On these engines, do not attempt to remove the shaft from the drive side; if you try to, you'll damage the shaft and journal. If the engine offers double thrust, you will find capscrews holding a bearing inside the crankcase. Remove these to pull out the crankshaft.

Check the crankshaft for bends or other damage. Check the alignment of the bearing journals, and inspect any gears for damage. Smooth down any rough spots or burrs. If you suspect that the crankshaft is out of round or unbalanced, have a machine shop check it, and replace it, if necessary.

Note: Never attempt to straighten a crankshaft, either in or out of the engine. Such attempts always lead to more trouble. If the shaft is mounted, you will damage the bearings and journals. In any case, you will weaken the shaft with microscopic fractures that could cause early failure and extensive engine damage if operated.

If the shaft is fitted with ball bearings, avoid removing them unless they must be replaced. If you must remove them, use an arbor press. To replace the bearings, heat the new unit in hot oil to change the press fit to a slip fit. Allow the cooling process to tighten the new bearing assembly onto the shaft.

Check the camshaft much as you checked the crankshaft. Clean the journals and oil passages. Have a machine shop check it for balance and replace as necessary. Cam lobes must be smooth and unscored. If they are only slightly damaged, they may be resurfaced to match undamaged lobes. This is another job for the shop, and you might be better off installing a new camshaft instead. Replace the camshaft if the bearing journals are worn or out of round, if the lobes are worn beyond easy repair, or if the shaft itself shows any signs of cracks, fractures, or excessive wear.

At this time, check all accessories that can be driven by the crankshaft, camshaft, or associated gears. These could include the oil pump, the governor, some types of fuel pumps, and so on. Clean these accessories thoroughly, and check all gears, pins, and bushings. Replace any distorted, damaged, or excessively worn parts. You'll probably need a service manual for your particular engine to perform these jobs properly, but in any case you should certainly acquire a shop manual before attempting a complete overhaul.

If you haven't already done so, overhaul the carburetor, fuel system, exhaust system, and ignition system in an order that is convenient in terms of reassembly.

At this point all of your checks and cleaning have been completed, and your new parts have been laid out to replace the old. Any necessary machine shop work has been done, and you have acquired over- or under-size parts to match the shop work. Begin reassembly with the piston and connecting rod. Replace the pin retainer or lock. If the pin is hollow, either end may go first on most models. If it's solid, insert the flat end first. Replace the pin lock with needle-nose pliers.

Install the piston rings on the piston in the correct grooves and direction. Oil the entire assembly, and use a ring compressor. Insert the piston and rod assembly into the cylinder with the rings compressed and the compressor loosened slightly.

Reinstall the crankshaft, cam gear, and camshaft. Check timing indicators and align accordingly. Oil the crankpin, and pull the rod against the crankpin, if your crank uses a pin. Assemble the connecting rod cap and torque its bolts to the manufacturer's specifications. Replace valves, springs, and retainers according to the instructions under Renewing Valves in this chapter. Renew cylinder head gasket and shield. Reinstall the fuel, ignition, and exhaust systems.

Note: To install oil seals on the crankshaft, use an insertion tool, which can be purchased when you buy new seals. Take care not to damage the shaft or threads.

With the engine fully reassembled, replace the oil, apply grease, and fill with fresh fuel. Avoid placing a heavy load on the rebuilt engine for a respectable period, at least five hours of use. Check the engine often for signs of error during repair procedures.

Yogi bartered for a broken chain saw, and Pappy is here to dig Parp's new grease pit. The high meadows are still clogged with snow, but the blue is back and the creek is running fast. We'll use Pappy's Cat & Hoe to clear debris, and Parp will do the saw after the sun goes down—he also has plants to catalog and a greenhouse to build. It looks like a busy spring, and that's without considering the annual Vise Grip Elk Dinner with Three-Legged Muskrat at the Hot Springs. Life is too short.

PART TWO:
The Grounds

CHAPTER FIVE

Lawn Mowers and Accessories

In 1812, Peter Gaillard designed the first grass mower, a device intended to make life easier for hay farmers. Hay is, of course, a grass, and Gaillard's invention began a long series of others that led through thousands of failures and many notable successes to the vast profusion of lawn mower designs available today.

Gaillard's mower and most of the mowers that came after it were hand powered. Although much can and should be written about the many fine, manually powered, reel-type mowers on the market today, Parp's concern in this book is limited to power tools. Fortunately for this book, most present-day mowers are powered by two- or four-cycle engines, or by electric motors. Let's begin our discussion of modern mowers by looking at the basic types and major designs on the market today.

LAWN MOWER DESIGNS

The first efficient lawn mowers were manually powered, reel-type mowers. The reel type dominated the market for many years, and it was natural that the reel type continued to be popular when coupled with internal combustion power. A manually powered reel type is still Parp's personal choice, but Parp resists progress to some extent, and the grass doesn't grow very fast in a rocky canyon.

The reel of a reel-type mower consists of several blades attached at both ends to drums that are, in turn, attached to wheels. The blades

are set in a pattern similar to that of a worm gear to prevent jamming and to facilitate efficient cutting. When a power source is attached, it spins the reel, often independently of the wheels. Many power reel-type mowers are also moved forward by the power of the engine. Yet, it wasn't long before designers realized that reel-type mowers could be improved upon by changing the blade action to rotary.

Today, almost all power mowers on the market feature rotary blades, although manual mowers are still of the reel type. A rotary blade is a simpler design that is dependent on the use of a vertical crank-shaft engine, either two- or four-cycle. The basic design features a single blade that is spun in a circle by the engine's drive shaft. The blade is attached directly, or almost directly, to the drive shaft.

Rotary blade mowers are actually less efficient cutters than reel mowers, as most cutting is done by the blade tips only. Blades fixed in a reel cut with the entire edge of each blade. However, the rotary design is more adaptable to power and much simpler mechanically, so it is more common. It's cheaper to buy and easier to maintain, too.

Power mowers of either the rotary or the reel design are useful for cutting large, fairly even lawns where rocks and other debris are not a constant hazard. Power mowers are also very useful for people who, for one reason or another, should not exert themselves with a manual mower. A strong, healthy person who uses a power mower on a moderate or small lawn is wasting fuel, materials, and money, says Parp. If you live in a rocky or very wooded area, a power mower can be dangerous and will probably present more and worse problems than it solves.

Types of Engines

Most large mower manufacturers produce machines that offer a choice between two- and four-cycle engines. The smallest mowers are commonly powered by two-cycle engines. Large, heavy-duty, or professional mowers usually incorporate four-cycle engines. The purchaser of a medium-size mower for normal duty can often choose either a two-cycle or a four-cycle power plant.

As we have seen, two-cycle engines are smaller and lighter than four-cycle engines. Also, many people prefer two-cycle power because they would rather not bother with a separate oil supply for lubrication. Two-cycle engines are usually less expensive, too.

Four-cycle engines, however, do have advantages in a mower application. They are much more efficient and dependable than two-cycle engines, and they can deliver more power per gallon of fuel. This can be a significant consideration if you want a mower with accessories, which add weight or otherwise use some of the power delivered by the engine. Self-propelled models and mulching models, for example, are less expensive to operate if they are powered by four-cycle engines. A riding mower should certainly be powered by a four-cycle engine.

Your particular situation will determine if you should purchase a four-cycle or a two-cycle mower. Many people mow small lawns with four-cycle-powered riding mowers. Others attempt to cut several acres with 18-inch, two-cycle models. In choosing between two- and four-cycle mowers, consider the size of your property, the difficulty of mowing it, the rough-

ness of the terrain, and your budget. Also consider the extent of your mechanical ability. If you have a moderate-size lawn and can choose either type of mower, you might select a two-cycle model because you feel more confident with two-cycle repairs and maintenance. On the other hand, you might choose a four-cycle model because of its efficiency and dependability and because you are willing to maintain and repair a more complex machine, or you have decided to let a professional mechanic do the repairs.

Terrain is probably the most important factor to consider in choosing between two- and four-cycle mowers. If your property is hilly or rough, a two-cycle engine could be best because it won't lose lubrication when operated at an angle. If you mow relatively flat terrain, you can be confident that a four-cycle engine will receive proper lubrication, and you'll gain its benefits without an excessive number of maintenance difficulties.

TYPES OF MOWERS

There are currently four basic designs available in power mowers. These are the rotary mower, the power reel mower, the riding mower, and the small tractor. Of these, the rotary mower is by far the most common choice for cutting residential lawns.

Rotary Mower

The design of the rotary mower is a direct result of the simplest approach to harnessing the power of a small engine. The engine is mounted vertically, and a simple blade is attached to the drive shaft. As the engine turns, it spins the blade in a rotary motion. The edges of the blade chop the grass by impact without the use of any kind of scissorlike action against another metal blade or surface. As previously mentioned, most of the cutting is done by the tips of the blades. Rotary mowers come in many sizes and degrees of quality and are suitable to many residential and commercial applications.

Power Reel Mower

A power reel mower is similar to a manual reel mower but is designed to use a small gasoline engine, usually a two-cycle, to spin the reel and, usually, turn the wheels. Some inexpensive models are available with as few as four blades. These models are best suited for cutting small yards of soft, thick grasses. Large lots and yards of thin, tough grasses are best maintained with mowers having seven or more blades. Blades must be kept sharp and clean. Any reel mower should feature an adjustable roller to control cutting height.

Riding Mowers

The riding mower also comes in many sizes and types, and its use is not limited to large estates or commercial situations. People whose health prohibits strain of any kind may choose a small riding mower for even the smallest residential lot. Riding mowers are generally available with 26- to 42-inch cutting units. Some models feature a vacuum action to lift clippings out of the cutter and into a grass catcher; this allows smooth cutting and clean bagging, even if the grass is wet. Some riding mowers have two power sources, one for cutting and one for traction. An adjustable seat is a more desirable feature than it may seem at first. Riding mowers are more complex to maintain than are most other types, but they often are built for heavier use and, therefore, are more durable if cared for properly.

Small Tractors

This is the top of the lawn-cutting hierarchy. Small tractors are much more expensive than any other type of mower but are, of course, much tougher, more durable, and more powerful than other mowers. They are also much more versatile because they can use such attachments as snow blades, snow and debris throwers, loaders, dozer blades, sweepers, sprayers, splitters, plows, tillers, cultivators, and spaders. The purchase of a small tractor is best justified by the need for one or more of these attachments. For these reasons, small tractors are often the best choice for rural dwellers, homesteaders, estate managers, and commercial grounds-care companies. Parp will probably pick one up as this book is being written. This book deals with small tractors in more detail in Chapter Nine.

Mower Sizes

Lawn mowers are sized by the width of the swath of grass they cut, the length of one rotary blade from tip to tip. Lawn mowers on today's market range from 18-inch models for average lawns, up to 55-inch (though most are 54-inch) professional models. The most common mowers are 19-inch and 21-inch walk-behind types, some of which are self-propelled.

Riding mowers are generally available in 26- to 42-inch sizes for the consumer market. Professional or commercial riders are available up to 54 inches in size (the most common are 48 inches), though these are usually limited to tractors with lawn-cutting attachments.

To choose the best size of mower for your situation, consider first the size of the area you'll be mowing most often. Then consider the obstacles. If you have a number of bushes, shrubs, or trees and you want to be able to mow around them easily, you'll need a smaller mower. If you have a large lawn or estate, you'll need a large mower, perhaps a riding model. If you have both a large lawn and a good number of shrubs or other obstacles such as tight corners or narrow strips, you might decide to purchase two mowers—a 19-inch walk-behind for close quarters, and perhaps a 30-inch riding mower for the large expanses.

MOWER ACCESSORIES AND FEATURES

The best of today's lawn-mowing machines also come with a good many useful accessories. Many companies offer an attachment that turns certain models into mulching mowers. A mulching mower or attachment cuts and shreds the mowed grass blades into tiny pieces that are supposed to feed the lawn without smothering it. Mulching is not always the best thing to do for a lawn, although it is good to return mulched grass to any lawn at least twice each year. Many people buy mulching mowers or attachments and use them constantly until the entire lawn turns brown. If you live in a southern or Pacific region where grass grows all or most of the year and is less susceptible to thatch or dead grass buildup, you could probably use a mulcher most of the time. You should, however, bag the cuttings during spring and fall mowings. In other areas where grass grows more slowly and seasonally, and where thatch buildup is more or less constant, you should probably bag the cuttings almost every time you mow and should mulch very infrequently. Like most other accessories for backyard tools, a mulcher is more limited than the advertising for them would have you believe.

A leaf shredder is a very useful attachment for people who have large lawns and shedding trees. The typical leaf shredder attachment increases the natural tendency of a rotary blade to create a vacuum. The vacuum action picks up leaves, light sticks, paper, and other debris, and the shredder cuts the material into small pieces. This means you can cut longer before emptying your bag. It also minimizes the raking you have to do before or after mowing in the fall.

Adjustable handles are a common feature on most quality walk-behind mowers, and indeed they are almost indispensable, especially if you are taller or shorter than average, or if your cutting area includes sloped or banked ground. Handles that fold down are handy when transporting a mower in a vehicle.

Any mower you select should have an adequate system for catching grass cuttings. There are two good basic designs of grass catchers in common use. The side-mounted grass catcher is most common on homeowner-type rotary mowers. The rear-mounted grass catcher, on the other hand, is popular among commercial lawn-care companies because it holds more without adding to the width of the mower and without affecting the mower's maneuverability or balance. The disadvantage of a rear-mounted grass catcher is that loose dirt and debris are thrown backward in the direction of the operator.

A self-propelled mower is useful for people who should avoid exertion, or for those who mow large or hilly lots. A power reel mower is easily engineered to be self-propelled because the engine belts can turn the wheels at the same time it spins the reel. Power reel mowers are suitable for many types of flat terrain and lawn, but if your lawn is hilly, you'll do best with a self-propelled rotary mower with rear-wheel drive. Front-wheel-drive mowers are somewhat easier to use because you don't have to engage a clutch in order to interrupt the drive—you simply push down the handle to elevate the front wheels. But, rear-wheel drive places most of the weight of the engine on the rear wheels and improves traction on rough or hilly terrain.

Parp has previously described the half-moon key, or Woodruff key, which is often used to fasten the flywheel to the crankshaft of a small engine (see Index). In quality rotary mowers, a similar device is used to fasten the mower blade to the drive shaft. This arrangement protects the drive shaft and engine from severe damage in the event that the blade strikes a heavy obstacle. If a machine without this feature strikes a heavy object, the force of the spinning blade is transferred back onto the drive shaft and can result in expensive and even irreparable engine damage. If the blade is fastened with a half-moon key, however, only the key will shear off; and the drive shaft will sustain no damage. You'll only need to replace the half-moon key—an easy job—in order to continue cutting. If you purchase a new rotary mower, Parp suggests that you obtain a few replacement half-moon keys for future use.

Other features that are desirable in any new mower include adjustable cutting height, easy-to-remove blades for sharpening, sturdy and simple controls within easy reach, and, of course, solid construction. This includes steel wheels and steel wheel bearings at least. Parp recommends all-steel construction in any mower type.

Safety Features

Many personal-injury accidents occur each year as a result of operating lawn mowers. Most of these accidents happen because people fail to learn or follow the simple safety rules related to operating a lawn mower. Every reputable manufacturer provides an owner's manual with each new machine, and these manuals always stress safe and proper operation and maintenance.

It is a fact of life that operating any power tool is, to some extent, potentially and sometimes even inherently dangerous. No government agency will ever change that, and Parp believes that government controls over the chain saw industry often, in fact, resulted in more accidents, not fewer. Many people tend to believe that the existence of a government agency relieves them of personal responsibility for their own safety. This, of course, is nonsense. Anyone who operates a power tool without first

Photo 5–1—Proper Positioning of an Exhaust System on a Lawn Mower

Photograph by Christie C. Tito.

learning the proper procedures and potential hazards is asking for trouble, and no government agency can protect that person from his or her own foolishness.

Parp believes that the demands of consumers in the marketplace and the integrity of most manufacturers will insure the safest machines possible. Major manufacturers of power tools were concerned about consumer safety and involved in safety research long before the government started making rules. If you purchase a new machine for its general high quality of materials, design, and construction, including safety features, you will have done much to assure the production of safe products and the discouragement of unsafe tools.

There are some particular safety features you should look for in a new lawn mower. Perhaps the most important is a rear deflector, which usually consists of a hinged flap suspended at the rear of the mower. It is designed to prevent flying objects and debris from reaching the operator. It can also stop your foot from reaching under the mower into the blade area.

There should also be a deflection guard at the discharge area. This should be designed to operate automatically and should not require removal in order to empty the bag or clean the machine. The guard should fall into place automatically whenever the bag is removed.

Finally, the exhaust system and muffler should be placed on the machine so that they do not burn the operator during normal operation, including bag removal. They should certainly be placed so that there is no danger of the grass bag being ignited by the exhaust heat or by sparks from the engine.

HOW TO USE A LAWN MOWER

You have just invested some of your valuable time in researching the mowers available on the market today. You've considered the size and terrain of the area you'll be cutting most and have selected a mower with features suitable to your situation and budget. Now you have the machine of your choice, and you're anxious to try it on your lawn.

Before you do anything else, sit down with your owner's manual and study it until you are familiar with all aspects of your new machine and all phases of its operation. Pay special attention to your manufacturer's safety recommendations, and decide from the start that you will follow these recommendations to the letter and at all times.

After you've become familiar with your owner's manual, go through it again while studying the particulars for your machine. Memorize the location and proper operation of all controls. Learn each step in the process of starting and operating your mower before you actually pull the rope or flip the switch. This familiarization can save you from making an error that could result in personal injury or damage to your machine. In particular, learn the location of any kill switch or safety cut-off that your machine incorporates.

If you buy a used mower and do not receive the owner's manual, try to obtain a manual. You can often do this through a dealer who handles your make and model. If this fails, call or write to the manufacturer and ask them to send you a manual. Include the make, model, and serial number of your machine with your request.

Before you start your machine, note the following general safety rules as well as any others that may be recommended by your manufacturer:

1. Operate your machine only after reading your owner's manual.
2. Do not operate any power tool while under the influence of intoxicants, or while taking medication that may make you drowsy or slow your reactions. Do not attempt to operate or repair a mower if you are tired or ill.

3. Never allow children or uninstructed adults to operate your lawn mower. Be sure all spectators are well out of the way.

4. Remove sticks, rocks, and other debris from the cutting area.

5. Never operate a lawn mower without all safety devices and shields in place. Never operate a damaged or defective machine.

6. Wear sturdy work shoes and long, close-fitting trousers. Never operate a mower while barefoot or when wearing loose-fitting clothing.

7. Keep fuel in a proper container. Do not store fuel indoors or near any source of heat or flames.

8. Fuel machine when cool. Do not smoke while fueling. Start and operate mower at least 20 feet from the fueling point.

9. Do not overfill the fuel tank. Clean up any spilled fuel.

10. Before starting, be sure all nuts, bolts, and screws are properly tightened and that all parts are securely attached.

11. Set cutting height for tallest grass first. Then lower cutting height to complete the job. Always make cutting height adjustments with engine off and all moving parts stopped.

12. While operating your mower, stay alert and watch your footing.

13. Keep all parts of your body away from the engine housing and the area of the cutting blade.

14. Do not operate your mower in the dark or when visibility is limited. Do not cut grass that is wet from the dew. Do not operate your mower in rainy weather.

15. When using a rotary mower on a slope, cut in rows from side to side. Do not push the mower up a slope in front of you, and do not operate the mower from above. Riding or tractor mowers should move up and down slopes to avoid tipping over on a side-hill run.

16. Disconnect spark plug cable before clearing obstructions or performing any repairs. Unless the spark plug is disconnected, most rotary mower engines can be started accidentally by turning the cutting blade.

17. Stop the mower engine before crossing open ground, driveways, sidewalks, roads, or grassy areas you do not intend to cut.

18. Allow mower to cool before storing or servicing. If you must tip the mower on its side, be sure to drain the fuel tank first.

19. Do not touch any part of the engine until you have shut it off and allowed it to cool. Hot engines and exhaust system parts can cause bad burns.

20. Know your machine, and always maintain it in like-new condition. Keep the engine and controls clean and in good working condition. Keep cutting parts clean, and securely and properly fastened. Replace parts with those recommended by your manufacturer.

Before using your mower, be sure it is properly and completely assembled. Your owner's manual should contain detailed instructions for completing the assembly of your mower. Rotary mowers, as delivered in the carton, will usually require that the owner assemble or attach the handle, certain operator controls and control cables, the grass bag, and, on electric-start models, the battery cables.

Riding-mower assembly required of the owner often includes the steering handles or wheel, the seat, the fuel tank, engine shrouds, the deck, and battery connections.

After assembly, double-check to be sure that all fasteners are tight and that all packing materials have been removed. The last step in preparing your mower is height.

Fuel and Oil

Most lawn mower engines require fresh, regular-grade, leaded gasoline. Consult your owner's manual, and be sure to use the fuel recommended by your manufacturer. If you have purchased a used machine, you can feel confident in using regular-grade fuel. Do not use high-octane fuel, which can damage your engine, and do not use lead-free fuel, which will cause your machine to run poorly, if at all. On four-cycle engines it can also damage valve seats.

If you have an owner's manual, it will also recommend the best types of oil and will instruct you on mixing the oil with the fuel (two-cycle engines only) or adding to a separate oil tank (four-cycle engines).

If you have a used machine and no owner's manual, first locate the fuel tank cap. Then look for an oil-filler cap. If you find an oil-filler cap, the engine is a four-cycle type. If there is no oil-filler cap, the engine is two-cycle.

If the engine is four-cycle, fill the fuel tank with fresh, regular-grade, leaded gasoline. If the machine was purchased used, discard any fuel that might be in the tank and refill with fresh fuel.

If the engine is two-cycle and you have no manual to consult for the manufacturer's specific recommendations, purchase a can or two of two-cycle engine oil. Then obtain a 2½-gallon fuel container and mix your two-cycle fuel according to the instructions printed on that specific can of two-cycle engine oil.

If yours is a four-cycle engine, however, you must still supply oil for the engine's lubrication, but separately from the fuel. Most four-cycle lawn mower engines do best when lubricated with a detergent oil such as SAE 10W–30 or 10W–40. If you lack the manufacturer's instructions, Parp suggests an oil of this type.

Locate the oil-filler cap. Chances are that an oil-level measuring dipstick will be attached to the oil-filler cap. Place the mower on a level surface to assure an accurate dipstick measurement. Then clean the area around the cap to prevent contaminating the oil tank and supply with dirt.

Add enough oil to the tank to bring it to full. Do not overfill, or engine damage can result, such as valve damage and excessive carbon deposits in the cylinder. Be sure that both oil and gas tank caps are securely replaced after filling, and wipe the machine clean of any spilled fuel or oil.

Your mower should now be ready to start.

Starting the Mower

With the mower assembled, fueled, and checked, you can now prepare to cut grass. First, be sure you know how to stop the engine once you have it started. In general, the following starting instructions will apply to most common rotary lawn mowers:

1. Attach high-tension wire (spark plug cable) to spark plug.
2. If the mower is equipped with a traction system, place the drive control in NEUTRAL or START *before* starting the engine.
3. Open fuel valve or valves. Also, some fuel tank caps must be turned to a certain position in order to open the fuel tank vent.
4. Place throttle control in FAST or START position.
5. Place choke control in CHOKE or START position.
6. Place foot on left side of mower housing. Keep the other foot clear.
7. Pull starter rope until you meet resistance. Then give a short, quick pull to start the engine. Repeat as necessary. All of this applies equally to electric-start machines except, of course, that

you will push a button or switch rather than pull a rope.

8. Set throttle control to slow. Open choke, if present, or set on RUN.

Instead of a choke control, many mowers have a primer system that supplies a rich fuel mixture for starting the engine. In this case, if the engine doesn't start after three tries, wait several seconds to allow the primer well to refill. Many primer systems are automatic or semiautomatic. Semiautomatic systems often incorporate a cold-weather starting mechanism, which is simply a method of filling the primer well at temperatures below 50°F. If your mower includes a primer assist of this type, push the button once only before attempting to start the engine at temperatures below 50°F.

If your mower is equipped with self-propelled drive, you must set the drive control mechanism to cut grass. Stand behind the handle (or, on a rider, sit down on the seat) and set the drive control on RUN or on the lowest speed. Operate your mower at full traction speed only on clean, smooth areas where the grass is of moderate height. Operating on slow speeds is safer and allows the mower to follow the ground contours better for a more even cut.

Always place the drive control in the NEUTRAL or STOP position when pausing or when you are finished cutting. If your mower moves forward under traction even when the drive control is set in neutral, the belt drive mechanism is too tight and must be adjusted for safe operation. The best policy for all repairs and major adjustments necessary on a new mower is to return it to the dealer or another company that is authorized to make repairs under the manufacturer's warranty.

Mowing Your Lawn

A properly maintained lawn grows thickly and evenly, with a strong, and widespread root system. Correct grass cutting promotes this kind of growth, provided the lawn receives adequate moisture and food. If your grass has grown overlong, as is often the case with new lawns, don't try to cut the grass down to the desired height on the first mowing. Instead, cut the grass down not more than a third of its height. If possible, allow a new lawn to grow to a height of 2½–3 inches, and set your mower to trim off only ½ inch on the first cutting. After that, maintain the lawn at about 2 inches in sunny areas and 2½–3 inches in shaded areas and on slopes.

If the grass is left too long, new grass blades and the lower portions of older grass blades will become unhealthy and discolored. If the grass is cut too short, the plants will use most of their food and energy to produce new blades rather than thicker root systems. In hot, dry weather, the grass should be left longer than usual and should be cut less frequently. Rather than maintain a rigid schedule, let the height and growth speed of your lawn determine how often you cut it.

It is better to vary the pattern of your mowing each time than to set a pattern and stay with it. This helps prevent uneven growth, minimizes thatch buildup, and prevents ruts from developing in wheel tracks. Whatever pattern you follow, always overlap each cut row by ¼ to ⅓ of your mower's cutting width.

MAINTAINING YOUR MOWER

As Parp stressed in the first section of this book, proper maintenance is necessary to keep power tools in safe and efficient operating condition and to extend the lives of your machines. Only through good maintenance will you receive the full benefit of your investment.

After each use, you should clean your mower thoroughly. Disconnect the spark plug cable and turn the mower on its side, spark plug up. Remove the deck from a riding or tractor mower, and remove the battery on electric-start machines. Remove all loose grass, dirt, and debris from around the blade and from all exposed areas. Clean the air filter or cleaning system after each use, and keep the area around the spark plug, oil cap, and fuel cap as clean as if new. Clean the deck and engine housing each time you cut, and clean the cylinder cooling fins whenever necessary. Don't neglect this last job, or your machine may greatly overheat, causing the engine to wear out much faster than it should, or even fail completely. Sharpen the blade, or have it sharpened, whenever it seems less sharp than it was when new. This takes care of the regular maintenance required to keep any mower in good condition.

Additionally, there are other matters to attend to periodically. These items are minimal, and the manufacturer of your machine will probably recommend other steps. Be sure to follow your manufacturer's maintenance recommendations as closely as possible.

Replace the air filter at the beginning of each season. Even so-called permanent air filters should be replaced yearly unless you use your machine very infrequently. Also, at the beginning of each season, check your fuel cap, oil cap, and oil filter to see if they need to be changed. A lawn mower will not run properly with a crushed or damaged fuel tank cap, and a damaged oil tank cap may prevent your engine from receiving proper lubrication. As Parp said before, be sure to use fresh fuel and oil at the beginning of each season. (For information on storing and removing from storage any power tool, see Index.)

You should inspect periodically the belt or chain drive for damage or wear. Chains should be cleaned in solvent, then oiled. Most mowers are designed so that the chain or belt, when properly adjusted, has about ¼ inch of slack mid-way between the pulleys. Occasionally, it's necessary to remove a link from a chain or turn an adjuster to achieve proper tension. Parp suggests you visit an authorized warranty station or mower mechanic for such an operation.

Your periodic maintenance should also include inspecting and cleaning the spark plug, spark plug cable, carburetor and carburetor linkage, muffler system and exhaust ports, and starting system (see Index).

Sharpening Blades

All lawn mower blades should be cleaned with solvent and inspected after each 15 hours of use. If the blade is dull or damaged—that is, bent, out of balance, chipped badly, or broken—it must either be sharpened to new condition or replaced.

At the end of each season, you'll do well to have your mower blades sharpened by a professional. This will allow plenty of time to have your mower ready for the next season. It is not easy to correctly sharpen any mower blade without proper equipment, but you can save some money on the bill by removing the blade yourself rather than delivering the entire machine to the shop. Removing a blade from a rotary or riding mower is not as easy as it may sound. The job is similar to removing a flywheel (described in Chapter Four), except that a blade is not quite as fragile as a flywheel. Whether you intend to sharpen your own blade or have it done by a professional, you should know how to remove the blade yourself.

To remove the blade, first disconnect the spark plug cable to prevent accidentally starting the engine. If you have an electric-start mower, remove the battery completely from the machine.

Remove the spark plug, and turn the engine by hand until the piston is all the way down in the cylinder. Then insert a length of clothesline or cloth to protect the piston from damage. Now turn the mower on its side so that you can easily and safely work on the blade itself.

Place a block of wood or rubber between the blade and the deck, or body, of the machine so that the blade cannot turn all the way around. Now, wearing heavy work gloves, turn the blade

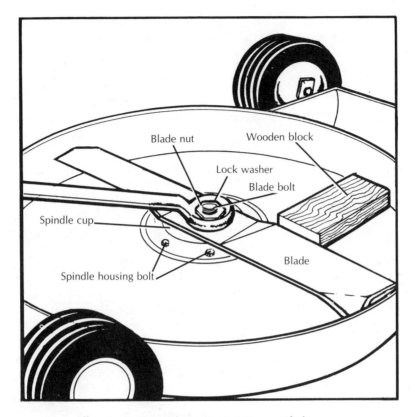

Illus. 5–1—Removing a Rotary Mower Blade

counterclockwise against the block. Hold the blade firmly against the block as you loosen the retaining nut. You may need an impact wrench to loosen the nut, and you may have to remove more than one nut. When you pull the blade from the shaft, look for the half-moon key that is likely to have been installed to protect the engine. If the half-moon key shows any sign of damage, replace it with a new one when you remount your blade. Be sure to keep all nuts, washers, and other parts in the correct sequence.

If your blade is bent or badly nicked, it should be replaced. Some nicked blades can be restored by a shop with a belt sharpener and the proper guides. If you wish to sharpen your own blade and it isn't badly nicked, you can usually

do the job with either a hand file or a blade-sharpening attachment made to fit your electric drill.

Sharpen your blade at exactly the original angle, usually 25°, and with a dulled edge rather than a sharp edge. Most manufacturers leave a 1/32-inch or 1/64-inch plane between the two sides of the mower blades. Be sure to sharpen both or all sides evenly so that the blade will be properly balanced when reinstalled.

Before you replace your blade, check the drive shaft, half-moon key, and key recess for damage. Place a straightedge across the bottom of the deck, against the drive shaft. Turn the engine by hand, and check to be sure the drive shaft neither leaves nor moves the straightedge

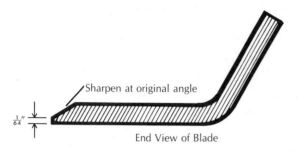

Sharpen at original angle

$\frac{1}{64}"$

End View of Blade

Illus. 5—2—Blade Sharpening Detail

as it turns. If the shaft is bent, it *must* be replaced to restore the mower to safe and efficient operation. A bent shaft cannot be safely straightened, as any bend causes invisible fractures in the steel. A shaft so weakened can easily break, presenting a serious hazard to the operator.

Riding mowers usually require special lubrication systems for the transaxle, which connects the transmission to the axle mechanism, or sometimes acts in place of the transmission itself. Check this lubrication system frequently, and service it according to your manufacturer's recommendations. All grease fittings should be serviced at least every 25 hours of actual use. Clean the fittings before and after greasing. Wheel bearings and steering linkage must also be greased periodically. If any moving part seems stiff, you should apply a light oil, but be sure to keep oil and grease off of any belts or other rubber or fabric parts.

Knowing that snow and cold have returned to Parp's canyon in the progress of this chapter will tell you how short his season of sun and foraging really is. Truthfully, though, these lawn mowers were interrupted by the passings of early trout, summer wood gathering, and autumn's hunting, not to mention a thousand miles of adventure. All of this may dismay an eager editor, but without it Parp would never have anything to say to anyone. Now he can look for that tractor he needs and hope to have much more to offer before good spring returns with a bounce and a laugh.

CHAPTER SIX:
Weed Trimmers and Brushcutters

Oh, Parp loves the frozen world and the wild, dead weeds that reach above the snow to stand golden in the winter sun. "Long live the weeds and the wilderness yet," said the poet Gerard Manley Hopkins. But neither Hopkins nor Parp is considering the groundskeeper in these sentiments, nor the domestic shrubs, young trees, and delicate grasses that must compete with wildness and weeds for water, sun, and nourishment.

When we consider our backyard or estate lawns, we cannot afford to gaze romantically on ragweed and thistle. We must kill or remove them, if possible, to allow for the needs of the plants that we prefer. Often, however, the weeds are stubborn and won't die—they won't "stay gone." They come back again and again, and all we can do is wish that they wouldn't grow higher than our pansies. They do grow higher, though, and they grow in places the mower won't reach, places that bring us to our knees to work stiff, slow clippers against tree bark or concrete foundations.

Most of us remember when clippers were the only weapon in the battle against close-growing weeds and brush. Perhaps the most significant new development in backyard tools in recent years is the flexible-line power trimmer, or string trimmer. This tool makes it possible to closely and precisely trim weeds and grasses that grow tall in places impossible to reach with a mower. The flexible-line trimmer can be used directly against trees, buildings, birdbaths, and outhouses without damaging bark, paint, or structures.

The best ideas are often simple ideas, and the best new developments in backyard tools are also often based on simple ideas or basic principles. The screw splitter developed by Art Stickler (see Index) comes to mind, as does the brushcutter developed by Stephen Hoff and the flexible-line lawn trimmer developed by George Ballas. Perhaps fortunately for us, but less fortunately for these and other inventors, basic ideas cannot be patented, and tools based on simple ideas are often difficult or impossible to protect under patent laws. As a result, many companies now produce screw splitters, brushcutters, and weed trimmers. Still, Stickler, Hoff, and Ballas are each in charge of their own companies, and each enjoys profits from the sales of the tools he developed. And, Parp says, the developers of new tools often take the lead in both sales and refinement of their new products and thus enjoy wide consumer support despite their lack of protection in some areas under patent laws. The public tends to stick with original inventors, although this support often appears to be unconscious.

The grass in Houston, Texas, grows year-round and, like grass everywhere, has no regard for the wishes or convenience of homeowners. It grows best in those places most difficult to reach with a mower, and against surfaces easily damaged by a scythe. In 1974, a man named George Ballas was actually cutting his own

Houston grass when he suddenly grew impatient with the problem of trying to trim around his oak trees. The mower wouldn't reach it, the clippers were too tedious, and the scythe would injure the trees.

Instantly, Ballas was stuck with one of those ingenious yet exceedingly simple ideas. He knew that nylon monofilament line could cut the grass but would not cut into the trees. But how could he set a piece of nylon line into motion fast enough to cut the grass, yet still be able to control it?

In a nearby trash bin he found an empty popcorn can. He punched holes in the can and threaded the holes with pieces of nylon fishing line. Then he removed a blade from his circular power lawn edger and attached the popcorn can in its place. When Ballas started the edger's motor, the can spun, causing the attached filament to fly out due to centrifugal force. The can made a terrible noise, but it held together, and the nylon cut the grass.

In just a few minutes, Ballas easily and neatly trimmed the grass around his oak trees without the slightest damage to them. Thus began the huge flexible-line trimmer business and the taming of one of the most difficult and tedious of groundskeeping chores.

In a short time, Ballas got together with a machinist friend, and they developed a flexible-line trimmer based on his original concept. It was soon on the market as the *Weed Eater*, and Ballas's idea has grown, of course, into an enormous business with wide public acceptance. Other flexible-line trimmers were soon marketed by McCulloch, Black & Decker, John Deere, Toro, Echo, and other companies in the outdoor power equipment field.

TYPES OF WEED TRIMMERS

Most weed trimmers available today use the same principles as George Ballas's prototype. They work by swinging, at high speed, a flexible monofilament string attached to a drum. The force of the drum's circular motion causes the string to strike off grass, weeds, and soft vegetable stalks without tearing up tree bark, fence posts, and other tougher objects the string hits. In some models an electric motor, run either by an extension from house current or by batteries, spins the drum with one, two, or sometimes even three monofilament lines. These lines are arranged symmetrically, like the blades of an airplane propeller.

Photo 6–1—Weed Eater Gasoline Trimmer/Edger Model XR–50

Courtesy Weed Eater, Inc.

Most string trimmers store the excess line on a small drum in the hub of the trimmer. When you tap the bottom of the trimmer on the ground, it allows more string to unwind. A cutter blade built into the housing of the trimmer cuts off the frayed tip of the string. Thus, when the string breaks or wears down on the end from hitting concrete steps or other rough surfaces, you can tap the trimmer to run out more and have it trimmed to length automatically.

Larger string trimmers are frequently powered by small two-cycle gasoline engines. These may be mounted on the trimmer at the top of the handle to drive a gearbox at the bottom with a flexible drive shaft that's similar to an oversize cable on a speedometer. Or, they may be mounted on the trimmer at the bottom of the

wand and drive it either directly or through gears. Homelite models use the hollow wand as a fuel tank.

Ballas's early trimmers were all powered by electric motors. Trimmers are now available from many manufacturers, in every price range, with optional electric motors or small two-cycle engines. There are heavy-duty trimmers with an edger capability and hard-blade accessories, and there are battery-powered trimmers costing less than $20 that are no larger than an ordinary broom. Some feature an automatic line dispenser, while others include a manual line advance system. Trimmers are available that will cut paths anywhere from widths of 6–18 inches. Some trimmers feature interchangeable heads for versatility. All quality trimmers do a good

Table 6–1: Weed Trimmer Selection Chart

Weed Trimmer Type	Trimmer Capabilities
Economy model: electric motor, smaller than 2 amp., lightweight, 8-inch path	Grass trimming only, on small, patio-size lawns or limited areas between buildings
Homeowner model: electric motor 2–3 amp., lightweight, 10–14 inch path	Trimming grass and light weeds on small- to medium-size lawns
Large electric model: 3–4 amp. motor, 14–16 inch path, capable of edging	Trimming, edging, sweeping, and mowing on most lawns
Heavy-duty electric: 5 amp. motor, 14–16 inch path, accepts hard blades capable of edging and pruning	Trimming, edging, sweeping, mowing, scalping, cutting heavy weeds, and pruning
Lightweight gasoline-powered: 12–30 cc. two-cycle engine	Trimming, edging, sweeping, mowing, scalping, cutting heavy weeds, and pruning any size lawn without power cord
Homeowner gasoline model: 20–50 cc. engine, capable of pruning and brushcutting, with attachments	Trimming, edging, sweeping, mowing, scalping, cutting heavy weeds, and pruning any size lawn without power cord
Pro gasoline model: up to 86 cc. engine, with attachments and power for heaviest brush and weeds	Trimming, edging, sweeping, mowing, and scalping. Extended professional and heavy-duty use on weeds, fields, and thick brush; for clearing use and pruning

job of trimming grass and weeds in hard-to-reach areas and are a very worthwhile addition to any power tool collection.

Since the many makes and varieties of trimmers available today can perform a number of jobs, the first step in selecting a new trimmer is to determine your particular needs. If you have a small, patio-size lawn with no heavy weeds, the simplest, most basic electric models will serve your purposes—provided you select a quality machine with a dependable motor. If your estate requires edging, pruning, ground-level scalping, and beveled, decorative slopes, you will need one of the more elaborate models, probably gasoline powered with interchangeable heads, including saw blades and other attachments. Table 6–1 lists many of the trimmer types currently available and the jobs they can perform. Simply determine which terrain situation is most like your own, then check Table 6–1 to find the most suitable model for your needs.

SAFE USE OF WEED TRIMMERS AND BRUSHCUTTERS

Many people mistakenly assume that using a nylon trimmer is as safe as eating apple pie in the kitchen. It is true that the spinning line is less likely to cut your leg off than a chain saw, but there are some very real hazards, as there are when operating any piece of power equipment.

Read your owner's manual and follow its safety rules to the letter, and then some. Besides the safety suggestions applying to all power equipment, enumerated in Part One (see Index), here are some special considerations for trimmers and brushcutters.

1. Select a safe design. The handle and controls of any trimmer or brushcutter should be proportional to the machine's power. Parp favors large, two-handled control bars as opposed to the popular loop-type handle because the double grip, in conjunction with a harness suspension system, provides positive protection against bodily contact with the cutting apparatus. Look for solid construction and balanced design. Better materials, such as steel and other metals, indicate better construction and, usually, a more safety-conscious manufacturer, not to mention greater durability—a safety factor in itself.

2. Wear sturdy shoes, eye and head protection, long trousers, and gloves at all times, regardless of whether the manufacturer recommends them. Unfortunately, some manufacturers place convenience considerations ahead of safety by rationalizing that a specific machine is light or not particularly dangerous. Beware of this attitude. Cover yourself for safety.

3. Use the machine according to the instructions in your owner's manual. Never attach metal blades or metal wire in place of the flexible line on machines designed as trimmers only. Always use the line or blades specifically recommended by your manufacturer.

4. Check the handlebars, cutting head, and other parts to be sure they are undamaged and correctly fastened before use. If these parts are loose or damaged, they can cause severe personal injury.

5. Adjust handlebars to fit your size and needs. Using the handlebars in a cramped, extended, or uncomfortable position can be hazardous in that the cutting head can be too close to your feet, or so far away that balance is upset and control is difficult.

6. Properly adjust the carrying harness or strap, and inspect it frequently for

damage or wear. Pay special attention to any hook or fastener used on the strap or harness. These sometimes become damaged or fatigued in ways that are not immediately noticeable. This can present a real danger if the strap or harness breaks or comes loose during operation.

7. Never carry an operating trimmer or brushcutter without the harness properly worn and adjusted.

8. Frequently inspect the cutting head guard. Be sure it is not damaged or loose. Do not operate a trimmer or brushcutter with a defective guard.

9. Check muffler screws, nuts, and other fasteners periodically, especially after the first few uses of the machine. These fasteners often loosen on new equipment after some use.

10. On multiple-line trimmers, keep the lines all the same length, and don't try to do without one line unless this practice is specifically approved by your owner's manual. Operating one line shy will throw the machine out of balance.

11. Be sure hard blades are sharp and undamaged.

12. Be especially careful of bystanders and passers-by. There is a tendency to think of the flexible-line trimmer as a safe, harmless machine. Dangerous debris can be propelled considerable distances with enough force to injure the unsuspecting.

13. Never gaze directly into the orbit of the cutting head of any trimmer or brushcutter.

14. Never touch the cutting head while the machine is under power.

15. Do not operate an electric trimmer in the rain or in any damp or wet location.

16. Use an outdoor extension cord only. A common standard is a minimum 16-gauge wire up to 100 feet and a 14-gauge wire for greater distances.

In addition, follow all the usual safety precautions that apply to operating, fueling, maintaining, and repairing any power tool.

HOW TO OPERATE TRIMMERS

"Long live the weeds and the wilderness yet"—at least in a few places. Parp's friend, the author, found wilderness in the weeds and woods of railroad easements and industrial backyards—Massey-Ferguson, in fact. Pray, let the wilderness be when you can.

Use the right tool for the right job. Most trimmers and similar appliances are designed, intended, and recommended for one particular job under certain specific conditions. A lightweight, flexible-line grass trimmer is exactly that. The hazards of operating any machine are greatly increased by improper or incorrect application. Be very careful to follow all the instructions and recommendations in your owner's manual. If you operate a used machine for which you cannot obtain an owner's manual, the general information below may be helpful.

Operating an Electric Trimmer

All flexible-line grass trimmers powered by household current are equipped with a short power cord called a pigtail. The shortness of the cord assures that the connection between the unit and the household extension will always be within easy view and reach of the operator. To attach the extension, tie it in a simple knot with the pigtail. Do not plug in the extension before connecting the extension to the pigtail. To do so, of course, would place a live current into your hand. Always tie and connect the pigtail and the extension before connecting the extension to the power source.

Also, before connecting to power, check the trimmer for loose fasteners or a loose power head, and correctly adjust line or cutting parts. Be sure everything is tight and in good repair before applying power.

After checking and connecting, proceed to the area to be trimmed. Adjust your harness system and hold the control handles, or hold the handheld unit upright and in a comfortable position, with the cutting head well away from your body.

Most trimmers are designed to cut from the left side of the cutting head. This causes the clippings and other debris to be thrown away from you. Most trimmers should be held at a 30° tilt away from the ground. Do not force the cutting line into the work area. Allow the tip of the line to do the cutting while progressing in a steady rhythm. When trimming near young trees or other easily damaged objects, use the shortest line length available, and operate the unit at a slow speed. Always cut from right to left, tilting the machine slightly to the left. Move into vegetation slowly and cut around sharp corners, posts, and metal fences last to save line.

If your machine is equipped with a typical semiautomatic line advance, you need simply tap the center of the cutting head lightly on the ground while the unit is running. This will feed new line from the spool. A line limiter on most machines will then cut the line to the proper length.

If your machine has no feed mechanism, you must manually advance the line. To do so, turn the machine off, and disconnect the power. Withdraw the required amount of line through the exit hole and, if necessary, clip off the worn or damaged line. Reconnect the power source, and continue trimming.

To mow small areas that are inaccessible to a lawn mower with the typical grass trimmer, simply hold the cutting head parallel to the ground. Do not press the cutting head into the ground.

Some trimmers may also be used for edging. Be sure your machine is designed for this purpose before using it in this manner. For edging, the unit must be adjusted so that the cutting head is perpendicular to the ground when the handle or control bar is held in a normal position. Most often, this means that you must adjust the handle or control bar, usually by loosening a wing nut or other fastener and repositioning the handle to the back side of the unit's main shaft. This causes the line (or blade, on machines so equipped) to cut straight down toward the ground. Again, allow the tip of the cutting line or edging blade to do the work without excess force.

To scalp an area, use the unit in its trimming position, with the cutting head held at the same 30° angle. Allow the tip of the cutting line to strike the ground, thus removing all unwanted vegetation clear to the ground. Be especially watchful for observers, and insist that they stand at least 30 feet away. Cut on the left side of the head so that all debris is thrown away from you.

For sweeping, extend the line to its maximum recommended length. Hold the cutting head parallel to the surface being swept, and move the unit from side to side while moving slowly forward. Do not attempt to move large objects, such as sticks, stones, and the like with this sweeping motion. Stop the machine, and remove large objects by hand.

Again, do not attempt to clean or adjust any machine while it is under power. Always disconnect the power source before performing any adjustment, maintenance, or repair.

Operating a Gasoline Trimmer

Most of the operating details above also apply to gasoline-engine trimmers. However, a few special considerations are necessitated by the engine.

Remember that the muffler and exhaust area is usually hot enough to deliver a painful, even serious, burn. Be especially mindful of this fact when making any adjustments to the handle or machine. Most units are designed so that you reach under the housing to loosen the wing or collar nut for handle adjustments. This keeps the muffler away from your hand and arm.

When the trimmer is operating, bring the engine to the desired speed before actually cutting. On the other hand, avoid operating the machine at full speed when you are not cutting, and never operate the engine at a speed higher than necessary for the job.

When pausing or stopping, allow the engine to return to idle while not cutting. When you turn the engine off, hold the OFF button or switch until the engine completely stops running. Be sure you know how to turn off the machine before you start cutting.

Operating a Brushcutter or Pruner

When you attach hard blades to your machine, remember that the blade will turn in the same direction as the drive shaft. If you are unsure, turn the engine off, and slowly pull the starter cord. Watch the flywheel or the drive shaft itself, then install the blade so it faces the same direction in which the engine turns.

To attach or remove blades on most machines, look for a notch or slot in the cutting head and another in the deflector cup or housing. Align these notches, and insert a screwdriver to lock the head in place. Then simply remove the nut or fastener that holds the blade or spool. Most blade or spool fasteners use a right-hand thread and must be turned counterclockwise to loosen and clockwise to tighten.

When using a brushcutter to clear an area, move the unit in large, semicircular swings of 6–7 feet while advancing approximately 5 inches with each swing. The best brushcutters are equipped with body harness suspension systems that allow you to swing them with your hips rather than with the arms and hands. As you work, avoid tangling the machine in the material you have already cut. While clearing or cutting

Photo 6–2—The Hoffco Brushette

An attachment that converts a chain saw into a brushcutter. Courtesy Hoffco, Inc.

under any heavy load, operate the unit at full speed.

When pruning, avoid overextending your arms; this places you off balance. Cut slowly into each limb without forcing the machine. Parp urges you to wear boots, a hard hat, safety goggles, and ear protection while pruning or brushcutting.

Maintenance

Please see Chapter Two for complete information on using and maintaining the two-cycle engines used to power trimmers and cutters.

Most trimmers utilize a flex shaft for transmitting the power from the motor or engine to the cutting head. These flexible steel shafts require adequate lubrication. Most manufacturers recommend lubricating flex shafts about once for each 20 hours of use. Some manufacturers supply lubrication holes, or zerks, to which you apply a lithium lubricant or other specified lubricant. For many machines, you must remove the shaft entirely and cover it with a thin coat of lithium grease, which is moistureproof and less susceptible to deterioration.

Removing the shaft is usually a simple operation that begins with loosening the collar nut and removing the drive shaft housing from the engine. You then pull the flex shaft out of the shaft housing, or tube, and apply the lubricant. When the flex shaft is correctly reinstalled, it will turn. The flats on the drive shaft must engage the flats in the clutch housing.

Remember to clean the air filter frequently on units powered by gasoline engines. Trimming and clearing work usually throws enough dust to clog a filter in an hour or two.

CHAPTER SEVEN:
Blowers and Throwers

Now that we've mowed the lawn, trimmed the weeds, and cut the brush, we have a yard full of leaves, clippings, and twigs to deal with. The sidewalk and porch are littered with tiny green slivers, many of which stick like wet tissue to concrete, rake, and broom. The rear bagger on the mower caught most of the organic debris, but not the stuff thrown by the weed trimmer or the trash that seemed to come from nowhere as we ran the brushcutter. Among the leaves and clippings are torn candy wrappers, old cigarette filters, and unidentifiable bits of damp fluff. So much trash over so much space. It will take forever to sweep it all together so that we can collect it conveniently for disposal.

Now is the time for another new invention, the power blower, or power broom. With this handy backyard tool, you can create a powerful wind that you can direct across walks, porches, and similar expanses. The wind quickly removes all but the most stubborn debris and can be used to collect everything into a single pile, ready to pick up.

POWER BLOWERS

A power blower is one of the most useful and versatile of the new power inventions. Whether powered by an electric motor or by a two-cycle gasoline engine, the blower can be used to clean screens, walls, windows, garages, vehicles, gardens, hedges, and other shrubbery. It will sweep sidewalks, patios, driveways,

Photo 7–1—Backpack-Mounted Power Blower

Courtesy Deere and Co.

porches, swimming pools, eaves, and troughs. It can rake leaves, pine needles, grass clippings, and most litter and debris. It can also be used to dry up a puddle or to dry off a car. Once you own a power blower, you'll really wonder how you ever got along without one. Every day you think of new jobs that are made possible or much easier by your power blower. Many models also double as sprayers for garden or orchard use, or even as flamethrowers for burning off unwanted growth, controlling field and forest fires, and for other agricultural uses.

Many power blowers are backpack models. This configuration utilizes a two-cycle gasoline engine mounted in a backpack with a hose and attachments that extend to your arm and hand for easy control.

Other blowers are smaller and less powerful and can be carried in one hand. Blowers of this design usually incorporate a top-mounted

Photo 7–2—Handheld Power Blower

Courtesy Echo Chain Saw Division, Kioritz Corp. of America.

engine or motor fitted with a handle. A tube or hose extends downward to direct the airflow. Many handheld blowers are powered by electric motors and are chiefly intended for light-duty domestic use on patios and small lawns and walks.

Mechanically, there is very little to a power blower. An engine or motor turns a fan that is connected to the drive shaft. The airflow is directed through a tube or hose, and it exits from one of the various attachments to perform any one of a number of tasks. The remaining parts of a blower are usually not owner-serviceable and are usually replaced on failure. Indeed, the power blower is such a simple device that one wonders why they weren't on the consumer market long ago.

The first power blowers were developed for commercial use by professional groundskeepers and maintenance crews at golf courses, airports, stadiums, zoos, and similar public facilities. They were used commercially for many years before certain outdoor power equipment manufacturers, notably Echo, Inc., introduced them to consumers during the 1970s.

Now the power blower comes in several design and model types, ranging from small, handheld electric units through solid, gasoline-engine-powered homeowner models, up to professional-quality, heavy-duty backpack machines designed for rugged, extensive use under all conditions. Any of these models may interest the reader, so Parp will now review the various types available, their limitations, and their best applications.

The Electric Broom

The typical electric broom is an economy-model power blower driven by an electric motor. The motor is mounted at the top of the unit and usually delivers 7–10 h.p. Operator handles are usually incorporated into the motor housing itself and, with an average weight of about 8 pounds, the typical electric broom is the lightest and handiest of all power blowers. The electric broom possesses all the usual advantages and disadvantages of any electric appliance. Since it emits no exhaust, does not use gasoline, and is relatively quiet in operation, the electric broom is safe and convenient to use indoors or in enclosed areas where a gasoline engine would be dangerous. On the other hand, it cannot be used in rainy or wet conditions, but who sweeps the walk in the rain, anyway? Very often, the air blast from an electric broom does not equal the blast from a gasoline-powered blower, but it usually exceeds 100 mph in any case, and that is quite adequate for sweeping walks, porches, patios, and small yards. It should never be used to dry puddles or vehicles, or any time your feet or hands are likely to be wet. Nor should it be used for removing snow or for spraying. An electric broom is just that; it has no other recommended application.

In choosing an electric broom, look for a motor of about 8 or 9 h.p. built around a permanent magnet. Check for convenient handles—two are best—and an air blast of about 100 mph. The unit should be very light, yet solid in appearance and feel. If it weighs more than 8 pounds, you might as well choose a gasoline model if your requirements justify the investment. Electric models are, of course, cheaper, some only half as much as a gasoline-engine model, and some even less. They are a good value since, for this particular application, an electric motor is more appropriate than an engine-powered model. A good electric broom should certainly carry a one-year warranty.

Handheld, Gasoline-Engine Power Blower

The typical handheld, gasoline-engine power blower is intended for general sale to consumers. It is designed to perform most cleaning and sweeping jobs for which an air blast can be effective, and its only limitations are that it should not be used indoors or in enclosed areas, and that it is not handy or powerful enough for extended or rugged use. A common configuration is a two-cycle engine of about 12–14 cc. mounted at the top of a blower tube equipped with at least one handle. As with the electric broom, the hose is usually an inflexible tube that is rigidly fixed to the engine housing. This design makes it somewhat less versatile than a backpack-mounted blower with a flexible tube, but it is handier for most relatively quick jobs such as sweeping, cleaning, and drying in areas not too difficult to reach. Some handheld models—the Echo PB–200, for example—have a larger engine of up to 21 cc. and an auxiliary supporting strap that's worn over one shoulder. With an auxiliary supporting strap, a flexible air hose can be used. The blower should include a stand or legs so it can be rested on the ground as desired. Some handheld blowers also can be used for spraying with the addition of an optional liquid-spray container and fan-type spray nozzle.

When you select a handheld, gasoline power blower, look for one that is lightweight, usually about 7–10 pounds. Be sure that you can manage it with the supplied handle configuration and, above all, be sure that the muffler and exhaust parts are safely situated away from the operator's hands and body. The maximum air blast should be between 100–140 mph. Interchangeable heads are a desirable feature but are not commonly available for handheld models. An ON/OFF or ignition kill switch should be conveniently located on the handle itself.

Unfortunately, some rather shoddily manufactured lightweight power blowers are flooding the consumer mass market today. In some cases, the engines on these units barely outlast the manufacturer's warranty. Parp recommends that you avoid discount department store brands and that you purchase your power blower from a reputable, outdoor power equipment dealer

who represents a major manufacturer. Your best bet is to select a blower from a manufacturer who has a good reputation as a builder of other power equipment. Echo, John Deere, Stihl, Amerind-MacKissic, Allis-Chalmers, and other equipment manufacturers produce especially usable lightweight power blowers.

Backpack-Mounted, Gasoline-Engine Power Blower

These are the real workhorses of the power blowers designed for general consumer, non-professional use. They are, of course, considerably more expensive than either the handheld electric or gasoline-powered models and, like all gasoline-powered equipment, cannot be used indoors or in enclosed areas. However, the engines on these are larger, more powerful, and more dependable than the necessarily smaller

Photo 7–3—Fingertip Throttle

Offers good access for easy operation of a backpack power blower. Courtesy Echo Chain Saw Division, Kioritz Corp. of America.

engines or motor used on handheld units. They are generally capable of running for longer periods of time and, thanks to the backpack suspension system, are comfortable to carry and convenient to use for extended periods. A flexible hose is a necessary feature on any backpack blower. The engine should be 18–40 cc. and should include an extension for a tube-mounted, fingertip throttle and stop switch so that the operator can easily turn the backpack unit off without reaching behind him. The base of the engine should include a stand or legs for resting on the ground. The fuel tank should have a capacity of one liter or more, and the engine should be equipped with an anti-vibration system of some kind, preferably rubber shocks. The backpack straps must be adjustable and should be well padded. An auxiliary spray system and interchangeable nozzles are desirable as optional features.

The wind blast on these machines is not usually measured as velocity per hour, as it commonly is with smaller machines. Instead, the output of the unit is normally measured by volume—that is, by cubic feet per minute (cfm). Using this system, a good, medium-duty, backpack power blower should deliver at least 200 cfm, with 250–300 cfm a more desirable volume.

A good, powerful, backpack-mounted, gasoline-engine power blower can handle an amazing variety of jobs, from cleaning and drying vehicles and residue moisture in emptied swimming pools to easily chasing pounds of refuse out of tangled hedges and shrubs. A quality unit is well worth an investment of a little more money and the commitment to carry a little extra weight.

Gasoline-Engine Commercial Power Blower

The commercial, or heavy-duty, power blower differs from the consumer model chiefly in the size of the engine, durability, and fuel capacity. Many homeowners with country lanes or estate-size lawns and extensive shrubbery will do well to select a heavy-duty blower because of its greater power and extended range. The fuel capacity of a commercial blower should be adequate for two hours of continuous operation. The engine should be about 40 cc. in size and it definitely should be set in anti-vibration mountings. The vibrations of an engine this size can damage the operator's back unless the vibration is isolated by a good system of flexible shocks. Exhaust should be directed down and to the rear of the operator. The maximum air volume should exceed 300 cfm, with a desirable maximum volume being 350–400 cfm.

You cannot expect the unit to be light; the average weight is right around 25 pounds. The backpack system must include padded, adjustable straps, and the strap fasteners should be replaceable, as they have a tendency to break after about 100 hours of use. If one breaks, replace all of them. When selecting a heavy-duty blower, be sure that the hose is flexible and will accept interchangeable nozzles. A solid-state ignition, while not owner-serviceable, will usually minimize ignition failures caused by dust, dirt, and moisture. A heavy-duty, washable, and replaceable foam-type air filter is another desirable feature.

Most commercial blowers are intended for blowing only and do not double as sprayers. If you need a heavy-duty machine that is also capable of spraying both liquid and granulated substances, the next machine is for you.

Gasoline-Engine, Heavy-Duty Power Blower/Sprayer/Duster

This design differs from the type described above only because, in addition to blowing, it is capable of spraying powders, liquids, or granular materials. A truly professional machine, this type is quite expensive and is probably of consumer interest chiefly to farmers, foresters, and keepers of large estates. A 40 cc. engine is the standard, supported by a good, padded back-pack system and anti-vibration engine mounts. The maximum air volume should exceed 600 cfm and is best at 650–700 cfm. Interchangeable nozzles are a must, and among them should be a fan-type nozzle for blowing and misting (or wide-angle liquid spraying), a specially designed, granule-spreading nozzle, a double or Y-head nozzle for spraying a double row, a dusting nozzle, a dusting hose, a liquid pump, and a flamethrower nozzle for forest or field fire-fighting and selective agricultural burning.

As you can see, this type of unit is the ultimate in versatile backpack power blowers. The Echo DM–9 Power Duster/Mist Blower is Parp's choice of this type. It is versatile, durable, and of excellent quality. The DM–9 options include a 40-meter dusting hose that allows two people to dust an entire crop in a very short time. The substances are emitted from tiny holes scattered the entire length of the hose. (Parp recommends using organic substances only.) With a unit like this, one or two people can quickly and safely perform many difficult tasks in forestry and agriculture that formerly would have required a week or more of crew time. **Caution:** When spraying, misting, or dusting, the operator and all nearby persons should wear a respiratory system protection device or a breathing mask.

Heavy-Duty Leaf Blower

Each of the blower types described above is either handheld or backpack mounted. Most are powered by lightweight, two-cycle engines. Another type of blower specifically designed for rugged, professional maintenance might be of interest to homeowners with extensive walk areas, large patios, swimming pools, tennis courts, or parking lots. This type of blower is powered by a large four-cycle engine and looks somewhat like a large lawn mower. The engine and the blower unit are mounted on wheels. Mower-type handlebars extend up to the operator's level.

These units typically weigh about 100 pounds or more and ride on rather large pneumatic tires. The fuel capacity is about three times that of the handheld- or backpack-type blowers, allowing for extended use between refuelings. The air blast is also much greater, and provides enough force to move huge piles of wet or dry leaves, cardboard, and trash. Amerind-MacKissic currently manufactures two excellent models, the LB–516 and the LB–816. The 516 is powered by a 5 h.p. Briggs & Stratton engine, and the 816 has an 8 h.p. Briggs & Stratton engine. Both engines are powerful, dependable, and easy to maintain. These machines, of course, are not as versatile as a handheld or backpack blower, but they do a better job on heavy trash and extensive cleaning. They are also useful to paving contractors for clearing debris from new driveways and parking lots before sealing.

ELECTRIC MOTOR PRESSURE WASHER

An electric motor pressure washer is a rather specialized machine primarily designed for use by farmers, ranchers, and others who have the problem of cleaning tractors, combines, and other large pieces of equipment. A pressure washer is actually a scaled-down, industrial-type pressure cleaner designed for portability and individual use. The typical pressure washer uses electric motor power and a hydro pump to direct a liquid cleaner through a nozzle at high pressures. In selecting an electric pressure washer, look for a pressure of 700–1,000 psi and an output of about 2½–3 gallons per minute. Completely double-insulated electrical parts are necessary and a shut-off switch and other remote controls should be arranged so that the operator can easily reach them while using the cleaner hoses. The pump must be acidproof and should have a double inlet to allow hot and cold fluids to be introduced, either simultaneously or separately.

The Allis-Chalmers Power-Clean Model 803 is a fine example of a pressure washer suitable for home, agricultural, or light industrial use.

SNOW REMOVAL EQUIPMENT

Snow removal is another grounds-maintenance problem that has been made easier and safer by recent developments in outdoor power equipment. A moderate amount of snow can be cleared with any of the stronger gasoline-engine blowers mentioned above. But for heavy snow and areas larger than a small walk, a machine especially designed for snow removal is a better bet. Some companies simply market their standard blowers as snow blowers, including those described above. Other companies produce heavier equipment made primarily for this purpose. The features on these machines should include a winterized engine, a multispeed transmission, and some method of breaking up the snow to be removed.

Snow Throwers

A fine example of a heavy-duty snow thrower is John Deere Model 826. The 826 is a walk-behind, mower-type machine with an optional waterproof cab attached to the handle to cover the operator. It is powered by a winterized 8 h.p. Tecumseh Snow King engine and is capable of clearing a 26-inch path.

The 10 h.p., 32-inch path John Deere Model 1032 is another good heavy-duty snow thrower. The 826 and the 1032 both offer features that are desirable in any snow thrower. The power system is a two-stage design with a low-speed auger that breaks up and collects the snow, then feeds it to a higher-speed discharge blower. The transmission provides five forward gears, plus reverse. This kind of multispeed transmission is necessary in a snow thrower, because snow can be either deep and heavy or light and fluffy. It is very helpful to be able to match the speed of

your machine to the toughness of the snow you're clearing.

The tires used on snow throwers should be large with fairly deep treads. The carburetor should be well enclosed by sheet-metal housings or a rubber encloser to protect it against moisture and freezing. The air filter should be specially designed for winter use. The carburetor should include a primer system for easier starting on cold days, and the fuel tank ventilation must be designed to resist ice buildup and internal freezing.

You should also look for special safety devices on a walk-behind snow thrower. The auger, or snow-breaker, is potentially dangerous, and the machine should feature an auger brake that stops the collection mechanism when the auger drive is disengaged. A safety mechanism should also prevent the starter from working unless the auger is disengaged. The clutch design should be such that the machine stops moving forward if the operator's hands leave the controls.

Snow Blowers

A snow blower is typically simpler than a thrower, and it, again, is shaped more or less

Photo 7–4—Snow Blower

Photograph by Christie C. Tito.

117

like a lawn mower. A common design uses a large, rubber paddle wheel to scrape up snow and direct it through chutes that may be adjusted to blow the snow in either direction. It does not have an auger for breaking up hard snow. The average snow blower will clear an 18- to 20-inch patch and will blow the snow 10–18 feet away. Again, a winterized engine with a protected carburetor and fuel vents is desirable.

Tractor Snow Removal Attachments

As with many other jobs, snow removal is made much easier if you own a small tractor (see Chapter Nine). Many snow-clearing attachments of various kinds are available for most of the small tractors on the market, especially the better-known makes. Parp would not suggest that you buy a tractor just to remove the snow from your walk or drive, but if you have enough other needs to justify investing in a small tractor, then you should also purchase a blade, blower, or thrower attachment for winter use on snow and ice. A blade, of course, is a simple steel attachment that fits onto the front of a tractor at an angle. It pushes the snow to one side and clears down to the level of ground or concrete. Various other blower and thrower tractor attachments are also available, and both generally do an excellent job of clearing snow.

MAINTENANCE AND OPERATION

The secret of success in doing your own maintenance work on a snow thrower or snow blower is the same as that for any other piece of backyard equipment. Before all else or anything else fails, find yourself a manual and read it. You can avoid a lot of damage this way.

Since these are winter machines, they never break down or need maintenance when the weather is warm enough to make working on them comfortable. Thus, it's a good idea to perform some maintenance functions, like replac-

ing a broken skid on your snow thrower, in the summer if possible. This summertime maintenance check also gives you time to order needed parts and have them arrive before you actually need the snow thrower or snow blower again. Of course, repairs will have to be made in the cold if the machine breaks down during operation. But preventive maintenance in warm weather should reduce these occasions significantly.

Before thinking about looking at any of the machinery on your snow thrower or snow blower, remove the spark plug wire from the engine, and tape it to a spot where it cannot contact the spark plug. You won't have to worry about the engine starting up by accident while you are working on it.

First, check out the engine following the four-cycle instructions in Chapter Three. Also, always use multi-viscosity oil in your snow blower for easier starting in cold weather. Spray bared metal parts, such as the edge of the auger, with antirust oil or paint.

Any machine used in the winter or in wet, snowy conditions naturally requires more attention than other machines. People often fail to clean a snow blower's air filter because the machine is not exposed to the dirt and dust one encounters on a fall or summer day. However, any air filter or fuel filter can become clogged with moisture even more quickly than with dirt. Moisture will not pass through a good fuel filter system and will soon cause the machine to stop completely, even if it doesn't freeze solid.

Fuel and air filters on winter-use machines should be washed and rinsed in clean gasoline, then hung in open air to dry after each use of the machine. Also, the entire engine and all external parts should be wiped dry after use, especially around the carburetor and spark plug.

Many snow throwers use a V-belt to carry the drive from the engine to the transmission that runs the auger. Often this belt is arranged to be used as the clutch that idles the engine.

The drive is engaged by tightening up on a third pulley. Those belts do wear, and unfortunately they are usually connected in the middle of the machinery, which makes them hard to change. For example, a friend of Parp's owns an ancient Hahn-Eclipse machine, and he has to remove the transmission to get a new belt around the shaft—there is no other way to do it. If you have to do the same, it's a straightforward disassembly job that's easy to do by following the diagram of the machinery in your owner's manual. It just takes some time. Since it was such a time-consuming task for Parp's friend, he installed two belts instead of one to replace the tired belt. He wired the second belt up out of the way of the one that is actually working so that, when it breaks, it will be a simple matter to cut the old belt and drop the second one into place on the pulleys. This is one practice that you should make sure you can do on your machine, however, before proceeding with it.

If you've never examined your snow thrower's belt, or if you think it's worn, check it out. Be sure that the spark plug wire is off before you look at the belt. Move the belt by hand by turning the engine with the starter cable or by turning the auger. Look for signs of wear, cracking, or other general fraying. If the belt shows any fatigue at all, change it.

Most snow throwers have shear bolts on the drive axle. These are special, weakened bolts made of soft steel that are designed to shear off if the auger eats a rock or branch. Replacing them is easy and obvious but is only possible if you have spares on hand. They are available from your snow thrower dealer.

While getting spare shear bolts, you might also buy an extra master link for any drive chains and some Woodruff keys for drive pulleys.

Chain drives are like bicycle chains and work the same way. Your manual will tell you what the tension on the chain should be and how to adjust it. Most machines have locking bolts and adjusting bolts on the shaft at one end

of the drive chain. Loosen the locking bolts or nuts, and then screw the adjuster in or out until the chain has the recommended tension. Usually it should be about as tight as a bicycle chain, with about ¼ inch of sag in the middle of the run. You should also lubricate the chain. By using motorcycle chain oil, you can spray it on; it will congeal, and it will stay on the chain rather than being slung off as the machine runs.

Snow throwers vibrate, and sooner or later they manage to shake loose most of their screw fasteners. It's a good idea to go over the machine every time you use it to check for loose screws. Using an anaerobic, thread-locking compound reduces this tendency, but you should still check every bolt you can reach after every hour or so of operation.

Operating Snow Removal Equipment

Several factors combine to make snow removal and other winter jobs especially hazardous. It is well known that many people overexert themselves with winter chores and consequently suffer accidents, heart attacks from too much strain, and respiratory problems caused by breathing too much cold air. The presence of power equipment does not lessen these hazards at all. In fact, many of us are more inclined to overexert ourselves simply because we think the machine is doing all the work. Allow yourself to become accustomed to winter activities gradually, and always avoid overexertion. That last stretch of snow can wait until tomorrow, or next week.

Fires related to power equipment are also more common during winter than in other seasons. This is partly because people often rush to get in out of the cold, or they are reluctant to perform hazardous jobs outside, such as refueling, or washing air and fuel filters. Very often, a person falls victim to a fire because he has brought a machine indoors immediately after use and then has spilled fuel on the hot engine. Be especially careful to follow all safety precautions when using any power equipment in wintry conditions.

In addition, anyone can slip and fall on ice or snow while operating a snow thrower or blower. For this reason alone, wear protective clothing and boots, be well acquainted with your machine, and keep all other people well away from your work area.

The discharge from a thrower or blower is also potentially hazardous. Quite a few children and adults have been seriously injured when an operator mischievously aimed a thrower or blower discharge chute in their direction. Such accidents sure take the fun out of power equipment and those fine winter days.

It is better to keep your snow thrower or snow blower out in the cold rather than in a warm garage, because outside snow is less apt to melt on it and then freeze up, which will stop the machine from operating. Spraying floor wax onto the auger and inside surfaces of the discharge chute will help to keep snow from sticking to it and keep moving parts from rusting shut over the summer.

Brush snow off the machine and out of its workings after each use. Before starting, be sure that the auger paddle blades are free to turn, not frozen in place or blocked by ice from partially melted snow. Remember to remove the spark plug wire first. After freeing the blades, reconnect the spark plug, set the choke, and start the engine. Let it warm up for a few minutes before you begin removing snow.

If you have a gravel driveway, set the auger high so that it doesn't pick up much gravel with the snow. Unless you practice this basic trick, you'll forever be replacing the Woodruff keys on the transmission and putting in new master links to reconnect broken chains.

Parp has wandered off in mid-sentence to reveal his favorite ice-fishing spot to our new town marshal, and he probably won't be back until the end of the week. This leaves a lonely author in a deep canyon with only a guess as to how Parp wants to approach the garden section of this book. Oh, well. Maybe we all need a break. A long soak in the hot springs is good therapy for writer's cramp, and other professional ailments not to be specified here.

See you in the garden.

PART THREE:
The Garden

CHAPTER EIGHT:
Tillers
and Shredders

YARD AND GARDEN TILLERS

A tiller is a garden machine designed for digging, cultivating, aerating, and mixing soil in order to minimize resistance for growing vegetables, flowers, and lawns. The typical tiller is a simple design that consists of a power source (engine) mounted over revolving tines. Handlebars with operating controls extend to a convenient working height above rear wheels. The wheels are usually free and are not driven by the power source. Instead, the engine rotates the tines, which pull the machine forward while digging or cultivating.

The tines operating depth in the soil is determined by the adjustable setting of the wheels. Wheels set high allow the tines to churn deep in the soil. A low wheel setting causes the tines to turn the soil at a shallow depth.

Tillers are most often used to prepare the soil before planting. The tines can cultivate shallowly in a frequently planted area, or they can dig quite deeply to break new ground. The tines of most tillers can be adjusted or partially removed for various gardening needs.

A tiller is a useful power tool for anyone who gardens at all seriously. Without a tiller, ground must be broken and cultivated by laborious shovel work—work that is often too difficult for many people to do thoroughly. A tiller improves the quality of a garden and its produce simply because the soil is better prepared for growing. Most tiller users feel that the machine pays for itself in increased and improved garden

crops. Plants grow better because the roots can spread and descend more easily through the broken and well-mixed soil to reach nourishment and moisture. If you decide to mulch or add sand, gypsum, or peat moss to a new garden area, a tiller makes the job much faster, easier, and more complete.

You control how deeply your tiller digs into the soil by adjusting a depth bar up or down. The depth bar puts a drag on the tiller and holds the machine back so that the tines will dig in before moving forward. With a shallow setting, you can till a path around trees, shrubs, and flower gardens, as well as along a sidewalk. Once you own a tiller, it is easy to maintain these cleared areas for convenient mowing. A tilled area around trees also allows water and nutrients to reach the roots more effectively and helps to prevent bark damaged caused by mowing too close. Tilling also saves hours of trim work that must otherwise be done by hand.

Shallow tilling around sheds or immovable eyesores provides areas for planting flowers or ground covers that do not require mowing or trimming. This helps to eliminate those weeds that always seem to grow at the edges of such obstacles. Your landscape maintenance is much easier and, of course, it's a simple matter to till again whenever necessary or when you want to plant new flowers.

Difficult-to-mow areas around air conditioners, fences, rock borders, and swimming pools also can be tilled instead. One of the most difficult and annoying yard jobs is trying to mow close to such areas without your mower's discharge chute deflector or side-mounted grass bagger snagging on the obstacles. Tilling a border around these areas can even prevent injuries that may otherwise occur if you are tempted to remove important safety devices from your mower.

The most common use of a tiller is seedbed preparation for a vegetable garden. Although most tillers have removable tines to make narrow rows, you'll need all tines in place so that you can till a wide swath. If the area is now in sod, place the depth bar in a shallow setting for the first pass, then increase the tilled depth with each successive pass until the soil is well mixed to a depth of about 8 inches (12 inches would be better if your tines churn that deep). Soil mixed thoroughly to this depth makes for a healthy vegetable garden.

To keep your tiller on an even keel, leave an untilled strip of earth between passes. Otherwise, you'll find yourself digging a ditch on one side of each pass that will cause your tiller to lean off balance. When you've covered the garden area, go back and till the untilled strips to break the ground crust. Also, till again in directions 90° from your original paths. If you first tilled in an east-west direction, now go north to south. After tilling, rake or harrow to break up any remaining clumps, but do not granulate the soil. Rain causes finely broken soil to crust, thus making it difficult for plant sprouts to push through. If your soil is a heavy clay, use your tiller to mix in sand, gypsum, or peat moss.

When you plant, space your seed rows somewhat farther apart than the narrowest setting of your tiller tines. This way you can use your tiller to cultivate and kill weeds between rows all summer. To cultivate lightly, set your depth bar at 1½–2 inches, or at the shallowest setting on your machine. This shallow cultivation will control weeds and loosen the soil without damaging your plants' roots.

In the fall, you can use your tiller to prepare your garden and flower beds for winter. The soil should be tilled to a coarse, open texture that allows it to breathe and absorb moisture and nutrients that otherwise might run off with the melting snow.

If you use a mower that collects and mulches grass and leaves from your lawn, you can also till this mulch into your garden soil. Be sure the mulch is fine enough to prevent clumping. Fine mulch from your yard will decompose quickly and will add significant nutrients to the soil, especially through the winter months.

What to Look For in a Tiller

A standard front-tine tiller is a light machine in relation to the chores it must perform. Accordingly, weight distribution is particularly important. The machine should be designed with most of its weight riding on the working tines, which must both dig and pull the machine forward. A properly balanced machine has the engine mounted directly or almost directly over the tines. If the engine's weight bears down on the wheels instead, the front-tine tiller is very difficult to operate.

The tines themselves must be made of best-quality, high-carbon steel and should be adjustable for width, either by moving or removing some of the blades. Some inexpensive tillers utilize low-grade steel tines that break or bend out of shape easily.

The best mechanism for transferring the engine's power to the tines is a chain drive. Belt drive mechanisms often slip under strain and wear out much more quickly than chains. The entire chain drive mechanism should be encased in a metal shroud and should operate continuously in an oil bath. Any exposed parts of drive mechanisms must be cleaned constantly.

A simple clutch mechanism is the best design for starting and stopping the forward motion of the machine. Some method of locking the clutch control in position is a useful feature. The clutch control and an engine speed control should be attached to the handles within easy reach, and they should be easy to operate. For cultivation, it is handy to have a machine that you can operate from one side to avoid walking directly behind the tiller in the cultivated earth.

Photo 8–1—A Front-Tine Tiller

Rodale Press photograph.

Rear-Tine Tillers

Rear-tine tillers are larger and heavier than the standard homeowner machines discussed above, and they are generally used by people who farm or garden larger areas of ½ acre or more. These machines do not have the engine mounted over the tines. The wheels are larger, with heavily lugged tires designed to slow the machine's forward movement. With the weight of the engine on these retarding wheels, a quality rear-tine tiller is a heavy-duty machine designed to till or cultivate deeply into the earth with less effort than the lighter, front-tined tiller.

Rear-tine tillers obviously present more of a hazard to the operator than do front-tine tillers because the cutting tines are rotating much closer to the operator's feet. Any rear-tine tiller should be equipped with tine covers. The rear of the tine covers should be hinged so they will clear the ground as the tiller digs in. Chain drive is essential in a machine of this type, as are good balance and adjustable handlebars with conveniently located controls.

Tiller Attachments

Most tiller manufacturers also offer various attachments to make their machines more versatile. A furrowing blade is the most common attachment offered by the better manufacturers. In some cases, such as the Mighty Mac tillers made by Amerind-MacKissic, the furrowing blade is attached in place of the depth-control drag bar and can be adjusted for seed row depth. This allows the gardener to prepare furrowed seed beds while tilling at the same time.

Other companies, such as Snapper, offer large-diameter lugged wheels that are put on in place of the tines when using furrowing or other attachments. This configuration provides greater traction but allows only one operation at a time.

Some tillers also can be used with optional hilling attachments. A hilling attachment is used to fill in furrows, and it requires the use of a

125

Photo 8–2—A Rear-Tine Tiller

This garden tiller can be operated from one side. Rodale Press photograph.

wheel kit to replace the tines. Both the width and the depth of the hilling blades should be adjustable.

Tiller Maintenance and Operation

Most tillers are powered by commercial four-cycle engines, many of which are built by Briggs & Stratton. See Chapters Three and Four for maintenance and repair information on these engines, or service the engine as recommended by your manufacturer in your owner's manual. Always service your tiller before operating it. Remember that fresh fuel of the proper grade and a correct oil level in the crankcase are critical in four-cycle engines.

Engine problems aside, the most common cause of problems with tillers is improper or inadequate lubrication of the transmission. Always check the transmission for lubricant level before using your tiller. Use only the lubricant

recommended by your manufacturer, and maintain the level indicated on the machine or in your owner's manual. In the absence of manufacturer's instructions, fill the transmission to overflowing with SAE 90 gear lube or SAE 50 motor oil.

At the beginning of each season and at 20-hour intervals thereafter, check all bolts, nuts, screws, and other fasteners for tightness. Replace missing parts with manufacturer-recommended pieces before using the machine. Be sure that all shields and other safety devices are properly in place and correctly fastened.

Most tillers are equipped with some kind of skid device. The purpose of the skid is to drag in tilled soil and slow the forward movement of the tiller. If you are breaking new soil or doing your spring tilling, adjust the skid to its lowest setting, and place the wheels in their highest position. This adjustment usually requires you to keep a constant pressure on the handlebars to make the skid drag properly. To increase your speed and decrease the tilling depth, simply lift the handles slightly.

To cultivate between the rows of an established garden, position the wheels at their lowest setting and raise the skid fully up. It helps to reduce your tilling width to approximately 12 inches by removing or adjusting the tines as necessary.

The engine always should be set at as slow a speed as possible for the job at hand; this makes tiller operation much smoother and thus, less difficult. The machine should be allowed to do the work without excessive effort on the part of the operator. Less than half-speed is best; a tiller's engine should never approach full speed under load.

When rocks or similar objects become jammed between the tines and the tiller frame, immediately release the clutch control. Do not attempt to use the engine's power to clear the wedged object. Instead, shut the engine off. With the clutch disengaged, lift up on the handles, and push the tines down with your foot. If this fails to dislodge the object, you may have to loosen the tines.

If your tiller is equipped with a belt drive, the belt will stretch during use, and periodically it will be necessary to compensate for this stretching. Occasionally, this will be necessary with chain drives as well, as even they will stretch in time. You can compensate for belt or chain drive stretch on most machines by adjusting the idler pulley. To do this, first loosen the idler shaft, then pull up on the idler arm. You'll now have to adjust the clutch cable or rod, usually with some kind of adjustment link, collar, or cable clip. Do not overtighten the clutch cable; simply tighten it enough to remove the slack. Then retighten the idler shaft.

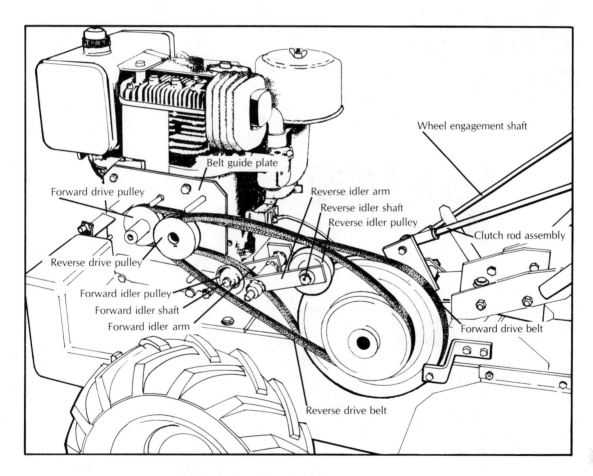

Illus. 8–1—Idler Pulley Adjustment

This tiller model has two drive belts and two idler pulleys. Adjust both idler pulleys as you would on a tiller with only one.

With some machines, it's actually necessary to move the engine forward in its mounts to properly adjust belt or chain drive tension. To do this, loosen the bolts that attach the belt shield to the engine. Then loosen the engine mounting bolts (there are usually four of these on this type of tiller), and slide the engine forward, which will tighten the belts. Retighten the engine mounting bolts and the belt shield bolts. Some machines require both of the procedures described above in order to adequately tighten the drive belt or chain.

Rear-tine tillers require further caution and instructions. Never attempt to operate a rear-tine tiller with the wheels disengaged and, while operating, never push down on the handles with enough force to raise the wheels off the ground.

A rear-tine tiller requires that the wheels be engaged and in contact with the ground for safe control and proper forward motion. The wheels actually retard the forward motion for safe control. Without the backward force of the wheels, the tines will drive the machine forward too quickly. For this reason, the tines are installed with their treads reversed for maximum resistance so as to slow the machine adequately. Always keep the tires and wheels in the position in which your manufacturer installed them.

Most rear-tine tillers allow for wheel engagement adjustment. If your wheels tend to slip down so that the tines are too high and disengage from the soil, you'll probably have to adjust the wheel engagement ball plunger to hold the wheel engagement shaft tighter. Many machines

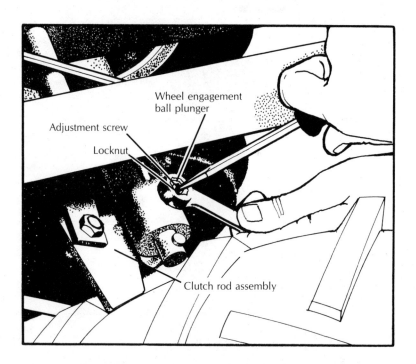

Illus. 8–2—Wheel Engagement Adjustment on Rear-Tine Tiller

use a locknut and screw adjustment to accomplish this. Loosen the locknut 2 or 3 turns, and turn the adjustment screw in until it seats against the wheel engagement shaft. Do not overtighten, or you'll damage the spring mechanism that keeps the wheels in place for operation. When the adjustment screw is seated, turn it back ¼ turn, and tighten the locknut.

These instructions are general and are intended to help in the absence of an owner's manual. If your manufacturer's instructions are different, of course, follow them instead.

Drive Belt Problems

Minor stretch problems in front-tine tillers and smaller machines have been covered above. Larger machines and rear-tine tillers occasionally develop other belt problems because there are often more belts (for reverse drive and other gears) and because the mechanisms are more complex. Any belt-driven tiller that is left out in the weather or exposed to radical changes in temperature will develop belt problems in time.

Before attempting to troubleshoot and correct any belt problem on a larger, framed ma-

Table 8-1: Tillers and Shredders Drive Belt Troubleshooting Chart

Problem	Possible Cause(s)	Remedy
Slips out of forward drive	Belt shrinkage	Reposition engine and readjust linkage
	Incorrect linkage adjustment	Adjust linkage or cable clips
	Worn linkage or linkage fasteners	Replace linkage or fasteners as required
	Clutch rod spring too tight	Adjust spring retaining device to lighten spring load
Does not engage forward drive	Clutch rod spring too loose	Adjust spring retaining device to increase spring load
	Belt shrinkage	Reposition engine and readjust linkage
Slips in reverse	Inadequate tension on reverse belt	Adjust reverse idler pulley
Does not engage reverse drive	Shrinkage in reverse belt	Reposition engine and readjust linkage
Forward or reverse drive belt smokes	Pulley out of alignment	Engage appropriate drive, and straighten belt by moving pulley as required
Smoke and noise from belts—engine stalls	All belts are too tight	Reposition engine and readjust linkage
Smoke and squeals from belts	Belts slipping, loose	Reposition engine and readjust linkage

chine or on a rear-tine tiller, check to be sure that your engine is mounted securely and is in the correct position for the length or size of your belts. To do this, remove the guard, or shield, over the belts, and press the belts down as far as they will go. The forward idler pulley should only move ¼–½ inch. If it moves more than that, the engine must be repositioned to the rear, usually only about ⅛ inch. Loosen the engine mounting bolts or the engine base plate (depending on design), and move the engine as necessary. You must then readjust the linkage to keep the clutch engaged in forward drive. You may now use Table 8-1, the Tillers and Shredders Drive Belt Troubleshooting Chart, to determine your problem.

SHREDDERS AND COMPOSTERS

Parp says that a shredder is one of the handiest backyard tools you can own. The Kemp Shredder Company (see Appendix C for address) has a partial list of things you can accomplish with a shredder. The list includes making compost in 14 days, turning organic garbage into humus quickly and without odor, making a more efficient mulch, making instant leaf mold, and making excellent seed and potting compost.

A good shredder is designed to shred, grind, or pulverize leaves, weeds, vines, brush trimmings, sticks, bones, phosphate rock, sludge, sod, soil manure, household garbage, and many other substances. If Parp started now, he could probably shred the entire town of Creede before the next hunting season.

As with other useful machines, there are several types and sizes of shredders available. While a few models are powered by electric motors, most are equipped with four-cycle gasoline engines (see Chapter Three). The smallest and simplest shredders are compost and soil shredders. These machines are designed to turn organic materials into compost, or humus, for gardening. A combination shredder/chipper is a larger, heavier machine designed to do all of the above, as well as turn branches up to approximately 3 inches in diameter into small chips that make excellent mulching material and are easily handled and stored. A combination shredder/chipper should be powered by a four-cycle engine of at least 4 h.p.

Shredder efficiency is measured in terms of the cubic yards of material the machine can shred per hour (cu. yds./hr.). Current models go from less than 3 cu. yds./hr. for smaller garden models, up to about 100 cu. yds./hr. for comercial soil shredders.

If you want a shredder primarily for light gardening or greenhouse use, look for a smaller machine, but be sure you choose a quality prod-

Photo 8–3—The Working Parts of a Soil and Compost Shredder

Courtesy Kemp Co.

uct. Look for solid construction, mobility, and ease of operation. The power should be a good four-cycle, 4 h.p. gasoline engine for outdoor garden use. For indoor greenhouse use, a quality electric motor of at least 1 h.p. and approximately 3,500 rpm is a good power plant. Four wheels are desirable on any shredder, but the smaller models designed for indoor use might have two front wheels and a metal leg at the rear.

A somewhat more versatile and efficient shredder should have a 5 h.p. gasoline engine and should handle 5–6 cu. yds./hr. of material. Kemp's Model K6 meets these specifications and is a sturdy, dependable machine. It is available with either two or four wheels.

If you operate a large greenhouse or a good-size garden, you might do well with a shredder that can handle 12 cu. yds./hr. A shredder in this range should have a 7–9 h.p. gasoline engine. These machines are a good investment for heavy users and will provide years of dependable service. A shredder of this type weighs 400–600 pounds, sometimes even more, so four wheels are certainly required.

Shredders for commercial use are manufactured, notably by Kemp, in the 20-to-30 or 30-to-40 cu. yds./hr. capacity ranges, and they are used commonly by professional groundskeepers, nursery operators, and wholesale florists. A 24 h.p. engine is efficient for machines of this size, which frequently weigh 1,800 or more pounds.

The largest shredders commercially available are primarily designed as soil shredders, with a capacity of 75–100 cu. yds./hr. A machine of this type should have an engine of 50 h.p. or more. These shredders can be machine-loaded and should include some mechanism for separating rocks from the finished material. Parp says the Kemp Model K101 is the best shredder in this range and is respected by professionals, many of whom use it exclusively.

Shredder/chipper combination machines do not have quite the design variations that standard shredders do. The chipper hopper should be separate from the hopper used for leaves, mulch, and soil, because a different design is required for the blades. A typical light combination machine weights 180 pounds, is approximately 45 inches long by 38 inches tall, and has a 4 h.p. engine. A medium-duty machine might weigh 300–400 pounds with a 5–7 h.p. engine. The heavy-duty shredder/chipper weighs 400–500 pounds, is 50 inches high and 60 inches long, and is powered by an 8 or 9 h.p. engine.

There are few attachments made for the types of shredder/chipper manufactured at this time, although Parp says Kemp's Sweep-N-Shred is especially useful. This machine attaches to most Kemp shredders and is actually a large vacuum machine that can suck piles of leaves and light material directly from the ground into the hopper of the shredder.

Operating a Shredder

Shredder operation is similar to working with any other power tool. The usual safety precautions apply, including keeping children and bystanders clear, using these gasoline-engine-powered machines outdoors only, and finding a safe, level area in which to operate the machine. You should never leave a running shredder unattended, of course, and you should keep yourself and others away from the discharge area during operation. Follow your manufacturer's instructions for maintenance and operation, and never attempt to shred material not recommended in your owner's manual. If you have a used shredder with no instructions, refer to Part One of this book for engine operation, maintenance, and repair, or to Appendix A for information on electric motors.

If a part comes loose inside your shredder, with extreme care you can examine it to see if you can determine what it is and if you can

Photo 8–4—Operating a Shredder/Chipper

Be sure to wear safety glasses. Leather gloves are the only kind that should be worn when handling rough materials; cloth gloves could get caught on a thorn and be pulled into the machine. Courtesy Kemp Co.

repair it easily yourself. If not, you should have the machine repaired by a professional before you use it again.

Never operate any shredder without a belt guard or shroud correctly in place. Obviously, attempting to clear or remove jammed material with your hands could result in tragedy.

Before you start your shredder after leaving it unused for a time, always make a visual check of the hopper. A baseball may have landed inside, or a cat may be sleeping there on top of unshredded material. These things do happen.

Your shredder will operate more smoothly and efficiently if the material is relatively dry and if you feed the material evenly and not too quickly. If you have to shred wet material, it helps to mix dry material with it for easier shredding.

A compost tumbler is a useful gadget for shredder owners. Of course, many simply turn shredded organic materials in their compost heap or bin into good compost for the garden or greenhouse. Either way, a shredder makes composting much faster, because a greater area of the material is exposed to the bacterial action that breaks it down to produce fine compost.

CHAPTER NINE:
Small Tractors

The small tractor is an amazingly useful and varied machine—it will do most of the jobs performed by many of the backyard tools discussed in this book, and many others in addition. It can be used as a mower, spreader, roller, tiller, cultivator, seeder, aerator, thatcher, harrow, leveler, and dozer blade for both earth and snow.

With certain attachments or options, a tractor can also be a wood splitter, generator, blower, and cut-off saw, which can be either fixed or on a flexible shaft. In fact, a small tractor can be used to run many kinds of hydraulic and direct-drive machinery not mentioned here. Both major types of wood splitters—the screw splitter and the hydraulic splitter—may be driven by the power of a small tractor, saving hundreds of dollars that would otherwise have to go for separate engines or motors.

If you have a large lawn of 1½–2 acres or more, you'd be smart to purchase a lawn and garden tractor just for the mowing. A 20 h.p. tractor can mow a full acre of grass in less than 30 minutes. A good riding mower requires more than twice as much time for the same work. If you have 3 acres of grass, you can complete your weekly mowing in less than an hour and a half—the same amount of time the average homeowner spends on a small yard each week.

Mowing is only a small part of the story. When the snow gets really deep, or when spring rains threaten to flood your newly seeded garden, or when you need to move something really heavy, then the tractor really shines. Of all the

Photo 9–1—Lawn Tractor

For mowing medium-size lawns of ¾–1½ acres. Courtesy Deere and Co.

134

big chores you expect to do, it's the odd, unpredictable jobs that make you glad you own a tractor (like straightening that light pole your teenage son backed into with the family car).

TYPES OF SMALL TRACTORS

Small tractors are generally of two types. The first is the lawn tractor. The lawn tractor is usually a machine of 8–12 h.p. designed primarily for mowing medium-size lawns of ¾–1½ acres or so. A lawn tractor may be equipped with a blade and used for light to moderate snow removal.

The other type is the small garden tractor, called a lawn and garden tractor. These are usually powered by heftier engines of approximately 15–25 h.p. and are designed to do most of the jobs mentioned at the beginning of this chapter. They usually include Power Take-Off (PTO) capability for running other machines, and they are designed to accept a wide variety of optional attachments. They are sturdier and more powerful than tractors primarily designed to mow lawns. When used as mowers, lawn and garden tractors generally cut a much wider swath than lawn tractors and in less time. They are also much more stable and efficient than lawn tractors under more difficult circumstances—on steep slopes, for example, or on hilly or rocky terrain.

If you have a large garden, the greater horsepower and heavier weight of a lawn and garden tractor makes it much easier to operate a tiller or plow attachment. Garden tractors may also include such features as hydrostatic drive* (so you don't have to shift gears), power steering, two-speed rear axles, heavy hitches, electric or hydraulic equipment lifts, and greater operator comfort with better seats, footrests, and the stability of a heavier machine.

*Caution: Pushing or pulling a hydrostatic tractor will damage the transmission. Do not use another vehicle to push or pull the tractor in gear, or at speeds above 10 mph.

For the purposes of this chapter, we will limit our discussion to machines that fit Parp's working definition for a general utility lawn and garden tractor. This means that the machine (1) must have all removable attachments, (2) must have provisions and capability for accepting and handling such ground-engaging attachments as moldboard plows, tillers, disks, or cultivators, and (3) must have a device to lift and control these attachments.

DESIRABLE FEATURES

Now that you know what kind of machine you're looking for, consider some important features you want to find in a garden tractor that you plan to have for many years and expect to operate for hours and days on end. Let's start at the front.

The basic material should be steel. Fiberglass bodies look great when they're new and seem solid enough, but a working tractor vibrates enough to weaken fiberglass in time, as well as crack the finish on a glass surface. Solid steel is easier to patch, repair, or bump out, and will hold its looks longer than a fiberglass body under constant use.

The engine is best protected if it is mostly but not entirely enclosed by a steel hood. If the engine is fully enclosed, it is likely to overheat during hard use. If the engine is fully exposed, the operator is also exposed—to both unsafe noise levels and to debris that may be sent flying from the engine as dirt enters from the front. The hood should be completely removable for easier engine service when you have to do a big job. There also should be plenty of room to work without removing the hood.

Examine the engine mounting system in any tractor you consider buying. Simple metal-to-metal bolted mounts transmit most of the engine's vibration to the frame and body of the tractor and to the operator. Excessive, undamp-

Photo 9–2—Lawn and Garden Tractor

In addition to mowing larger areas, a lawn and
garden tractor can also be used to till, cultivate,
and seed the garden. Courtesy Allis-Chalmers.

ened vibration will certainly wear you out fast,
create great stress on the machine and its parts,
and eventually be harmful to your skeleton and
nerves. The best mounting systems include solid
rubber vibration dampeners to improve your
tractor's performance and to assure your comfort, health, and safety.

The frame should be heavy-gauge welded
steel rather than light-gauge stamped and riveted
steel. Stamped steel frames are more likely to
bend or flex on rough terrain and may eventually
distort so much that the tractor will not operate
or drive properly. For the same reason, a forged
steel front axle is preferable to one made from
lighter materials.

Under the front end, the steering mechanism should be at least partially protected from
terrain and climate. The steering wheel should

be as large as is practical and should be padded to absorb vibration.

Step plates should be large enough to provide good footing when you climb into or out of the tractor with wet, muddy, or snow-slick shoes. The surface of the step plates and floorboards should be textured or stippled to prevent slips, and there should be plenty of foot space on the floorboard so you don't get caught if you have to bail out.

Speaking of safety, headlights and taillights are good to have on a tractor. Many people don't think of these features; some tractors come with no illumination at all. It's likely that you will need to operate your tractor at times when natural light is low, especially when removing snow on early winter mornings. For your own protection and that of others, headlights and taillights are a good investment.

Hydrostatic transmissions are fairly common on today's better small tractors, and they are also a good investment. A hydrostatic transmission is pedal-operated with one foot, leaving your hands free for steering and other operations. As you press the pedal down, the transmission automatically shifts into a higher gear, and the tractor operates at a greater speed. Decreasing pressure on the pedal shifts the tractor back into a lower gear for slower operation but with more torque or power.

Snapper offers a memory device for the transmission, and other manufacturers also might offer similar devices. This device allows you to set a certain working speed and then maintain that speed constantly by simply holding the pedal to the floor rather than having to hold it suspended in a certain position. Holding the pedal halfway or so becomes very tiresome, and the memory ability is a worthwhile feature to look for on a tractor.

A two-speed transaxle is also a valuable feature. Along with the transmission, this rear axle doubles the available operating speeds for better control. Some operate automatically, and others have a separate lever to control the ranges of operating speeds. It gives you a low range for power and close-in work and a high range for speed when transporting materials or changing job locations.

The drive train should be in-line from the engine to the transaxle, not a mess of twisting belts and pulleys that will reduce your engine's efficiency.

The engine's exhaust system should be designed to direct fumes and heat away from the operator and should be situated so that you're unlikely to burn yourself by bumping into the muffler. The muffler should be efficient enough to reduce the engine's noise effectively.

PTO capability at both the front and the rear of the tractor allows for much greater versatility than does a rear PTO only. A front PTO is especially useful for operating snow throwers and similar equipment. The rear PTO should be live, or independent of the tractor's clutch system; otherwise, the attachment will stop or slow every time you stop or slow the tractor. Some manufacturers offer three live PTOs as an option on larger tractors. The PTO itself should be a standard American Society of Agricultural Engineers (A.S.A.E.) PTO with a splined shaft, so that it will accept any manufacturer's attachment that fits A.S.A.E. PTO standards.

Speaking of standards, A.S.A.E. has also approved certain hitch design specifications that most manufacturers follow. Obviously, you don't want to replace or adapt every accessory you've collected when you decide to buy a new tractor, or change brands. And you may like a cart, or whatever, made by someone other than the manufacturer who built your tractor. The common A.S.A.E. hitches are a one-point sleeve hitch and a three-point category O hitch. Most manufacturers of tractors and accessories can supply any machine or accessory with either of these hitch designs. If your tractor uses a "house" hitch, a hitch design used only by that manufacturer, your options are clearly limited.

A hydraulic lift system is best for long-term dependability and heavy-duty service. Some manufacturers offer dual hydraulic lift systems, the best combination available. This type of system permits simultaneous but independent operation of both front- and rear-mounted accessories. The lift system should provide both a float capability (that is, you can adjust it during operation), and also locked positions that keep the lift immobile, either up or down, during operation. It should also have a depth control for groundbreaking implements.

The operator's seat should be ample and comfortable. It's best if it's padded, and it should be hinged to cover a storage area. You'll want to be sure your tractor has sufficient out-of-the-weather storage space for tools, owner's manual, garden plans, spare parts, gloves, and the like, especially if you store your tractor outdoors.

There should be fenders over the rear tires so you won't be splashed by water, mud, and snow. The fenders should be wide and should provide plenty of clearance for mud-clogged tires.

Most modern small tractors are powered by air-cooled, four-cycle engines. This is by far the best choice for a tractor engine, no matter how many cylinders it has. Air-cooled engines avoid the concerns about antifreeze or coolants, broken radiators and hoses, and freeze-cracked engine blocks.

The dashboard, or control panel, should be equipped with real gauges, not idiot lights. These should include an ammeter to check your battery's charge, a fuel gauge (sometimes located on the fuel tank), an oil temperature gauge, an oil pressure gauge, and an hour meter (to tell you the lapsed time of actual tractor work for maintenance scheduling). In addition, the control panel might include a choke control, a throttle control, and controls for independent PTOs.

If your tractor is equipped with a limited slip differential on the rear wheels, you'll have better control and maneuverability in mud or snow, and more control on tight turns. This system provides automatic, controlled traction to put more drive force on the wheel with the best traction on a slippery surface.

After all of this, you might consider the tractor's design, appearance, and color. You might also check with a local farm implement mechanic to determine price and availability of parts, ease of maintenance and repair, and general reputation of the manufacturer.

Choice of Tractor Size

Perhaps the most common complaint among users of small tractors is that they bought a tractor that is too small to meet their needs, or that they got carried away by tractor fever and bought one too large to operate on their property. The best suggestion Parp can make to anyone who is considering the purchase of a tractor is to take your time. Look at as many models as you can before you decide to buy. And don't just look—operate the machines as much as possible, both to get a feel for tractor operation before you own your own and to learn how much space a tractor needs to operate with good clearance. Determine your present and forthcoming needs, and choose a tractor that meets these needs but does not go too far beyond them. There's nothing worse than a beautiful machine locked in a shed because it's too much for the yard or garden.

TRACTOR ATTACHMENTS

All major tractor manufacturers provide a wide variety of tractor attachments. If the manufacturer uses A.S.A.E. hitches, connections, and specifications, the equipment will also fit tractors from other manufacturers who meet the same standards. This increases competition, decreases prices, and encourages the development of new, laborsaving features and improvements. It also provides the consumer with a wider choice of attachments.

Mower

Probably the first tractor attachment chosen by most owners is a mower. Mowers for tractor use come in various sizes, from about 30 inches up to about 60 inches. Except for highway strip and large grounds reel mowers on commercial tractors, all tractor mower attachments are of the rotary design and usually fit underneath the tractor between the wheels. Rotary mower attachments should be engineered to follow the contours of the ground to minimize lawn scalping.

Tiller

The rotary tiller attachment is used to prepare seedbeds by lifting and blending garden trash, soil, and compost into an aerated mixture that holds moisture and nutrients for healthy garden plants. The tiller attachment should be equipped with enclosed ends and a hinged, floating tailgate to keep debris and stones from flying around.

Front-End Loader

A front-end loader is extremely useful for moving earth, trash, logs, and other heavy material, and dumping them where you want them. The loader should have float capability and should be operated by an independent, PTO-driven hydraulic system.

Cultivator

A rear-mounted cultivator works both sides of seed rows to turn over nutrient-stealing weeds and grasses. It creates better soil aeration and water absorption. The tractor's wheels should, of course, ride between the garden rows.

Grader Blade

A grader blade is another rear-mounted attachment. You can set it for either a right angle or a left angle for spreading soil, gravel, or other materials. You should also be able to reverse the blade for backfill work or turn it over for building terraces.

Front-Towing Hitch

If you own a boat, another vehicle, or a piece of equipment that you must sometimes position in an exact spot, a front-towing hitch can be a very useful attachment.

Sickle Bar Mower

A sickle bar mower is used to clear weeds, brush, and heavy grass. It usually attaches to the side of a tractor and should be adjustable to cut both above the horizontal, as with a hill, or below the horizontal, as in a ditch. The best sickle bar mowers include a breakaway system, which releases the pressure automatically when an obstacle becomes stuck in or against the mower bar.

Moldboard Plow

A moldboard plow turns sod and buries garden trash in the preparation of a garden area. It leaves a broken, rough surface that slows wind erosion and water runoff. The plow's gauge wheel should be adjustable for depth.

Snow Thrower

A snow thrower is, of course, a front-mounted attachment. A good one will remove even the heaviest wet snow quickly and easily. The discharge chute, or spout, should be adjustable so that you can deposit the snow where you want it, out of the way.

Dozer Blade

A dozer blade can be used as a snowplow for long drives, or for moving relatively loose dirt or gravel. You should be able to position it either at a right or left angle, and it should include a breakaway release to protect the blade from obstacle damage.

Weather Enclosure

Some manufacturers offer a weather enclosure for their own tractors. Most enclosures are intended only to shield the operator from wind, snow, and rain, and they are not sturdy enough to provide protection if the machine turns over.

Dumpcart

Here is a most useful accessory. Many people make their own, but all major tractor manufacturers offer sturdy utility models that will operate smoothly for many years. To get the best use from a dumpcart, it should handle at least 300 pounds and up to 1,000 pounds of material. The corners and edges should be smoothly rounded for your protection. The endgate should be both hinged and removable, and it should be a true dumpcart—that is, there should be some convenient method for dumping the cart's load. With a dumpcart, cut-off saw, and hydraulic splitter (see Chapters Ten and Eleven), you can cut, split, and haul wood from areas difficult to reach by car or truck, thereby making the worst woodgathering chores very easy to handle.

Thatcher

A thatcher removes dense, built-up thatch from your lawn, which improves the health and growth of your grass. If you have a lawn of an acre or more, this attachment will save a lot of labor and time.

Earth Auger

Some tractor manufacturers, notably John Deere, offer both earth augers and posthole diggers for use with their tractors. They sure are handy when it comes time to open up a spring or put in a new fence.

SUPPLEMENTARY ATTACHMENTS

That about covers the typical range of attachments offered by most tractor manufacturers. In addition, there are many handy attachments and accessories that are manufactured by smaller, independent companies that do not build tractors. We'll cover some of the best of those devices now and include sources as well.

Rotary Broom

This is a polypropylene brush 5 feet wide for sweeping hard surfaces. It can be used to clear dirt, leaves, trash, and light snow. Contact Jenkins Equipment Co., Inc., 2720 Baker Rd., Dexter, MI 48130.

Backhoe

Brandly Manufacturing Co. (P.O. Box 187, Frederick, OK 73542) offers backhoe attachments made especially for garden tractors. They manufacture 8-, 13-, or 16-inch buckets that can dig up to 6 feet into the ground.

Vacuum Sweeper

Some tractor manufacturers offer their own sweepers, but one of the best independent companies is E-Z Rake, Inc., 1001 S. Ransdell Rd., Lebanon, IN 46052. They make a 70 h.p. combination sweeper/collector that sweeps up grass clippings and trash, and collects the material in a huge covered cart.

Broadcast Spreader

Many companies make spreaders for distributing seed and organic materials over large areas. A good model that adjusts to cover areas from 5–20 feet is sold by Brinly-Hardy Co., Inc., 324–T E. Main St., Louisville, KY 40202.

Tractor Cabs

The Original Tractor Cab Co., Inc., Arlington, IN 46104, manufactures basic, one-piece fiberglass tractor cabs with tinted windows, which are for weather protection only. Cozy Cab, Litchfield, MN 55355, makes roll-over protective cabs with safety glass windows and removable doors. Cozy Cab also makes a simpler, four-post protective cover. This consists of a four-post roll-bar, shade roof, and seat belt.

Trencher

This attachment allows you to dig trenches 3–4 feet deep. A good one is the Bulldog Model

260, made by Bulldog Enterprises, Inc., 7800 Elm St., N.E., Minneapolis, MN 55432.

Power Sprayer

The H. D. Hudson Manufacturing Co., 500–T N. Michigan Ave., Chicago, IL 60611, makes an excellent tow-behind power sprayer of various capacities up to 30 gallons.

Tractor Rakes

You can do all kinds of difficult landscaping jobs with a 4-foot or 6-foot rake from Arps Corp., New Holstein, WI 53061. These are very sturdy, heavy-duty units adaptable to almost all models of small tractors.

OPERATING A TRACTOR

If you buy a new garden tractor, you will surely receive an owner's manual that, in most cases, will be more complete and instructive than owner's manuals for most other backyard tools. Most good dealers will also give you a certain amount of personal instruction and will specify the most important cautions and safety procedures. For this reason, Parp urges that you make any new tractor selection and purchase through a professional farm implement dealer. You may pay slightly more than if you find a tractor in a department or discount store, but the predelivery instruction and the after-purchase service will more than make up for any difference in price.

If you have purchased a new tractor, be sure to study your owner's manual carefully and become well acquainted with all the adjustments and operating procedures before attempting to operate your new equipment. This also applies to any accessories or attachments with which you are unfamiliar.

If you have acquired a used tractor without an owner's manual, contact your manufacturer to obtain a manual before using your equipment.

If you cannot obtain an owner's manual, the following general suggestions may be helpful, but do not consider them a replacement for the specific information that can be supplied only by the owner's manual for your particular equipment.

Tractor Safety Rules

Many of the following rules apply to all power equipment and may have been previously mentioned in this book. For the sake of clarity and safety, they are repeated here.

Without doubt, there is one single most important safety rule regarding the use of any power equipment that applies even more so to tractor operation. *Never attempt any repair or adjustment and never add fuel, oil, or any accessory or attachment to a tractor that is in motion or while the engine is running.* Failure to follow this basic precaution results in several thousand serious personal injury/accidents each year.

1. Become familiar with the controls and proper use of your tractor and equipment before using them. Read your owner's manual, if available.
2. Never allow a child to operate a tractor. If you are instructing an older child, do not leave her or him unsupervised.
3. Do not allow anyone to operate your tractor without complete instruction and supervision.
4. Do not allow passengers on your tractor. Be sure that all observers are at a safe distance and that they do not distract you during operation.
5. Be sure your tractor and equipment are in good operating condition.
6. Keep all safety devices, shields, and covers in place and in good working condition.
7. Use only attachments or accessories approved by the A.S.A.E. for use with your tractor.

8. Be sure to direct discharge of materials away from all bystanders.

9. Handle fuel with caution. Use approved containers.

10. Never remove fuel cap from or add fuel to a hot or running engine.

11. Never add fuel indoors.

12. Never run the engine indoors for more than a few minutes. Be wary of exhaust fumes. Open the doors if you start your tractor in a garage or barn, and get the tractor outdoors quickly.

13. Clear your work area of obstacles that might be picked up and thrown by attachments.

14. Disengage all attachment clutches and PTOs and shift into NEUTRAL before starting the engine.

15. Wear sensible work clothes. Your clothing should not be loose or torn.

16. Wear work boots or heavy shoes. Never operate a tractor while barefoot or in sandals or canvas shoes.

17. Disengage all attachments when not in use or when transporting materials.

18. When leaving the tractor unattended, disengage power to attachments, lower all equipment, shift into NEUTRAL, set the parking brake, shut off the engine, remove the key, and block a wheel. All of these precautions should be taken every time you leave the operator's seat for any reason, such as to unclog attachments or to make any repair or adjustment. If you must refuel, allow the engine to cool first.

19. After striking an obstacle, stop tractor and attachments (see rule 18) and inspect for damage. Repair any damage before proceeding.

20. When mowing on rough ground or in tall weeds, set mower at highest cutting height.

21. Do not operate mower in wet grass.

22. Do not operate mower without deflector or grass collector properly in place.

23. Keep hands and feet out from under mower or other attachments.

24. Stay alert for holes in the terrain or other hidden hazards, such as rocks, groundhog burrows, buried cables, logs, and so on.

25. Operate mower in daylight only. If you must operate other attachments such as a snow thrower before or after daylight, be sure you have adequate artificial light.

26. Do not start or stop suddenly when operating on a hill or when going uphill or downhill.

27. Go slowly on slopes and when making turns, to prevent tipping or loss of control. Avoid sharp turns when possible. Execute necessary sharp turns very slowly. Be extremely cautious and slow when changing directions on a slope.

28. Operate only up and down the face of a slope. Never drive across the face of a slope. Do not start or stop suddenly on a slope.

29. Use extra care when pulling loads or using heavy equipment such as a backhoe. Attach hitch properly, and limit loads to those you can safely control. Do not turn sharply. Be careful when backing up. Use wheel weights when recommended for attachments.

30. Garden tractors are not designed or recommended for street or highway use. Watch for pedestrians and traffic when crossing or operating near roads or rails.

31. Keep all nuts, bolts, and screws tight to be sure equipment is safe. Check attachments frequently, especially mower and attachment blades.

32. Keep engine clean of grass, leaves, or excess grease.

33. Do not change engine governor set-

tings, which can result in overspeeding the engine, causing rapid engine damage.

34. Do not run engine while standing, or with seat deck raised.

35. Disconnect ground (−, or negative) terminal when servicing electrical system. Keep smoke, fumes, and sparks away from the battery, especially when charging. Do not overcharge battery.

36. Do not store gasoline-fueled equipment inside a building with a heat source.

37. Pay careful attention to all caution labels and instructions that appear on your tractor or attachments. Locate and know these labeled caution plates before using equipment.

38. Avoid accidents by thinking before you act.

Checks before Starting

Before starting and using your tractor, check the following points.

1. Be sure the crankcase is filled to the full mark with recommended engine oil. If manufacturer's recommendations are unknown and unavailable, use an SC or SD type of detergent engine oil. Use Table 9–1 to determine correct oil viscosity.

2. Be sure all nuts, bolts, screws, pins, covers, and shields are properly in place and correctly tightened.

3. Adjust the operator's seat so you can safely reach all controls from the operator's position.

4. Fill fuel tank with a good grade of fresh gasoline—unleaded or regular—according to your manual's specifications. Do not use stale or premium fuel, and *do not* mix oil with gasoline.

5. Check oil drain plugs for tightness.

6. Check for leaks at all fuel system connections.

7. Be sure that wheel bolts are tight and tires are properly inflated.

8. In addition to normal daily maintenance and service, check the "hours worked" indicator to determine other necessary maintenance procedures according to Table 9–3, Small Tractor Maintenance Schedule, further on in this chapter.

Table 9–1: Correct Oil Viscosity According to Air Temperature

Air Temperature	Oil Viscosity
Above 30°F	SAE 30
30°F to 0°F	SAE 10W–30
<0°F	SAE 5W–30

Starting the Engine

1. Seat yourself in the operator's seat. Many tractors have a dead man's safety switch under the seat. The operator must be seated on the tractor to start or run the engine. Never start the engine unless you are seated in the operator's position.

2. Be sure the parking brake is engaged.

3. With standard transmissions, place gearshift lever in NEUTRAL position, and disengage PTO clutch controls. On hydrostatic tractors, place hydrostatic control in NEUTRAL position and disengage PTO clutch controls.

4. Depress the clutch-brake pedal and apply brakes. Keep clutch disengaged until engine is started.

Illus. 9–1—Location and Function of Typical Tractor Controls

A	Front Lift Control	Operates front hydraulic lift cylinder when latter is installed on tractor. Used to raise and lower front-mounted attachments.
B	Rear Lift Control	Operates rear hydraulic lift cylinder. Used to raise and lower center- and rear-mounted attachments.
C	Hydrostatic Control Lever	Controls direction and speed of tractor.
D	LIGHTS Switch	Switches tractor lights on or off
E	ENGINE Speed Control	Operates engine throttle to adjust engine speed.
F	Choke Control	When pulled out, closes engine choke for starting and warmup in cold weather.
G	Brake Pedals	Two pedals, left and right, operate separate brakes on respective rear wheels. Pedals should be locked together when operating tractor at high speeds.
H	IGNITION Switch	Operates with key to start, run, or turn off engine.
I	Parking Brake Lever	Locks brake to hold tractor in parked position.
J	Clutch Pedal	Operates traction clutch. Used to disengage transmission from engine for cold-weather starting or emergency stopping.
K	REAR CLUTCH Switch	Operates electrically controlled clutch for rear PTO (Power Take-Off). Used to turn rear-mounted attachments on and off.
L	FRONT CLUTCH Switch	Operates electrically controlled clutch for front PTO (Power Take-Off). Used to turn front- and center-mounted attachments on and off.
M	Shift Lock	Used to lock transmission shift lever (item N) in selected gear position.
N	Gear Shift Lever	Shifts transmission gears to control tractor speed range.

144

5. If engine is cold, pull choke control all the way out, or place in CHOKE position.
6. Set engine speed control on SLOW or START position.
7. Turn key to start engine. As engine warms, push choke control all the way in, or place in RUN position.
8. With engine running, set the engine speed control between ¼- and ½-speed.
9. Be sure the path you're going to travel is clear of friends, pets, and other obstacles.
10. Release parking brake.
11. With clutch engaged, for hydrostatic tractors, push hydrostatic control to clear the neutral notch, or place gearshift lever in desired gear. Move hydrostatic control slowly forward to move tractor forward, or pull lever back to move to the rear. With other transmissions, select gear, then move speed range control lever to high or low range.
12. Release clutch-brake pedal to place tractor in motion.
13. With hydrostatic tractors, adjust engine speed control for desired engine speed, and adjust hydrostatic control for desired ground speed.
14. To change standard transmission gears, stop the tractor completely, and depress fully the clutch-brake pedal.
15. To stop, move hydrostatic control lever to neutral. To stop faster, and to stop standard transmission tractors, depress clutch-brake pedal fully.
16. *Before leaving tractor seat,* disengage PTO or stop attachment, and stop tractor motion. Set engine speed control to SLOW. Set parking brake and lower attachment fully. Turn off engine and remove key.

Wheel Weights

Most tractor manufacturers supply wheel weights for use with tractors above the smallest size lawn tractors. Wheel weights are used to increase the stability of a tractor when using certain attachments, especially the backhoe and similar heavy equipment, or under certain operating conditions.

Wheel weights should always be used when operating the tractor on hills with slopes of 11° or above. The usual standard is one weight for each rear wheel. Front and rear wheel weights are recommended when using the tractor to operate a backhoe or front-end loader. They're available at your farm implement dealer.

Engine Speed and Gear Selection

Selecting and shifting gears is one tractor operation that some people find difficult or confusing. It may help to consider the operation of the transmission separately from the problem of engine speed.

The transmission gears are shifted by moving the gearshift lever. The gearshift lever has as many positions as there are combinations or functions of gears, including NEUTRAL and, sometimes, PARK. Many small tractors have three gears; some have six gears.

The gearshift lever of a three-speed tractor transmission has three gear positions and neutral. The following gear position guide will also clarify the more complex transmissions.

Neutral disengages the transmission for the rear wheels. NEUTRAL is for starting or parking the tractor, and for moving it under other than its own power. Always place the lever in the NEUTRAL position when moving the tractor under other than its own power, and never exceed 10 mph in this operation.

First Gear is for the slowest tractor speeds. Use it to go up and down slopes, over obstacles and ditches, when operating on rough ground, and when maximum pulling or pushing power is required.

Second Gear is for medium speeds and pulling power. Use it when first gear is not required, on moderately smooth, fairly level terrains.

Third Gear makes the tractor move quickly. Use this when traveling over smooth, level ground or pavement. Never use third gear on any slope or hill, or on rough ground.

Selecting the correct combination of engine speed and transmission gear for the job at hand is the most critical factor in safe and efficient tractor operation. It is impossible to fully represent every type of tractor engine and transmission here, but the following chart, Engine Speed/Gear Selection, should be helpful to tractor owners who have no owner's manual, or whose manual is incomplete in this respect. The author is grateful to the Allis-Chalmers Corporation for the information on which Table 9–2 is based.

Table 9–2: Engine Speed/Gear Selection

Attachment	Engine Speed Control	Transmission Gear Selection	Hydrostatic Lever Position	Approx. Ground Speed (mph)	Required Accessories and Options	Recommended Accessories and Options*
Transporting Tractor	S — F	1 / 3 — ②	N / R — F	3–6		
	S — F	1 / ③ — 2	N / R — F	5–10		
Center-Mounted Rotary Mower (Smooth, level terrain; normal grass)	S — F	1 / 3 — ②	N / R — F	4–6	Hitch assembly for mid-mounted attachments.	Front turf tires and wheels; rear turf or high flotation tires and wheels.
Center-Mounted Rotary Mower (Rough or sloping terrain; heavy or wet grass)	S — F	① / 3 — 2	N / R — F	2–3	Hitch assembly for mid-mounted attachments.	Front turf tires and wheels; rear turf or high flotation tires and wheels; rear wheel weights.
	S — F	1 / 3 — ②	N / R — F	3–4		

Table 9–2—Continued

Attachment	Engine Speed Control	Transmission Gear Selection	Hydrostatic Lever Position	Approx. Ground Speed (mph)	Required Accessories and Options	Recommended Accessories and Options*
Sickle Bar		1,3 — ②		2–5	Hitch assembly for mid-mounted attachments.	Rear wheel weights for side hill mowing.
Stationary PTO		1,3 — Ⓝ — 2		0	Rear PTO.	
Snow Thrower (Light snow)		1,3 — ②		2–4	Hitch assembly for front-mounted attachments; hydraulic cylinder.	Tire chains; rear wheel weights.
Snow Thrower (Heavy or wet snow)		① ,3 — 2		1–2	Hitch assembly for front-mounted attachments; hydraulic cylinder.	Tire chains; rear wheel weights.
		1,3 — ②		2–3		
Snowplow and Dozer Blade		① ,3 — 2		2–3	Hitch assembly for front-mounted attachments; hydraulic cylinder.	Tire chains; rear wheel weights.
		1,3 — ②		3–5		
Rear-Mounted Grader Blade		① ,3 — 2		2–3	Three-point hitch.	Tire chains; rear wheel weights; front weight; front bumper.
		1,3 — ②		3–5		
Rotary Tiller		① ,3 — 2		1	Three-point hitch; rear PTO.	Front weight; front bumper.
		1,3 — ②		2–3		

[Continued on next page]

Table 9–2—*Continued*

Attachment	Engine Speed Control	Transmission Gear Selection	Hydrostatic Lever Position	Approx. Ground Speed (mph)	Required Accessories and Options	Recommended Accessories and Options*
Mounted Plow				1–4 2–3	Three-point hitch.	Front agricultural tires and wheels; front weight; rear wheel weights (two sets); front bumper.
Cultivator				2–3 3–5	Three-point hitch.	Front agricultural tires and wheels; rear agricultural tires and wheels; rear wheel weights.
Front-End Loader				1–3 3–5	Front high capacity tires and wheels.	Tire chains; rear wheel weights and/ or calcium chloride in tires; rear high flotation or agricultural tires.

*Use front weights whenever you operate rear-mounted attachments on slopes. Use rear wheel weights when needed for traction or counterweighting and to operate on slopes greater than 20 percent (11.3°). Never operate on slopes greater than 35 percent (19.3°).

REFER TO YOUR ATTACHMENT OPERATOR MANUAL FOR ADDITIONAL INFORMATION.

Driving a Tractor

The first time you operate your tractor, you should do so on level ground only, and not in wet conditions. Be sure the tractor and all safety equipment are functioning properly before moving the machine. Start off in first gear, or in low range, and at a slow engine speed. Make wide, slow turns, and avoid all slopes and obstacles. When you have a feel for driving and steering the tractor, practice starting, stopping, and starting again. Then increase your engine speed slightly, and practice some more. Gradually advance by selecting faster transmission speeds.

Stopping

Hydrostatic tractors can be stopped most easily by simply moving the hydrostatic control lever to NEUTRAL. This will slow and stop the tractor rather gently. If you must stop on a slope, do not depend on the hydrostatic transmission to hold the tractor. Most garden tractors have a double-lock brake system. To stop, just press down on the brake pedal, or both pedals if there are two, and engage the parking brake while holding the pedal or pedals all the way down. The foot brakes will then be locked down when you remove your foot, and the locked brakes will hold the tractor securely on any slope that is safe for a garden tractor (less than 30–35 percent, or 19°). Be sure to release the parking brake lever completely in order to unlock the foot brakes before attempting to move the tractor again.

If your tractor has two brake pedals, you should lock them together during operation, especially if you expect to use the tractor at higher speeds. Never stop the tractor by depressing only one of two brake pedals, especially when traveling at higher speeds or on slopes or rough terrain. Use the brake pedals separately to aid in making slow turns. Depressing the left pedal in a left turn, or the right pedal in a right turn, gives the operator more control during delicate maneuvers. Except when using a brake as an aid in turning at slower speeds, both brake pedals should be depressed equally and at the same time to avoid losing control. If your brake pedals do not lock together, you can depress both simultaneously and equally with one foot by placing your foot over the gap between the two pedals so that your foot contacts both pedals.

Checks during Operation

As with an automobile, indicators on the dashboard warn you when your oil pressure is insufficient, your battery charging system is malfunctioning, and your engine or transmission is running too hot. If your crankcase is correctly

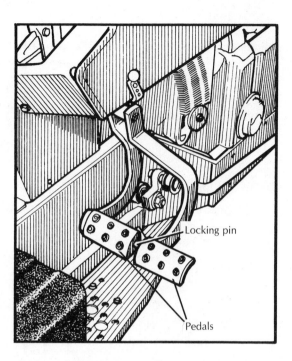

Illus. 9–2—Double Brake Pedals and Locking Pin

filled with the proper lubricant and your oil pressure gauge or idiot light indicates low pressure, you probably have a serious engine or oil system problem that must be repaired before the machine is used further. Never continue to operate a tractor if the gauge or light warns of insufficient oil pressure.

If a gauge or light indicates that your hydrostatic transmission is too hot, stop the tractor by placing the hydrostatic control lever in NEUTRAL, but keep the engine running at full speed to cool the hydrostatic lubricant. When the gauge shows that the transmission oil temperature has returned to normal, stop the engine and clean the oil cooler. If the cooler is quite dirty, you can assume that its inability to work properly caused the high temperature and you can continue to work in the same gear. If the cooler is not dirty, you should shift to a lower gear before proceeding. If the cooler is dirty, you should change the transmission lubricant and replace the internal filter (if any), especially if the oil has been overheated and smells of burning.

Operating Conditions

When you operate a tractor in dusty, cold, or hot conditions, you should take further precautions for safety's sake.

Dusty Conditions

1. Keep engine fins and cooling fan screen clean.
2. Service air cleaner more frequently than usual, often enough so that an unobstructed flow of clean air can enter the carburetor freely.
3. Change oil more frequently, approximately every 10–16 operating hours.

Cold Conditions

1. When the temperature is below freezing, use the engine oil of the appropriate weight (5W–30 or 10W–30), even if you must change ahead of schedule. Warm the engine thoroughly before changing oil.
2. Use fresh fuel. Fill the fuel tank after each day's work to minimize condensation.
3. Always disengage the clutch when starting the engine.

Hot Conditions

1. When the temperature is above 85°F, take extra care to keep engine cooling fins, fan screen, and transmission oil screen clean. Keep engine free of debris, grease, oil, or anything that might obstruct free airflow.
2. Use SAE 30 oil, or heavier oil if manufacturer recommends it.
3. Check battery fluid level more often than usual. Fill up with distilled or soft water when necessary.

MAINTENANCE AND REPAIR

By now you know how Parp feels about maintenance. If you don't take care of your tools, they won't work—like Parp's nice new chain saw. Someone filled the chain oiler with grit. Now the pump's damaged. Parp has done the same himself, but he usually avoids such errors these days. They're too expensive and troublesome.

Tractors, especially, require exact maintenance, precisely because they are brawny machines designed for heavy use, even in muddy conditions. Your tractor will do well in mud or other adverse conditions provided you clean it between such uses. Otherwise, one day soon it will refuse to go near mud.

Small tractors require maintenance if they are to continue operating efficiently and dependably. Certain maintenance services should be performed daily—that is, each time the tractor is put to use, either before starting (see Checks before Starting, page 143) or at the end of the day's work.

Other maintenance checks and services must be performed at regular intervals. This emphasizes the importance of an "hours worked" indicator, which is usually an optional feature. Table 9–3 is a maintenance schedule designed by Parp to apply to most aspects of maintenance required by most tractors, as intended by the various tractor manufacturers. Not all checks and services will apply to all small tractors, and some tractors may require some maintenance not mentioned here. Whenever possible, follow your manufacturer's instructions. Of course, perform all maintenance checks and services with the tractor's engine off.

It would take an entire book or more to cover all maintenance and repair procedures for all the small tractors in use today. However, most small tractors are reasonably similar, so most of the procedures specified for a particular model will apply, with minor modification, to most other small tractors.

Table 9–3: Small Tractor Maintenance Schedule

Required Service	Before First Use	Daily— Before or After Use	Every 5 Hours	Every 25 Hours	Every 100 Hours	Every 200 Hours	Every 400 Hours
Check fuel supply	√	√ before					
Check for loose or damaged parts, shields, nuts, screws	√	√ before	√				
Check engine oil level	√	√ before	√				
Clean or replace air filter				√			
Check transmission oil level	√			√			
Check tires and tire pressure	√			√			
Check battery fluid level	√			√			
Change engine oil and filter				√			
Lubricate tractor and mower	√			√			
Clean transmission oil cooler			√				
Clean mower or other attachments		√ after					
Lubricate attachments	√			√			
Clean battery and cables					√		
Inspect spark plug(s)					√		
Clean engine cooling fins					√		

[*Continued on next page*]

Table 9–3—*Continued*

Required Service	Before First Use	Daily— Before or After Use	Every 5 Hours	Every 25 Hours	Every 100 Hours	Every 200 Hours	Every 400 Hours
Sharpen mower blades				√			
Repack front wheel bearings							√
Have planetary assembly repacked					√		
Clean fuel filter				√			
Service breaker points							√
Clean entire engine					√		
Check ignition timing							√
Check valve-to-tappet clearance							√
Have cylinder heads serviced							√
Have starter serviced							√
Clean crankcase breather					√		
Clean and adjust linkage						√	
Replace fuel filter						√	
Check drop housing oil level	√				√		
Check traction clutch belt tension					√		
Change transmission oil and filter							√
Change air filter						√	

Parp describes below some repair and maintenance procedures common to most garden tractors. Most common engine procedures, such as checking the crankcase oil, have been discussed in Part One, so they will not be repeated here.

Transmission Oil Cooler Cleaning

This job does not apply to any of the other backyard tools and many of the smaller tractors discussed in this book, but it is critical to the protection and efficient operation of lawn and garden or larger tractors. If the cleaner and the rest of the transmission oil cooler is not cleaned every 25 hours, or more often if necessary, the tractor will overheat and soon will cease to function.

When cleaning the transmission oil cleaner, a filter inside of the cooler, take care not to damage the cooler fins. Do not use a hard tool such as a screwdriver or hammer. Refer to Illustration 9–3, showing a typical tractor's transmission oil cooler, and follow these steps:

1. Raise tractor hood.
2. Remove loose debris, grass, and dirt with a large, clean paintbrush.
3. Use air pressure or a garden hose to clean between the cooler fins. To get under the cooler, remove the hold-down screws on both sides, and lift the

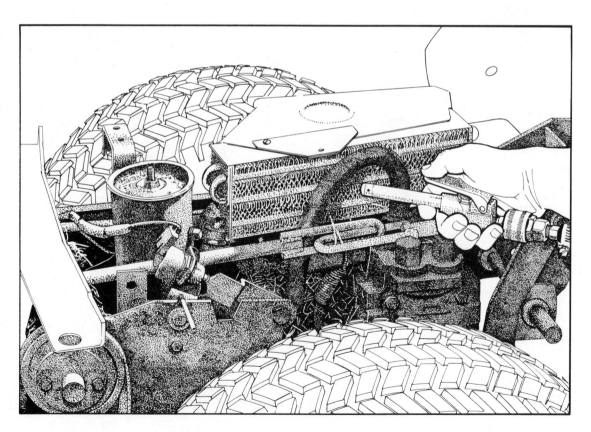

Illus. 9–3—Cleaning the Transmission Oil Cooler

Use compressed air to clean dirt from cooling fins.

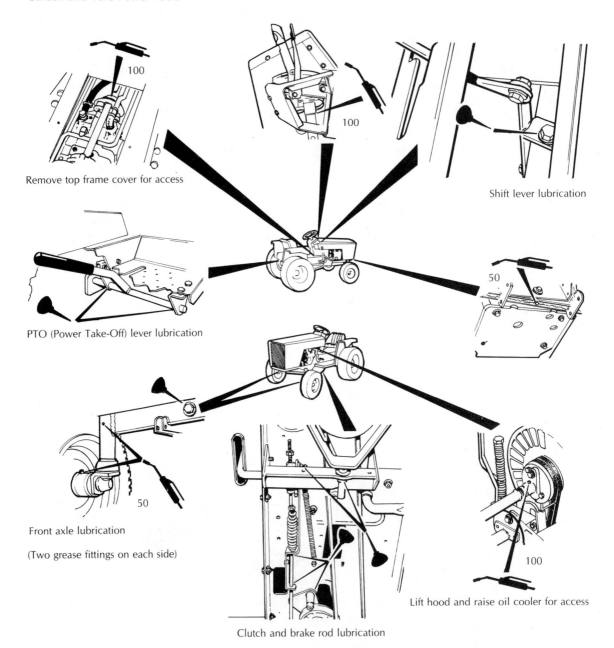

Remove top frame cover for access

Shift lever lubrication

PTO (Power Take-Off) lever lubrication

Front axle lubrication

(Two grease fittings on each side)

Clutch and brake rod lubrication

Lift hood and raise oil cooler for access

Note: Keep grease and oil off belts and pulleys.

Illus. 9–4—Typical Tractor Lubrication Points

The oil can symbol indicates lubrication necessary with oil. The grease gun symbol indicates the use of a lithium base automotive grease. Numbers signify the number of hours between lubrication. To grease, wipe part clean with rag, apply 3 to 5 shots of grease, and wipe up residue.

left side of the cooler slightly. Clean the bottom side of the cooler with air pressure, if available. Retighten hold-down screws. **Caution:** Wear eye protection when using air pressure for cleaning.

4. Use solvent to remove oil or grease. Do not use gasoline.

Engine Air Filter Cleaning or Replacement

Although this procedure is required for any engine and is already covered in Part One, tractor filters are often heavier and are designed to be more permanent than the air filters on many other small engines. Note that to clean most tractor filters you should use preferably air pressure, or soap and warm water. Dishwashing detergent works well. Do not use solvent. Clean after every 25 hours of use.

1. Raise tractor hood.
2. Loosen fastener, usually a thumb screw, on filter clamp.
3. Push clamp *toward* engine.
4. Remove air filter inlet cover and filter element. **Note:** Take care not to contaminate passages or parts usually protected by the filter assembly.
5. Clean air filter inlet and filter element with air pressure or soap and warm water.
6. Dry filter inlet and filter element before reinstalling. **Note:** Replace filter element at least after every 200 hours of operation or whenever element is dirty or damaged during cleaning.
7. Install filter element. Look for direction arrow. On many tractors, the arrow on the element must point toward the engine to show the direction of the airflow.
8. Install inlet cover. Secure with clamp and fastener.

Tractor Lubrication

Illustration 9–4 depicts some typical tractor lubrication points. Lubricate after every 50–100 hours of use.

Rear Wheel Drop Housing Oil Level Check

Check the drop housing oil level after every 100 hours of use.

1. Remove the check plug from drop housing (see Illus. 9–5).
2. Oil level in housing should be even with the bottom of the check plug hole. Add SAE 90–W transmission oil through check plug hole until full.
3. Replace and tighten the check plug.
4. Repeat procedure for drop housing of opposite rear wheel.

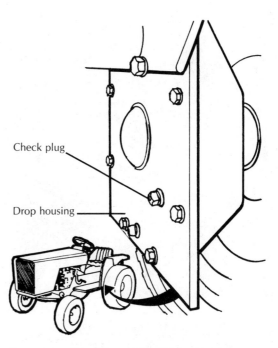

Check plug

Drop housing

Illus. 9–5—Check Rear Wheel Drop Housing Oil Level

Fuel Filter Replacement

Most tractor engines are equipped with a standard in-line fuel filter. This filter should be changed every 200 hours, or whenever operating conditions are extremely dusty, or when the filter is clogged by contaminated fuel. The fuel filter is usually held in place by two ordinary or spring-type hose clamps (see Illus. 9–6).

1. Use pliers to open and slide hose clamps away from fuel filter.
2. Pull ends of fuel filter out of hoses, one side at a time.
3. Insert ends of new fuel filter into hoses. Look for direction indicator. The arrow must point toward the carburetor unless otherwise indicated.
4. Use pliers to open and slide hose clamps into place.

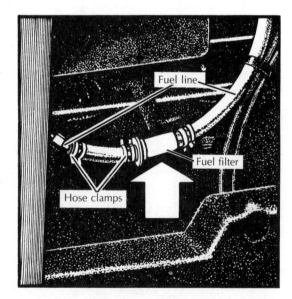

Illus. 9–6—In-Line Tractor Fuel Filter

When checking for sediment buildup, look at the point where the fuel line from the tank connects to the filter.

Crankcase Breather Cleaning

The crankcase breather allows excess pressure to escape from the crankcase of the engine and is therefore an important aspect of the engine's cooling system. When the crankcase breather becomes badly clogged, the engine can be severely damaged. You must disassemble the crankcase breather assembly in order to clean it properly. It should be cleaned after every 200 hours of use (see Illus. 9–7).

1. Remove hose clamp and hose from breather.
2. Loosen clamp screw and clamp.
3. Disassemble breather assembly (see Illus. 9–7).
4. Soak cover, screen, and mesh in a nonflammable automotive solvent. Be sure the plastic balls in the cover are free to move.
5. Carefully dry all parts.
6. Reassemble breather. Use a new O-ring.
7. Reinstall hose and clamp. Tighten screw to tighten clamp.

Governor Linkage Cleaning

Clean the governor linkage after every 20 hours of use.

1. If possible, use compressed air to blow loose dirt off the governor linkage.
2. Using a small, soft brush, carefully wash the linkage with a nonflammable automotive solvent to remove grease and oil. Be sure to take particular care not to damage or distort the linkage or its fasteners (see Illus. 9–7).

Engine Fins Cleaning

The engine cooling fins are the heart of the air-cooled engine's cooling system. Although some mechanics and manufacturers recommend cleaning the fins every 200 hours, Parp

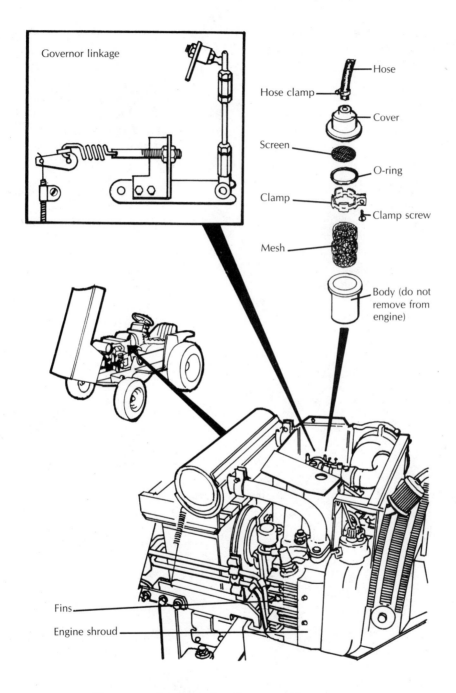

Governor linkage

Hose

Hose clamp

Cover

Screen

O-ring

Clamp

Clamp screw

Mesh

Body (do not remove from engine)

Fins

Engine shroud

Illus. 9–7—Crankcase Breather Assembly, Governor Linkage, and Engine Fins

advises 100 hours, or more often if they become very dirty, muddy, or extremely greasy.

1. Remove engine shrouds from both sides of engine.
2. Use compressed air or a brush and nonflammable solvent to clean engine cooling fins. Also clean the shrouds.
3. Replace and secure cleaned engine shrouds.

Repacking Front Wheel Inner Bearings

Repack your front wheel bearings after every 400 hours of operation.

1. Jack up front end of tractor, and block safely for wheel removal.
2. Use a screwdriver to pry off the grease cup (see Illus. 9–8).

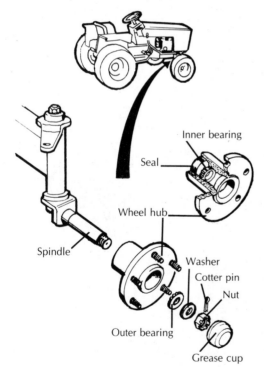

Inner bearing

Seal

Wheel hub

Spindle

Washer

Cotter pin

Nut

Outer bearing

Grease cup

Illus. 9–8—Parts and Assembly of Tractor Front Wheel Bearings

3. Remove cotter pin, nut, washer, and outer wheel bearing. **Note:** Keep bearings separated in order to return each to its original place.
4. Remove hub from spindle.
5. Carefully pry seal from hub. Do not scratch seal in hub. Inspect seal, and replace if worn or damaged.
6. Remove inner bearing.
7. Using a good solvent, wash the wheel spindle bearings, and the inside of the wheel. Wipe dry with a rag.
8. Coat seal and spindle with a quality wheel bearing grease. Keep grease clean.
9. Lubricate bearing completely with grease. Pack grease into spaces between rollers.
10. Install inner bearing in hub. Press new seal into hub.
11. Install hub on spindle. **Note:** Take care not to damage the seal.
12. Install outer bearing and washer. Install nut loosely.
13. Tighten nut slightly and spin wheel. Repeat until wheel drags slightly when spun.
14. Loosen nut enough to align nearest cotter pin holes.
15. Check for wheel wobble. If wheel wobbles excessively, repeat steps 13 and 14.
16. Install new cotter pin and cleaned grease cup. Wipe off excess grease.
17. Repeat procedure for the other front wheel.

Changing Transmission Fluid and Filter

After every 400 hours of service, you should change your tractor's transmission fluid and filter. Your transmission should be warm when you drain it. Run the tractor five minutes or more

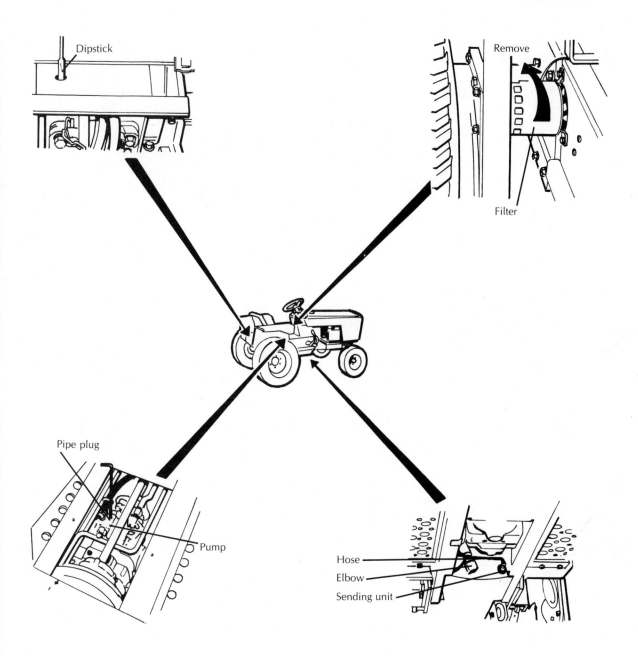

Illus. 9–9—Changing Tractor Transmission Fluid and Filter

before draining the transmission. The tractor must be parked on a level surface with the parking brakes locked.

1. Remove cover from bottom of tractor frame.
2. Disconnect temperature-gauge sending unit wire and remove sending unit. Fluid will leak when sending unit is removed.
3. Remove spring clamp and hose from elbow. Then remove elbow. Fluid will drain.
4. When fluid stops draining, replace elbow, spring clamp, hose, and sending unit. Reconnect wire.
5. Remove and discard filter.
6. Clean filter mounting bracket of tractor. Use a clean rag.
7. Coat seal at inner end of new filter with transmission fluid.
8. Install new filter. Hand-tighten only.
9. Clean surrounding area and remove transmission dipstick.
10. Pour manufacturer-recommended transmission fluid through dipstick hole. Go slowly and check level with the dipstick frequently, until full. **Note:** Because of the need for more pressure in the transmission when using a backhoe or trencher, Allis-Chalmers and other manufacturers recommend adding one additional quart of transmission fluid to keep the level 1 inch above the normal full mark for this use.
11. Charge transmission fluid pump.
    a. Disconnect wire marked B+ from ignition coil.
    b. Remove cover from center console of tractor. Remove pipe plug from pump. Pour transmission fluid through pipe plug hole to overflowing.
    c. Crank engine with battery until fluid flows from pipe plug hole with no

air bubbles. You may have to stop and add fluid several times. Wipe up spilled fluid.

    d. Install pipe plug, console cover, and bottom frame cover. Reconnect B+ wire to ignition coil.
    e. Run engine for short period, and recheck fluid level.

Clutch Free Travel Adjustment

If your clutch pedal depresses too easily all the way to the floor, or if it doesn't have the required free play (usually 1–2 inches at the top of its travel), you can adjust the free travel of your clutch.

To check the clutch free travel, first run the engine for 5–10 minutes. Measure the distance that you can easily move the clutch pedal with your fingers (see Illus. 9–10). The distance should be 1–2 inches. Adjust as necessary.

1. Stop engine, set parking brake, and remove ignition key.
2. Remove any center-mounted attachments.
3. Remove bottom frame cover.
4. Turn lockout nut (item H, Illus. 9–10) clockwise to *decrease* free travel, or counterclockwise to *increase* free travel.
5. Repeat check of distance and lockout adjustment until free travel is correct.
6. Replace and securely tighten bottom frame cover.

Clutch Belt Tension Adjustment

If the clutch belt tension is not adjusted correctly, the clutch belts will slip when the clutch is engaged (pedal released), or will continue to drive when the clutch is disengaged (pedal depressed). In either case, adjust clutch belt tension as follows.

1. Run the engine 5–10 minutes. Stop engine, remove key, and set brake.

2. Raise hood and oil cooler.

3. Check length of spring (item A, Illus. 9–10) from top of bracket (item I) to bottom of hex cap (item B). Compare with manufacturer's specifications.

4. Rotate hex cap (item B) to obtain correct spring length.

5. Measure gap between drive belt (item D) and belt stop (item E) according to manufacturer's specifications.

6. Loosen capscrew (item F) and move belt stop to correct gap. Retighten capscrew.

7. Check clutch free travel, as above. Adjust as necessary.

8. Reinstall oil cooler, and lower and secure hood.

Hydrostatic Neutral Adjustment

If the tractor moves forward or backward when the hydrostatic control lever is in NEUTRAL position, proceed as follows.

1. Stop engine, remove key, and set brakes.

2. Remove top frame cover. **Caution:** *Do not remove top frame cover while engine is running.*

3. Loosen locknuts (item A, Illus. 9–11).

4. Adjust turnbuckle (item B) about ½ turn. Go counterclockwise as viewed from above if tractor moved forward. Turn turnbuckle clockwise if tractor moved backward.

5. Start engine. If tractor creeps in neutral, repeat step 4 *with engine off.*

6. Once adjusted correctly, secure turnbuckle by turning both locknuts (item A) tightly against turnbuckle.

7. Replace top frame cover, and secure tightly.

Neutral Safety Switch Adjustment

The neutral safety switch should prevent the engine from starting when the hydrostatic con-

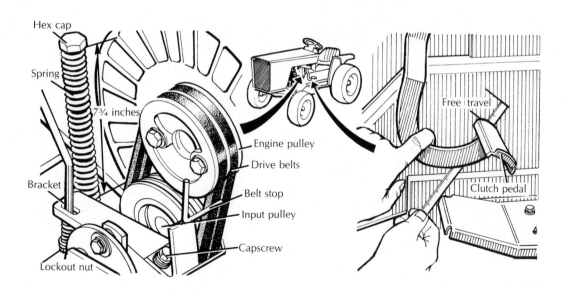

Illus. 9–10—Clutch Free Travel and Belt Tension Adjustments

Hex cap
Spring
7¾ inches
Bracket
Lockout nut
Engine pulley
Drive belts
Belt stop
Input pulley
Capscrew
Free travel
Clutch pedal

A Locknuts
B Turnbuckle

Loosen

A

B

A

Loosen

Illus. 9–11—Hydrostatic Neutral Adjustment

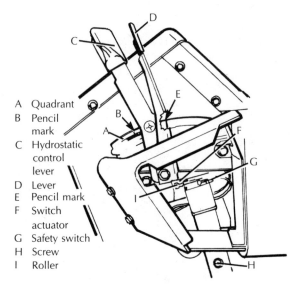

A Quadrant
B Pencil
mark
C Hydrostatic
control
lever
D Lever
E Pencil mark
F Switch
actuator
G Safety switch
H Screw
I Roller

Illus. 9–12—Neutral Safety Switch Adjustment

trol lever is in any position other than neutral. If it doesn't do this or if it prevents the engine from starting when the control is in neutral, adjust as follows. Perform as needed.

1. Stop engine, remove key, and set brakes.
2. Raise hood. Move hydrostatic control lever to NEUTRAL.
3. Make a pencil mark (item B, Illus. 9–12) on the quadrant (item A) $\frac{1}{16}$ inch from the rear edge of the blade on the back side of the hydrostatic control lever.
4. Place another pencil mark (item E) on the quadrant $\frac{1}{16}$ inch forward of the front edge of the block on the back side of the control lever.
5. Move hydrostatic control lever fully forward. Then move it slowly backward. The switch should click once as the front edge of the block passes pencil mark E, and should click again as the rear edge of the block passes near pencil mark B. If not, adjust as per remaining steps.

6. Move the control lever into NEUTRAL. The roller (item I) at the end of the switch lever should be centered on the switch activator (item F); if not, loosen the two switch bracket screws, and move the bracket. When the roller is centered on the activator, retighten the bracket screws.
7. Move the control lever forward until the front edge of the trigger lever (item D) is even with pencil mark E.
8. Loosen the screws that hold the activator (item F). Move the activator forward until the switch leaf arm almost touches the switch body. Then move the activator away from the switch until the switch clicks. Tighten screws to secure the activator in this position.
9. Return to step 5 to recheck. If necessary, repeat the adjustment procedure.

Front PTO Clutch Adjustment

The steps detailed here will serve as an example of the typical front PTO clutch adjustment procedure, but they apply specifically only to the Allis-Chalmers Model 720 tractor. The procedure likely will be similar for other tractors, but you will need your own manufacturer's specifications.

If the electrically operated front PTO clutch engages slowly or fails to engage at all, use the following procedure.

1. Turn off engine, remove key, and set brakes.
2. Tighten each of the four mounting nuts (item A, Illus. 9–13) ⅓ turn down (advance two faces of the nut). Be sure to turn all nuts equally.
3. With the engine stopped, insert a .010-inch feeler gauge through each of the openings (item B) in the clutch plate. Do not insert the gauge more than ¹⁄₁₆ inch. If it won't go that far, turn the

four mounting nuts counterclockwise ¹⁄₁₂ of a turn each, and repeat the check.

Placing Tractor in Storage

If you are going to store your tractor for an off-season, or for any extended length of time, proceed as follows:

1. Run the engine until the fuel tank is dry.
2. While the engine is still warm, change the oil and filter, if any.
3. Remove the spark plug(s). Pour an ounce of 10W–30 oil into each spark plug hole. Crank the engine a few times to distribute the oil. Replace spark plug(s).
4. Remove battery.
5. Lubricate tractor (see Illus. 9–4).

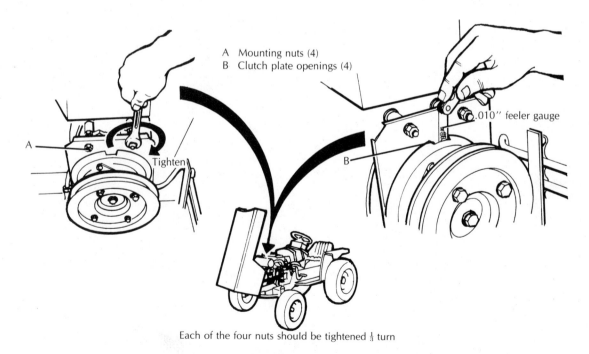

A Mounting nuts (4)
B Clutch plate openings (4)

Tighten

.010″ feeler gauge

Each of the four nuts should be tightened ⅓ turn

Illus. 9–13—Front Power Take-Off (PTO) Clutch Adjustment

Removing Tractor from Storage

If you used the above procedure to store your tractor for several months, follow these steps to remove it from storage.

1. Refill fuel tank with fresh fuel of the correct grade.
2. Clean transmission oil cooler, engine fins, and air filter as previously described.
3. Check fluid levels and tire pressure.
4. Reinstall battery, and charge as necessary.
5. Remove spark plug(s) and clean. Crank engine a few times to clear the oil from the spark plug holes. Reinstall spark plug(s).
6. Start as per normal starting procedure. Avoid high speeds or excessive loads immediately after starting.

Parp says that a small tractor is one of the most dangerous tools discussed in this book, especially to pets, children, lubricated visitors, and passersby.

Please be careful. See you in the woodlot.

PART FOUR:
The Woodlot

CHAPTER TEN:
Chain Saws

Parp fondly remembers less hectic decades, snowbound high in the Rockies with his infant son, when it was good to do all the firewood with a bow saw and an axe, week by week through the blazing falls and silent winters—a spiritual hibernation that prohibited gasoline as a ghastly affront and too heavy to carry that far on snowshoes, anyway.

Now there are after-school events, deadlines, and a progression of shifting editors. When Parp isn't cruising as a cop, he's talking to Love-of-His-Life Reporter, or sneaking an afternoon's hunt, or longhanding a way to pay the remaining bills. Clearly, a chain saw is now essential, and anything that facilitates the cutting, hauling, and splitting of Parp's only domestic fuel also helps Parp earn bread, enjoy his maturing towhead, and explain to Reporter why Town isn't tame.

Besides, firewood without a chain saw means smaller trees instead of healthy logs which, when split, yield five times the heat stored in a bow-sawed sapling. In other words, if wood heat is important to you, you need a chain saw. One can buy firewood, of course, and many wood users must buy it because they do not live in an area where firewood gathering is feasible. Buying firewood is really not very practical for anything other than occasional use in a fireplace, for amorous purposes. If you purchase firewood for the majority of your heating needs, it's likely your heat will cost as much as that supplied by other fuels, such as oil or gas.

However, if you live near a national forest or have access to a private woodlot, a good chain saw can help bring your wood fuel costs down. If you live near a rural or farming area, you may also be able to scrounge a fair amount of free or low-cost fuel wood by clearing areas for farming or new roads. Another source of low-cost fuel wood may be pieces from lumberyards, but you won't need a chain saw for these.

In addition to gathering firewood, a chain saw can be very useful in construction, especially if you're building your own house or outbuildings with logs. With a good chain saw and a mill, you can even manufacture your own rough boards and posts at far less than the retail cost, with the added benefit of making materials to fit your exact needs.

A BRIEF HISTORY

The history of the chain saw is significant chiefly because it reveals how saws of various manufacturers happen to be so similar in concept and design. The first chain saw was built by the German inventor Andreas Stihl in 1926. It was far from the sleek machines of today. It required two operators and was almost as difficult to maneuver as the logs themselves. But Stihl's machine revolutionized the logging industry and immediately launched widespread competition to develop a truly practical, lightweight, one-person chain saw.

By the end of the thirties, Stihl had developed most of the essential features of the modern chain saw and, protected by hundreds of international patents, had effectively left his competitors chewing bark and muttering to themselves.

Then came World War II. Stihl was a German citizen and his patents were, of course, immediately released and appropriated in the U.S. All of Stihl's basic designs were snapped up by U.S. and Canadian companies, and there were suddenly over a half-dozen brands of chain saws, all very much alike.

Since then, Stihl has gotten back into the business, and the chain saw has developed into one of the lightest, most efficient of all power tools. The basic concept is still the same, however, and many of the essential features found in common on all chain saws were originally covered by Stihl patents. Many other individuals, such as Charles H. Ferguson of Homelite and Arthur Mall of Mall Tool, also made important contributions to the development of the chain saw through the thirties, forties, and fifties.

There are now several excellent chain saws marketed by U.S., Canadian, and northern European companies; a good many mediocre saws from the U.S., Asia, and southern Europe; and cheap junk from everywhere, including some from the manufacturers of other saws in the excellent category. They are all very much of the same design because they still use many of Stihl's original concepts. They do, however, differ greatly in the quality of materials used, manufacturing processes, and durability and dependability. That's why it's good to be familiar with the outline of chain saw history—so you won't think that because they are designed similarly, they will all work equally well. They won't. (For a more complete history, see *Barnacle Parp's Chain Saw Guide*, Rodale Press, 1977.)

Remember, chain saws may all look very much alike, but the real differences become all too apparent after a year—or even one day—of hard use.

TYPES OF CHAIN SAWS

For all practical purposes, there are two basic types of chain saws. One is powered by an electric motor, the other by a two-cycle gasoline engine.

Electric Chain Saws

Electric chain saws have some real advantages. They are quiet, emit no fumes and use no hazardous fuel. If you intend to use your chain saw in your yard near a convenient power supply, a good-quality electric chain saw will serve you well. An electric chain saw is also handy on a construction site, powered by a generator. Most electric chain saws, however, are simply not of that quality. Those that you find marked $19.95 and stacked like boxes of toothpaste in dreary discount department stores are good for anchoring old rowboats in carp channels. Quality electric chain saws suitable for construction or serious firewood use are comparable in cost to similar saws powered by gasoline engines, and some may even cost more.

There are some good electric saws designed to be used with a 12-volt battery. Some of these saws are rugged, quality machines that will cut as much wood as a gasoline saw and just as dependably. But you must either use the saw near your pickup, or else carry a rechargeable marine-type battery into the woods. They say that's equal to carrying fuel, but Parp disagrees. You don't have to move your can of fuel every time you change cutting locations by 20 feet, and a 2½-gallon fuel can is much lighter than a battery, anyway.

A small electric chain saw from a good manufacturer can be a useful tool around the house. It will serve to trim backyard trees and can be used to cut small logs, up to about 4 inches in diameter, if you use it near a convenient power source.

Electric chain saws come equipped with a cutting attachment (bar and chain) that measures from about 8 inches for useless, cheap models up to about 18 inches on the professional construction models. The common homeowner models average about 12 inches—plenty adequate for tree trimming and light woodcutting in the backyard.

Parp sincerely hopes that none of his readers will ever be suckered into buying one of those discount mini-electrics with plastic sprockets and the pot metal bars. They're no damn good for anything, and they are unsafe.

Gasoline Chain Saws

Although there are drawbacks, Parp chooses a gasoline engine as the only really practical way to power a chain saw for serious wood-gathering and log construction purposes. A gasoline-engine chain saw is not limited by the availability of a power source; it can be carried into the woods and operated at any location. If you're cutting a fair amount of wood, you'll also have to carry a can of fuel and a supply of oil to lubricate the bar and chain. It is easy, however, to carry enough fuel and bar oil to operate a chain saw for days at a time. And you probably won't be cutting wood very far from your pickup or tractor and cart anyway, unless you're building a real primitive cabin deep in the backwoods.

A gasoline chain saw is powered by a two-cycle air-cooled engine that accomplishes an amazing amount of work for its small size. With an average 16-inch bar and a good saw, you can cut down and buck (cut into logs) a tree up to 32 inches in diameter. Gasoline chain saws come with bars ranging from about 10–60 inches, but the 16- to 20-inch size is by far the most popular and practical for anyone who is not a logger but is still interested in serious firewood cutting every year. A 14-inch bar will do well for most everyone, especially for meeting fireplace needs and occasional wood uses.

On the other hand, there are always trade-offs. A small saw is lighter and easier to handle, but it cuts wood less quickly and efficiently than a larger saw, thereby making for longer work sessions.

As a matter of personal choice, Parp much prefers a medium-duty saw of about 4 cu. in. engine displacement connected to a 20-inch roller nose bar and ⅜-inch semi-chisel chain. Any of a half-dozen saws from three or four particular manufacturers will do fine. The particular manufacturers Parp personally prefers are Stihl, Homelite, Husqvarna, and Jonsereds.

Displacement

When you go out to buy any backyard tool, you are likely to find the size of the tool's engine stated in cubic inches of displacement. This is partly because the horsepower of a small engine is often difficult to calculate and partly because displacement tells you more about the engine's actual size. Displacement refers to the volume of vaporized fuel that is compressed by the piston on its upward stroke in the cylinder. A displacement figure, therefore, gives you a good idea of the size of the cylinder and piston relative to other small engines of the same type.

Many manufacturers indicate the approximate displacement of an engine with the model number of the tool. For example, a typical chain saw with an engine displacement of 1.9 cu. in. might be called a Model 20. Most of us need only know that displacement indicates engine size for purposes of comparing similar tools from different manufacturers. Of course, displacement comparisons are useless when applied to tools of different kinds. A 3.5 cu. in. engine would be fine in a chain saw but would not do in a tractor.

CHOOSING A SAW

There are four basic classifications of chain saws. They are (1) mini-saws, (2) lightweight saws, (3) medium-duty saws, and (4) heavy-duty, or production, saws. Whether or not a saw is of professional quality is not related to its place in

Table 10–1: Chain Saw Selection Chart

	Mini-Saw	Lightweight	Medium-Duty	Heavy-Duty Production
Recommended cutting per year	1–3 cords	3–6 cords	6–10 cords	All day, every day
Dry weight of saw	6–9 pounds	9–13 pounds	13–18 pounds	18 + pounds
Engine displacement	1.8–2.5 cu. in.	2.5–3.7 cu. in.	3.5–4.8 cu. in.	4.8 + cu. in.
Fuel capacity	.7–.85 pints	.85–1.1 pints	1.2–2 pints	2 + pints
Bar lengths	8–12 inches	14–16 inches	16–24 inches	24 + inches
Chain pitch sizes	¼ inch	⅜ inch	⅜–.404 inch	.404 inch or ½ inch
Choice of attachments	poor	fair	excellent	good

these classifications but is rather determined by its ability to work all day, every day, with a minimum of coddling. Some very small saws of high professional quality exist that were designed primarily for use by professional tree trimmers. The Stihl 020 AVE Professional is one example. Others are made by Homelite, Husqvarna, and Jonsereds. These saws are excellent choices for those who cut a great deal of wood from trees that average less than about 12 inches in diameter (3–6 cords per year).

There also are large saws with heavy engines that are not much better than the tiny, cheap examples stacked at the sock shop.

If you can estimate approximately how much wood you expect to cut in a year, you will be better able to determine which class of saw best suits your needs. Parp cuts about 10 cords every year. That puts him at the high end of the medium-duty classification. The average homeowner who wishes to use a fireplace on occa-

sion will need less than a cord a year. Most firewood users fall someplace in between.

If you choose to buy a mini-saw, Parp recommends that you avoid the style with the handle mounted above the engine. Choose a model with a main handle extending behind the engine. This gives you greater control, easier handling, and safer operation.

Whatever class of saw you choose, be sure that its engine's displacement isn't too small for the weight of the saw. A 1.9 cu. in. engine just isn't enough for a 12-pound saw.

DESIRABLE FEATURES

There have been some changes in the features available on many saws, especially the smaller models, since *Barnacle Parp's Chain Saw Guide* (Rodale Press, 1977) was published. For example, many more saws now feature some vibration-dampening system. Formerly, this type of system was chiefly reserved for medium-duty and heavy-duty saws.

A well-balanced, easy-to-operate, and dependable chain saw makes for a less fatigued and frustrated, and therefore safer, operator. To find these features in a saw, look for one with good design made of quality materials. Pay attention to the little things, such as the quality and fit of the rubber grips on the handles, the sturdiness of the machine, and even the paint job. An efficient weight-to-engine displacement ratio (see Table 10–1, Chain Saw Selection Chart) and good balance are qualities of a good chain saw.

Vibration Control

Even the best manufacturer still sells some models that include no system designed to reduce or control the vibrations transmitted from the machine to the operator. Parp says a dampening system is one of the most important features to look for in a saw of any size. If you cut more than 2–3 cords of wood per year, it is extremely important to reduce vibrations because it's likely that some days you'll spend several hours doing nothing but cutting. Without an effective vibration control system your arms and hands will tire much more quickly, and Parp believes that even two hours of cutting with uncontrolled vibration can result in serious damage to the nerves, muscles, and tendons of your hands and wrists. Loggers who use chain saws all day in their work often develop traumatic vasoplastic disease (T.V.D.), commonly known as white fingers. The resultant nerve and blood-vessel failures of these unprotected professionals impair their grip upon any vibrating tools.

A good vibration-dampening system also greatly reduces chain saw fatigue and thereby promotes safer operation. When excessive vibrations weaken your hands, your grip is less secure, and an accident is much more likely. Now that dampening systems are available even

on mini-saws, Parp says not to buy a chain saw without one.

Automatic Oiling

There was a time when no logger would consider buying a chain saw with an automatic oiling system for the cutting attachment. They preferred a manual oiling system with a thumb-actuated pump. Now, few loggers will buy a saw without an automatic oiler, although many prefer a combination, and Parp agrees with the latter. A combination system uses an automatic oiler for dependable, constant lubrication of the bar and chain, coupled with a manual pump for tougher going. Unfortunately, few saws incorporate the combination, and you'll probably have to choose between automatic and manual. Choose automatic.

Hand Guards

Any chain saw should have two hand guards. The first extends up from the saw, in front of the front handle. The second is usually a widened lower portion of the rear handle. Both are important. The front guard protects against flying pieces of wood and can help stop your hand from hitting the chain if you lose your grip. The

Photo 10–1—Front and Rear Hand Guards on a Chain Saw

Courtesy Jonsereds AB.

bottom guard protects your hand from sticks and from the possibility of a broken chain snapping back against your fingers.

Trigger Interlock

This important safety feature is now available on virtually all new chain saws. It is a simple system designed to prevent accidental increases in engine speed that would result in activating the cutting attachment, an obvious hazard.

A trigger interlock system consists of a latch or safety lever that must be depressed before the trigger can be moved. This setup also means that you must have a full grip on the rear handle before you can press the trigger. If you're buying a new saw, it will surely have a trigger interlock system. If you're buying a used saw, be sure to look for this safety feature on any saw you consider.

Electronic Ignition

Electronic ignitions are rapidly becoming standard equipment on many chain saws. They have advantages and disadvantages. The advantages are that they make periodic service of points unnecessary, increase the efficiency of the engine, have no moving parts, are not susceptible to dirt, moisture, and oil contamination, and are much more dependable than standard ignitions.

The disadvantages are that they increase the purchase price of the saw and, if they do go bad, are much more expensive to repair, because the only real repair is to replace the whole system. On the other hand, electronic ignition failures usually occur while the saw is still new and covered by the manufacturer's warranty. If you get past the warranty period, your electronic ignition will probably last for many years.

Note: Do not confuse electronic ignition systems with electric starters. Electric starters add

significant weight to chain saws and are undependable, expensive, poorly designed, and inefficient. Parp says you shouldn't even consider an electric starter on a gasoline chain saw. Also, automatic sharpening systems add unnecessary weight, are inefficient, break down easily, and are a waste of money.

Replaceable Sprocket Nose Guide Bar

Most of the wear on a chain saw's guide bar occurs at the nose, where the chain, in spinning, is least efficient. A sprocket, or roller, with teeth matched to the chain holds the spinning chain away from the nose of the bar itself and speeds the chain around the nose. This greatly decreases heat, friction, and wear on the bar, chain, and engine, and it greatly increases the saw's all-around performance.

Many bars are designed so that you can replace the sprocket, or roller, when it becomes worn or when the bearings go bad. Parp recommends saws with this feature.

All sprockets require frequent greasing. Chain saw bar sprockets must be greased after each hour of use. The grease guns and grease

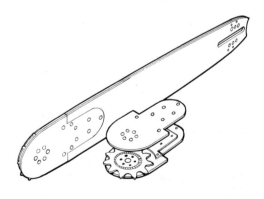

Illus. 10–1—Replaceable Sprocket Nose Guide Bar

for this job are inexpensive, readily available, and take up little space in a woodcutting tool kit. They're well worth the small bother.

Tool Kit, Carrying Case, and Chain Guard

Any new chain saw should come with an adequate tool kit that includes a combination wrench and screwdriver (for bar nuts, chain tensioning, spark plugs, and so on), a hook for fishing out the fuel filter line, a file and guide for sharpening the chain, a grease gun for the roller nose, a depth gauge, a device for locking the crankshaft when you change the chain sprocket, and an owner's manual. The salesperson should also throw in a can of two-cycle engine oil and a supply of bar and chain lubricant as recommended by the manufacturer, just to get you off to a good start.

It helps also to obtain a carrying case large enough for the saw, the items above, and an extra chain. If you don't receive an extra chain with your new saw, buy one and alternate the two chains to keep the wear on the sprocket and on each chain approximately equal. One sprocket should last through two chains, and that's a great deal of cutting.

TIPS ON BUYING A USED CHAIN SAW

It's still possible to get a bargain on a good used chain saw. Many dealers accept trade-ins to be reconditioned and sharpened before resale. Dealers will usually charge as much as they can for used saws in good running condition, but even this can save you a sizable chunk of change compared to the new price tag.

Good, hardly used chain saws are also quite commonly located through newspaper want ads and garage sales. Many people buy or receive chain saws and use them only once, twice, or even not at all. After such a saw sits in someone's garage for a year, it can become a real bargain. Some are never even filled with fuel, and these are the saws to watch for. If the chain is still sharp and the bar is clean and new looking, you can count on the saw being as good as new.

Test It First

If a saw has been used only once, it still may be virtually ruined, especially if the owner failed to use the proper mix of fresh fuel and good two-cycle engine oil. You should be able to tell by starting the saw and actually cutting a log with it. If the saw has been sitting for a few months or so, you should drain the old fuel and replace it with a correct mix before attempting to start it. You may have to clean the spark plug as well before starting.

What to Watch For

Before you buy a used chain saw, be sure that it fits your needs. It isn't a bargain if it's either too big or too small for your trees.

Avoid saws with engines and shrouds that are covered with old dirt and grease. Chances are the saw has overheated during operation and the engine may have few work-hours left. The saw may otherwise show signs of neglect or improper use, such as a bent or burned bar; battered chain teeth; a chain that won't turn or can't be tightened; missing nuts, bolts, or parts; and cracked or missing shrouds or handles. Any one of these problems may be minor and easily repaired, but they also indicate misuse of the saw and the likelihood of other problems developing soon.

Next to checking the engine itself, checking the function of the chain oiling system is most important. If a person uses good, clean bar and chain oil as recommended by all manufacturers, the chances are good that any saw's oil pump will function flawlessly far beyond the life of the engine. But old woodsmen who think they know something frequently fill their saw's oilers with old crankcase drippings, or worse. This old oil can quickly clog the pump and permanently damage its parts. Again, you could repair or replace the oil pump, but this kind of careless disregard indicates a slapdash attitude toward saw maintenance overall, and the saw is apt to have other problems.

To check the oil pump, start the saw in a safe area, and hold the tip about 3 inches from a piece of clean wood. As you rev the engine moderately, you should see a line of oil appear on the wood. If no oil flies from the end of the tip at half-throttle or so, the saw is either out of oil or the oil pump is not functioning properly. This applies to automatic systems only.

To check a manual pump, remove the bar and chain from the saw. Locate the hole in the plate near the fastening studs. Push the pump button, and watch for a squirt of oil from the hole. It should be quite strong.

For the same reason, check the air filter. A little dust or discoloration is unimportant, but if the filter has obviously been clogged with dirt or grease for a long period, engine damage is

possible, and general poor maintenance is certain.

Finally, examine the fuel line, the primary wire to the spark plug, the spark plug cover, and the starter rope. If any of them appear excessively worn or damaged, you'll have to replace the item. If all are worn or damaged, consider the saw a junker to be purchased for parts only, if at all.

HOW TO ATTACH THE BAR AND CHAIN

All chain saws have some fairly simple method of attaching the bar to the body of the machine. Usually, there are one or two large bolts protruding from the right side, near the front of the body. There are also corresponding holes in the bar and in the side plate that slips onto the bolts after the bar is in place.

Note: Soak a new chain in bar oil overnight before using. Clean a used chain in solvent, then soak in oil for at least one hour.

To begin, place the bar over the nuts, but do not fasten. Slip the chain behind the sprocket assembly, and place it on the bar with the cutting edges of the teeth pointing toward the tip on

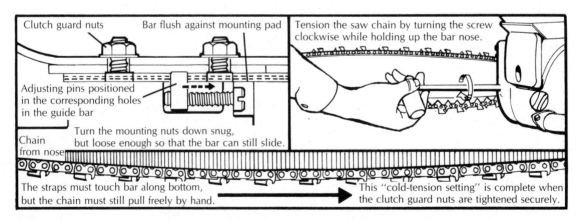

Illus. 10-2—Attaching the Bar and Chain to a Chain Saw

top of the bar and toward the saw on the bottom, with the drive links seated in the groove of the bar.

At this point, the bar is probably not flush with its mounting plate. That's because the chain tensioning device is probably not inserted into the corresponding hole in the side of the bar, near the tail.

Locate the chain tension adjustment screw, and turn it in until the hole in the bar matches the pin in the chain tensioning device. Be sure that the pin goes straight into the hole and that the bar is now flush against the mounting plate and appears straight.

Now mount the side plate, or clutch cover, on the mounting bolts. Install the nuts, and washers if supplied with the saw, and finger-tighten, leaving them each about one full turn loose.

Grasp the nose of the bar in one hand, being careful not to cut yourself, and pull up, not enough to lift the saw but enough to put upward pressure on the bar at the bolts. Turn in the chain tensioning screw until all the slack is taken out of the chain. Tighten the nuts, and check to see if the chain shows no slack but is still easy to move by hand. This movement with a minute slack is the correct cold chain tension.

OPERATING A CHAIN SAW

A chain saw is most frequently used to cut down dead trees and buck them into logs that can be split for firewood, and to trim damaged or problem limbs from living trees. Parp will concentrate on these procedures now. (For details on other procedures and chain saw applications, see *Barnacle Parp's Chain Saw Guide*, Rodale Press, 1977.)

Hazards

A chain saw is one of the most dangerous of all backyard power tools because the cutting attachment is always exposed while working and because the tool is small, easy to move, and unconfined by shrouds, shields, a large body, or other devices. A majority of chain saw injuries are serious, simply because the chain cuts so quickly through clothing and flesh. The saw usually inflicts a deep wound even before the victim realizes he's been injured.

Many injuries, perhaps most of them, occur when the operator momentarily forgets the danger and brings the running chain too close to a leg or foot. This is most likely to happen while cutting the limbs from downed trees. People tend to get a foot under the trunk while limbing the opposite side of the tree, or they might lean against the trunk while cutting toward themselves on the near side.

Illus. 10–3—Kickback

Kickback occurs when the chain contacts a solid object as it progresses around the upper quadrant of the bar nose.

Kickback path

175

Kickback is the single most common cause of wounds, accounting for approximately 30 percent of all chain saw injuries each year. Kickback is also most likely to occur during the limbing operation.

Kickback is caused when the chain moving along the upper nose of the saw contacts a solid surface, usually not the wood you are attempting to cut. When the chain is turning around the upper third of the nose, it is in the least efficient portion of its cycle. Since it can't cut efficiently, the teeth tend to catch in the wood, instantly stopping the chain. The power of the engine then sends the saw up and back, in an arc, toward the operator. Serious injury to the body, face, or head can occur.

The best way to avoid a dangerous kickback is to avoid cutting with the nose of the bar. Cut as close to the engine end of the bar as possible, and use your saw's bumper spikes to grip the wood whenever possible. If you must cut with the nose—when boring, for example—start the cut with the lower portion of the nose, and run the engine at full speed. As the chain cuts in, slowly raise the body of the saw to bore further.

You may also want to investigate one of the new anti-kickback chains that have just started

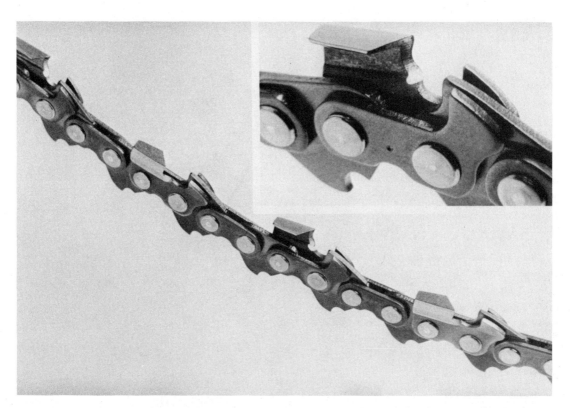

Photo 10–2—Cutter and Tripled Depth Gauges on Townsend Tri-Raker Chain Saw

Courtesy Townsend Saw Chain Co.

to appear on the market. The Townsend Saw Chain Company's Tri-Raker Chain (marketed under the Sabre brand name) is three times more effective in reducing chain saw kickback than a standard chain. The "triple-raker effect" is achieved by the addition of two more depth gauges in the same configuration as the cutter depth gauge. This increases the surface area on the depth gauge, which adds to its stability and prevents the raker from being buried in the wood. Yet, it still enables the chain to cut and bore with the same speed as a chain without anti-kickback features.

Recently developed guide bar designs may also contribute to the virtual elimination of kickback. Parp says Oregon Saw Chain Division (see Appendix C for address) carries the best-designed bars.

There are other hazards related to working with a chain saw. Some years ago, Parp and his old friend Muskrat were cutting Bull Pine in Weird Wood on Campbell Mountain—ancient wood of mystery. Parp was working in a clearing, cutting small pieces on the ground, an inherently dangerous operation. He wore no goggles in the July heat, nor head protection. Muskrat was also cutting small pieces on the ground, among the trees some 20 yards behind Parp, facing the other way. When Muskrat's chain caught on a small but very solid hunk of limb, the piece flew backward, grazing Muskrat's leg with a painful blow. The wood shard flew through the air with amazing velocity and thudded into the back of Parp's head. Unconscious on his feet, Parp threw his running chain saw to one side and staggered across the clearing. As he reached the edge of the gnarled forest, he fell, and a long, thin piece of ironlike Bristlecone went straight into his left eye. "Now nothing changes/that thick tear in the sky."

Always wear eye, head, and ear protection. Do not cut into small pieces of wood unless they are firmly held by a partner or a vise of some kind. Avoid cutting in dense brush, and clear any work area before you start your saw. Wear sensible, snug-fitting work clothes and gloves. Keep your head and body slightly to the left of the plane of chain rotation whenever possible. Take frequent breaks, and stop for the day whenever you become fatigued. Never add fuel to a hot saw, and always start your saw at least 10 feet from the refueling point. Never use a gasoline chain saw indoors or in any enclosed area unless there is plenty of ventilation.

When you use a chain saw to cut down a standing dead tree, there is always the danger that the vibrations will cause dead limbs to fall. Loggers refer to these limbs as widow makers. They can also be widower makers. They come down like spears and can penetrate inches of frozen ground—and most hard hats as well. Wool shirts don't even noticeably slow them down. Cutting down large dead trees is dangerous.

Whenever you work with a chain saw, keep a firm grip on both handles at all times and keep your feet far enough apart to maintain balance. Never work on an unstable or dangerous surface, such as a pile of limbs. Work close to your saw to maintain control, but keep the bar away from all parts of your body.

(For details on fueling, starting, running, and maintaining two-cycle engines, see Index.)

Practice Cuts

Before you go out to cut down Douglas fir trees or prune your pears, do some practice cuts in a safe area on safe material to become somewhat familiar with the operation and feel of a chain saw.

Get a good-size log and lay it on the ground, fully supported and secured against rolling. Stand on the uphill side of the log, start your saw, and allow it to warm up for a few minutes.

Hold the saw firmly in both hands with the engine at idle. Place the cutting attachment above the log with the nose slightly up. While you keep the chain off the log, lower the saw until you can engage the wood with the bumper spikes. Then squeeze the trigger as you pivot the saw on the bumper spike to bring the bar down to the log. Be sure the engine and chain are going full speed just an instant before touching the wood. Keep the engine at full throttle for as long as you're cutting. When you back out of the cut, release the trigger completely to idle the engine. Take several practice cuts at various places on the log, but do not cut through. If you wish to go ahead and buck the log into pieces, cut three-fourths of the way through from one side, then turn the log over to finish the cuts. Use a wedge to keep your saw from binding in the cut.

Cutting Wood with a Chain Saw

The manner in which a chain saw is used to cut a log or piece of wood is determined by the situation of the wood. The first consideration is safety, of course. You don't want to cut a log or tree that's going to roll or fall on anyone, or do any other damage. Before cutting, you must know how a log or tree is likely to react, and you must prepare for it to react in some other way as well. Another consideration is the effect of the cut on the wood itself. If cut improperly, a log, tree, or piece of wood very well may splinter and break in an undesirable way, especially when cutting for construction purposes such as a log cabin. But even when cutting firewood, splintered and jagged, broken logs are more difficult to split, carry, and use. It's also easy to pick up splinters from them, and they're simply less attractive than a woodpile of nicely cut logs.

For both safety and even cutting, stress is the factor we must consider first. Some examples follow.

When a log is placed on a sawbuck with one end protruding, a certain amount of stress is caused by the effect of gravity on the unsupported end. This stress is concentrated at that portion of the bottom of the log that is just beyond the support of the sawbuck. The bottom

of this portion of the log is under *compression*, while the top part of the log is under *tension*. If the saw cuts through the log from the top, the stress will increase, and a portion of uncut wood will break before the saw has a chance to cut all the way through. This will leave a jagged and splintered broken end, untidy and capable of inflicting minor wounds.

To avoid this occurrence, lessen the effective stress by beginning with an undercut of about one-third the diameter of the log. Finish the cut from the top, and there will be no splintering.

In fact, in any cutting situation with a chain saw, always cut on the compression side first and the tension side last.

When a log is supported on both ends, the compression side is the top of the log, and the tension side is the bottom of the log. Begin with a top cut, and finish with an undercut. Also, remember that when you're bucking a supported log into pieces, the pieces will fall. To avoid smashed fingers and a damaged chain saw, angle your cuts so that the logs fall away from the saw, not down onto it.

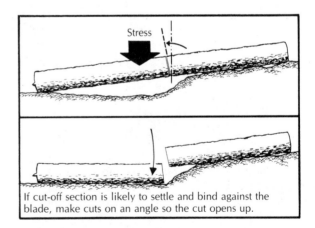

If cut-off section is likely to settle and bind against the blade, make cuts on an angle so the cut opens up.

Illus. 10–4—Angling Cuts on a Log

This cross-cutting technique prevents the log from pinching and binding the chain saw blade.

Cutting Standing Trees

Cutting down trees can be very dangerous, but the danger can be considerably lessened by using correct procedures. First, here's an all-important rule. Unless you are an expert logger, never attempt to cut any tree bigger than a sapling with the intention of making it fall in any direction other than the direction of its lean. If you are not an experienced faller, and you have a full-size tree that must be felled away from its direction of lean in order to avoid hitting your house or another obstacle, by all means call a licensed and insured professional. Do not do it yourself.

Remember, a good-size tree can always go in an unexpected direction. Plan for any possibility so that you won't be caught by surprise.

To fell a tree, first be sure that it cannot fall on any power lines, buildings, parked vehicles, or passersby. Determine its direction of lean and whether it is safe to fell the tree in that general direction and at that moment. Then clear the area all around the tree so that there will be nothing underfoot. Also clear a path of safe retreat to the rear and at a 45° diagonal on either side of the expected line of fall. Remember that the tree may well fall in exactly the opposite direction. Now you're ready to begin cutting.

There are two basic cutting operations in the felling procedure. They are the directional cut, or notch, and the felling cut, or backcut. The notch determines and controls the direction of the tree's fall. The felling cut removes enough wood from behind the notch to cause the tree to fall. The notch and the backcut must be made so as to leave a hinge of uncut wood (see Illus. 10–6).

Make the notch first. Crouch at the side of the tree, facing the direction of lean and the planned direction of fall. Aim across the top of your saw, along the front handle or falling sights, if provided. This will align your guide bar correctly.

Now cut down at an angle into the tree so

that your upper cut will end slightly below the level at which you wish to cut the tree. Cut about a third of the way into the trunk, never as much as halfway. Then make the lower cut horizontal to the ground and far enough to meet the bottom of your upper cut. Remove the notch of wood formed by these cuts.

Now go behind the tree and make a second horizontal cut from the other side, on a line about 2 inches above the horizontal cut of the notch. Do not make the backcut even with the

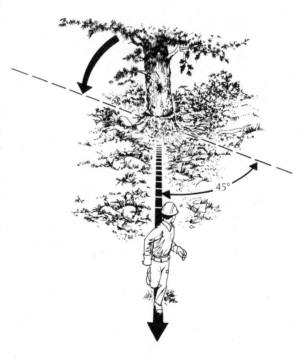

Illus. 10–5—Preparing the Cutting Area around a Tree

Clear undergrowth and debris from under the tree 45° on both sides of your planned retreat path. If the tree falls in an unexpected direction, you'll be able to escape without tripping.

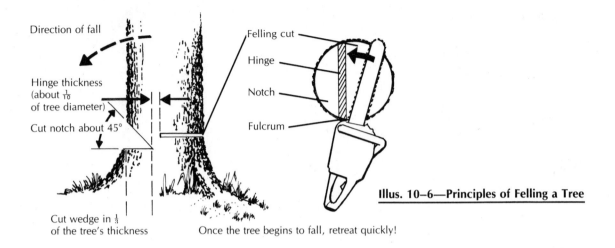

Direction of fall

Hinge thickness
(about $\frac{1}{10}$
of tree diameter)

Cut notch about 45°

Felling cut

Hinge

Notch

Fulcrum

Illus. 10–6—Principles of Felling a Tree

Cut wedge in $\frac{1}{3}$
of the tree's thickness

Once the tree begins to fall, retreat quickly!

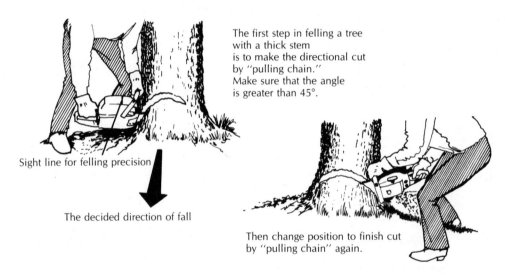

Sight line for felling precision

The first step in felling a tree
with a thick stem
is to make the directional cut
by "pulling chain."
Make sure that the angle
is greater than 45°.

The decided direction of fall

Then change position to finish cut
by "pulling chain" again.

Finish cutting initial wedge out,
making sure the lower cut
meets the upper one exactly.

Illus. 10–7—Cutting a Wedge to Fell a Large Tree

In felling a thick-stem tree, exercise extreme
caution to avoid kickback. Start your cut with the
underside of your saw, keeping pressure off the
saw tip. This is known as "pulling chain."

180

horizontal cut of the notch, or you will lose control of the direction of fall. Also, be sure not to take the backcut all the way through to the notch. Always leave a hinge of uncut wood on which the tree will pivot in the direction of the notch.

As your backcut approaches the notch, keep an eye on the top of the tree. When it starts to fall, turn off your saw and retreat along your planned escape route. Remember that the butt end of the tree may kick backward, and dead branches may fall or fly in any direction.

Limbing

Once your tree is safely down on the ground, it's time to cut off all the limbs and buck the stem into logs. The logs can be cut short, easy to handle and ready to be split for firewood, or they can be cut to a specific length for your building needs. Either way, the first step is the limbing.

Of all cutting operations, limbing is the most dangerous and results in the greatest number of personal injuries for professionals and amateurs alike. Since we are not considering or discussing professional methods, Parp will describe here only the safest, surest limbing method.

Start at the butt end of the tree. If you wish to use a logging tape to measure your lengths, attach the pin end of the tape securely to the butt. If the tree is lying diagonally on a slope, start work on the downhill side, and cut all the limbs from the uphill side first. In other words, keep the stem of the tree between you and the bar of your saw. Work close to the tree, with your tape playing out behind you. As you move from the butt end to the top end, cut all the limbs from the other side of the tree. Cut each limb separately and carefully. Do not reach under the tree with the tip of your bar, as it may reach clear to your feet. This is a common cause of accidents, particularly for overconfident saw operators. As you move up the tree, mark the trunk at desired lengths as indicated by your tape. (Parp recommends Spencer logging tapes, available from Spencer Production Co.; see Appendix C for address.)

When you reach the tip of the tree, move to the uphill side and reverse yourself, removing the limbs from the downhill side. Go slowly, and clear the cut limbs from your path as you advance. You may wish to buck each log section as you go. Be aware that the tree may roll downhill at any time, but the probability increases as you remove the downhill limbs. As each log section is limbed and bucked, it is very likely to roll when cut free from the rest of the tree.

During all stages of the limbing operation, be especially watchful for kickback. Try to cut carefully so that the tip of your saw doesn't contact other limbs or obstacles. Without losing balance, cut as much as possible with that portion of the bar that is closest to the body of your saw. Remember the stress and tension factors, and undercut large, heavy, free-hanging limbs before finishing with an overcut. If the end of the limb is pressed against the ground, you have a two-ended support situation, in which case the tension is on the underside of the limb and the compression on the top side. In that case, begin with an overcut, and finish with an undercut to avoid a bind on your bar and a whipping limb.

Note: Take time to be sure of your footing. Avoid standing on limbs or piles of brush. Definitely do not stand or walk on the trunk of the tree while limbing or while holding a running chain saw. This is a circus act that's best left for professional loggers only.

When your tree is limbed and bucked, stand on the uphill side of the tree, and roll the heaviest logs down first. Turn off your saw while doing this, even if you must occasionally restart it to remove missed limbs. Load your logs carefully to avoid straining your back—bend at the knees and lift with your legs by standing up with your back straight.

Pruning

To remove a dead or unwanted limb from a living tree, always start with a partial undercut a couple of inches out from the trunk of the tree. Then remove the limb by cutting from the top, a little further out on the limb, away from the trunk. Following this procedure will prevent the limb from splitting or breaking near the trunk and thus damaging the tree.

When the limb is removed, cut the remaining portion flush with the trunk, and paint over the wound with pruning paint.

CHAIN SAW MAINTENANCE

Of all the backyard tools discussed in this book, the chain saw is perhaps most susceptible to failure due to inadequate maintenance. If used correctly, a chain saw does all of its work at full engine speed; cutting at slower speeds will rapidly destroy the centrifugal clutch and will place terrific strain on the engine. Because the chain saw must operate at full engine speed whenever it is doing work, the air cooling system must always operate efficiently to prevent overheating.

This means you must keep the saw clean. A chain saw is constantly exposed to dirt, sawdust, and sticky sap that can clog the engine's air filter and the air passages, shrouds, and engine fins of the cooling system. Sawdust and dirt can also clog the oil pump and the oil port that distributes oil onto the moving chain to lubricate the cutting attachment. Without adequate lubrication, your chain will soon overheat and seize up; your bar will burn and easily can be permanently damaged.

To avoid these and other problems, clean your saw thoroughly after each 8 hours of work. On the starter side of the saw, you'll find a ventilated housing designed to allow air to be drawn in to the engine by the combination blower/flywheel. To clean it, remove it from the saw, and use an old toothbrush dipped in a moderate amount of solvent. Clean caked sawdust from the inside with a wooden scraper. Before replacing the housing, clean the flywheel with a rag slightly dampened with solvent, and wipe everything dry with a clean cloth. Follow this same procedure with all removable shrouds and with the engine's cooling fins.

After about every 20 hours of work, you should also disassemble and clean the muffler with solvent and a toothbrush.

Your daily maintenance should include a complete cleaning of the bar and chain. Use solvent and a toothbrush to clean the grooves and holes in the bar while you soak the chain in a can of solvent. You may have to use a screwdriver or knife blade to remove stubborn sawdust and sap from the grooves of the bar.

In the field, remove the air filter, and knock the loose dirt from it after each hour of work. At the same time, refuel your saw after it has cooled some, and fill the oil tank. Also grease the roller nose on bars so equipped, and be sure your chain hasn't become too loose or too tight; adjust as necessary.

(For two-cycle engine service and maintenance beyond the items mentioned here, please see Chapter Two of this book.)

Keeping It Sharp

To keep your saw cutting efficiently and straight, and to avoid unnecessary strain on your engine and your arms, you must keep your saw chain correctly sharpened. A chain saw needs sharpening any time it stops cutting quickly and easily; any time you hit the ground, a rock, or a similar obstacle; and any time the sawdust begins to look more like powder than like wood chips.

Two parts of a chain saw are involved in sharpening: cutters and depth gauges. A cutter is the sharp top edge of the chain that cuts the wood. The depth gauge is the flat part of the cutter link, which guides the cutter and keeps

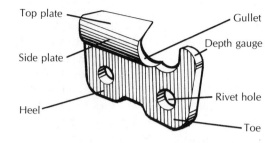

Illus. 10–8—Cutter and Depth Gauge on a Chain Saw Chain

it from digging too deeply (see Illus. 10–8).

It is possible to sharpen a chain satisfactorily with two handheld files (one for the cutters, the other for the depth gauges), but it's not easy to do it accurately without a good deal of practice. It is a great help to have a set of tools designed to make the job quicker and more accurate. These tools can be as simple as a handheld file guide to keep your cutters filed at the correct angle and a jointer to measure the depth gauge settings, or they may be elaborate power tools designed to do these jobs much more quickly and with extreme accuracy. Whatever tools you use, the basic job is the same, and the results should be, too. You should end up with all cutting teeth filed sharp, all at the same angle and of the same length, and with all depth gauges filed to the correct setting and uniformly rounded off so that the chain will cut smoothly. There are professional-shop-quality grinders that can sharpen a chain and set the depth gauges automatically in a few minutes, but the cost of these machines can be justified only if you are in business to sell a great deal of wood or to service other peoples' saws for a fee.

Sharpening Guides

Parp says without hesitation that the most commonly used, inexpensive file guide is the Granberg File-N-Joint, available in hardware stores. This is a good tool, and it will do an accurate job. Like the more expensive and somewhat higher quality Oregon File Guide, it clamps on the bar and holds a standard, handheld chain saw file at the correct angle, adjustable for any type or size of chain. Granberg also makes a motorized version for either 12-volt (v.) or standard household current that uses small, replaceable stones. Parp has used a 12-v. model for years and finds that the stones, moving parallel to the direction of chain travel, make for smoother teeth, no burrs, and better cutting. But the stones do wear and break quickly and are rather expensive to replace.

The latest breakthrough in sharpeners is the Gamń, from Gamń Enterprises (see Appendix C for address). This is a manually operated device, but it has several distinct advantages over any of the older designs. First, like the motorized Granberg, the sharpener works parallel to the direction of chain travel. It uses a carbide burr that turns with a crank instead of going back and forth. Again, this method makes for smoother teeth and smoother cutting with no burrs or irregularities. The carbide-cutting burrs should last virtually forever and will not lose efficiency with constant use. The Gamń is exceptionally well made from solid aluminum and is very rigid once it's clamped onto the bar. It has a device to hold the chain firmly and an adjustable stop for controlling the cutter length. Gamń has also recently developed an accessory device that retrofits to the sharpener and allows the owner to dress the depth gauges as well as sharpen the cutters.

If you use only one size of standard chain, Parp wholeheartedly endorses the Gamń sharpener as the best manual sharpener on the market today. It avoids all of the problems inherent in all other sharpening devices.

When to Sharpen

In use, a chain normally needs touching up after each hour of steady cutting. It needs complete sharpening after each 8 hours of steady cutting, or more often depending on conditions, the hardness and cleanliness of the wood, and accidents such as hitting the ground or a rock. Obviously, good sharpening tools can save a great deal of time and effort.

Chain Size

By far the most common type of chain and the most likely to be owned by readers of this book is the chipper chain. Chipper chain comes in various sizes, the two most common being ¼ inch, usually found on mini-saws, and ⅜ inch, found on almost all other saws. Other sizes and types of chain are mostly used by professionals, and even they use ⅜-inch chipper chain more than any other kind or size. Chances are that you use one of these two most common chains. Both require a round file for the cutters and a flat file for the depth gauges.

Steps in Sharpening

The first step in sharpening is to examine your chain for damage. This damage most frequently occurs to the cutters and the drive links that ride in the bar grooves. Replace, or have replaced, any damaged parts before you sharpen the chain.

When you sharpen a chain by any method other than an automatic bench grinder, it is best to leave the chain on the bar, or replace it after cleaning in solvent and inspecting for damage. Adjust the tension somewhat tighter than usual, but still loose enough to allow you to advance the chain with your gloved hand.

Next, use a ruler to find the shortest cutter tooth on your chain. Note that you measure a cutter by measuring the length of its top plate, to the tip. Sharpen the shortest cutter tooth first by filing lightly from the inside to the outside unless your filing device requires a different procedure. Consult Table 10–2, Filing Chart, to determine the correct size of file, and use only a file designed specifically for sharpening saw chain. Files are available at most hardware stores

and all chain saw shops. Be sure to file the tooth at the same angle as originally used by the manufacturer. In most cases, this angle is 35° from the perpendicular of the chain's length. About ⅕ to ⅒ of the file's diameter should be above the top of the cutter as you file. Remove only enough steel to sharpen the tooth smoothly or to remove any nicks. Move the file away from the cutter on the backstroke, and file only on the forward stroke. When the shortest cutter is sharp, file all the other cutters on the same side of the chain to match that tooth exactly. Then change sides, and file all the cutters on the other side of the chain, also to match precisely that first tooth. All teeth on both sides must be uniform in both length and angle. If the cutters are uneven, the saw will cut inefficiently and will not cut straight.

If all of the top plates are the same length, they will also be the same height. Remove any burrs with a piece of hardwood.

Dressing Depth Gauges

When you've finished all the cutters, check the height of the depth gauges with a jointer, or filemate. Most manufacturers supply these simple devices with every new saw. If you must purchase a jointer, be sure it is for your size of chain. If any depth gauge projects up through the slot in your jointers, file it level. Use only a flat, safety-edge file designed for this purpose, and file all depth gauges equally before rounding them off. Take care not to damage your cutters or any other chain parts with the flat file.

When all depth gauges are level and uniform, round off the front corners to restore the original shape. Depth gauges generally need to be lowered after every second or third complete sharpening to keep the cutters at the correct cutting height.

Touching Up on the Job

If you cut constantly for a couple of hours or more, even softwoods will dull a chain enough to require a complete sharpening. To avoid doing

Table 10–2: Filing Chart

Chain Size and Type	File Size and Type	Average Depth Gauge Setting	Notes
¼-inch chipper	⅛-inch or ⁵⁄₃₂-inch round file	.020 inch	⁵⁄₃₂-inch file best on new chain. Switch to ⅛ inch as chain wears.
.354 chipper	³⁄₁₆-inch or 5-millimeter round file	.025 inch	
⅜-inch chipper	⁷⁄₃₂-inch or ³⁄₁₆-inch round file	.020 inch	⁷⁄₃₂-inch file on new chain, ³⁄₁₆-inch file after considerable use. (Cutters shorter than .32 inch.)
⅜-inch S70 (Oregon) chipper	⁷⁄₃₂-inch round file	.025 inch	
.404-inch chipper	⁷⁄₃₂-inch round file	.030 inch	
⁷⁄₁₆-inch chipper	¼-inch round file	.030 inch	
½-inch chipper	¼-inch round file	.030 inch and .040 inch	
⁹⁄₁₆-inch and ⅝-inch chipper	⁹⁄₃₂-inch round file	.040 inch	
¾-inch chipper	⁵⁄₁₆-inch round file	.050 inch and .060 inch	
¼-inch Micro chisel	⁵⁄₃₂-inch round file	.025 inch	
.325 Micro chisel	³⁄₁₆-inch round file	.025 inch	
⅜-inch Micro chisel	⁷⁄₃₂-inch round file	.025 inch	
.404 Micro chisel	⁷⁄₃₂-inch round file	.030 inch	
.404 Super chisel	⁷⁄₃₂-inch round file	.025 inch	Oregon numbers 50, 51 and 52 may be filed with round file, but do not confuse with true chisel chains below.
.404 Super chisel, Oregon types 50AL, 51AL, 52AL	Beveled chisel chain file	.025 inch	Use ⁷⁄₃₂-inch round file to clean gullets.

(From *Barnacle Parp's Chain Saw Guide*, Rodale Press, 1977)   [*Continued on next page*]

Table 10–2—*Continued*

Chain Size and Type	File Size and Type	Average Depth Gauge Setting	Notes
Super chisel, Oregon types 9AL and 10AL	Beveled chisel chain file	.030 inch	Use 7/32-inch round file to clean gullets.
Oregon types 4AL and 5AL	Beveled chisel chain file	.040 inch	Use 7/32-inch round file to clean gullets.
Oregon types 16AL and 17AL	Beveled chisel chain file	.045 inch	Use 7/32-inch round file to clean gullets.
3/8-inch chisel other than types above	Beveled chisel chain file	.025 inch	Use 7/32-inch round file to clean gullets.
.404-inch chisel other than types above	Beveled chisel chain file	.030 inch	Use 7/32-inch round file to clean gullets.
1/2-inch chisel other than types above	Beveled chisel chain file	.040 inch	Use 1/4-inch round file to clean gullets.
3/4-inch chisel	Beveled chisel chain file	.050 inch	Use 5/16-inch round file to clean gullets.

the whole job too often, use plenty of clean, new bar and chain oil. Avoid cutting wood that is dirty or gritty, as abrasive materials dull a chain very quickly. Trees left after a logging or road construction project are frequently covered with sand and gravel.

Whenever you take a break (every hour, for safety's sake) check the edges of your cutters. If they aren't damaged or excessively dulled, you can usually restore them with two or three passes with a file. Just be sure to maintain the original angles.

Clutch and Sprocket Repair

One common repair procedure exists that is particular to chain saws: repairing the clutch and sprocket. The clutch and sprocket are the means by which the engine's power is transmitted to the cutting attachment. In other words,

these parts make up the drive mechanism. Naturally, these parts are quite susceptible to normal wear and tear, and they need to be repaired or replaced fairly regularly.

All modern chain saws utilize a centrifugal clutch, described in Chapter One (see Index). Since this clutch is of critical importance to the operation of a chain saw, Parp will now tell of it again, both general theory and specifics pertaining to chain saw use.

As its name indicates, this type of clutch is activated by centrifugal force. It assures us that the chain moves when we want it to and stops when it should. The sprocket is a simple gear mechanism that spins whenever the clutch is engaged. As the sprocket spins, its teeth engage the drive portions of the chain to move it forward.

When you start the engine, the crankshaft begins to spin. The faster the engine runs, the faster the crankshaft spins. Since the crankshaft is a turning mechanism, it possesses centrifugal force that tends to cause anything spinning on its axis to move outward, away from the axis.

A centrifugal clutch consists of a drum casing with a hub that fits over the drive side of the crankshaft. A bearing assembly allows the drive shaft to turn in the hub without turning the drum. Inside the drum, clutch shoes are attached by springs that tend to hold the shoes in, away from the drum. When the engine idles or runs slowly, the springs keep the clutch shoes from touching the inside of the drum. At idle, then, the drum stays still and the shoes turn within it, with the drive shaft.

As you increase the engine speed, centrifugal force overcomes the force of the springs and sends the clutch shoes outward until they contact the inside of the clutch drum. This causes the drum to turn, driving the sprocket and the chain.

The sprocket can be a separate gear assembly firmly attached to the clutch drum, or it can actually be an integral part of the drum itself. As the clutch shoes engage the drum, the drum turns the sprocket and drives the chain.

Note that if the engine operates at a moderate speed, just enough to cause the clutch to engage the drum, the shoes are pressed only lightly against the drum. This results in friction that will wear out the clutch shoes very rapidly. That's why you should cut wood at full engine speed only.

All of these parts can become worn or damaged by dirt, water, grit, or grease. The sprocket, of course, is continually exposed to shock as it strikes the drive portions of the saw chain. These parts must be serviced often enough to impel any chain saw owner to learn to do the job to avoid paying an expensive mechanic.

To disassemble the drive mechanism, first you must prevent the drive shaft from turning as you attempt to loosen the nut. Stihl and some other manufacturers supply special tools for this purpose. Most frequently, a plastic piston stop is threaded into the spark plug hole. When you turn the drive shaft, the piston stops against the plastic butt of the device, and the drive shaft can turn no further. This allows you to loosen the nut and remove the parts.

A suitable substitute tool for the plastic piston stop is a piece of clothesline pushed into the spark plug hole to fill the upper cylinder. Don't use a rope that can leave threads or pieces inside the cylinder.

Once the retaining nut is off, you'll probably find a clutch cover that might be held in place by a clip. Remove the cover, and examine the clutch shoes. If they're just dirty or oily, probably you can just wash them in solvent and replace them. If there is wear or damage, replace both clutch shoes and the clutch springs.

Also check the clutch bearings, usually a set of needle bearings in a needle cage. If they are rusted or damaged, replace them also. If they are in good condition, apply a high-quality, waterproof grease to the bearings and a drop of oil onto the crankshaft behind the clutch drum.

The sprocket is always installed immediately to one side or the other of the clutch drum. Examine the sprocket for wear. If the teeth are badly gouged or if the slots are damaged, it will have to be replaced.

Note that on some saws the oiler pump is driven by a pin that is set into the clutch drum. When you reassemble the drive mechanism, be sure the pin fits properly into its hole.

Ah, chain saws. There's no understanding Parp's irrational fondness for these noisy, dangerous, foul-smelling, mechanical beasts. But they have been an important part of an otherwise quiet and simple life in the Rockies. Maybe they just add a little suspense, besides making wood gathering easier and faster.

CHAPTER ELEVEN:
Power Wood Splitters

Winter again; from Bangor to Charlottesville, from Allentown to Cleveland, and from the Midwest to the Olympic Rain Forest, more homes than ever are partially or completely heated by wood. If you do the work yourself, wood is the most economical, most renewable source of home heat and the most comforting, especially on cloudy winter days. If you don't cut your own, wood is as expensive as most other fuels, or even more expensive. People charge by the hour to cut, gather, split, and stack firewood, and they include in their fee the costs of gasoline, repairs, and insurance for chain saws, trucks, and machine splitting. If you do all of this work for yourself, wood heat can be as economical as it is pleasant.

So, off you go with your pickup and your chain saw to a nearby national forest, maybe ten times each year. Each time, you return with a rick or so of good firewood in the round. Now you have to split those round logs into stove or fireplace-size pieces. How do you do it?

For everyday home use, Parp says to use an axe or other appropriate hand tools, such as a maul or a wedge and sledge. A little of this wonderful work every day through the year's different seasons is better than spending thousands on glitter-sprayed jogging suits or designer running shoes, unless you live in a town where such fashions are mandatory. Splitting wood by hand is the very best of exercise, and it sure takes the grunt out of the cabin plague days of January and February. Play Mozart or Elvis from a good speaker aimed at your woodpile, or just listen to the dear silence bitten by your axe blows. Even a certain President would heartily recommend it.

If you live in a very rural area, it's also a good idea to store a protected supply of good split wood for emergencies and sick days, up to a year's worth, not to be touched except when really fevered or when sleeping through a hellish blizzard.

There might be times when you end up with a huge load of green wood that you need to season before using. If so, it'll dry fastest if it's all split and stacked, bark side up. And if you have a surplus of split wood ready to burn, you can make extra money by selling it in the depths of winter to some less farsighted individual.

In these and other situations, almost anyone who uses wood might benefit by having a fast and dependable power splitter. It is certainly essential to any profitable firewood business; most people who buy firewood want it split, delivered, and stacked.

At present there are two basic types of power splitters. One uses a power source to turn a large, screwlike device. The power source may be an attached four-cycle engine, or it may be a vehicle with the screw attached to a rear wheel. Whatever the power source, the turning screw engages the wood and pulls it in as the screw penetrates. This soon splits a log into halves, each of which may then be split into quarters or smaller pieces.

The other type of splitter uses a power source connected to a pump that forces hydraulic pressure to drive a plunger that, in turn, forces a log against a permanent wedge until the log splits in half. Again, the halves can be split into quarters or smaller pieces. A hydraulic splitter can be a self-contained unit with its own four-cycle engine, pump, and hydraulic system, or it can have a pump and hydraulic system driven by an external power source, such as a tractor's Power Take-Off (PTO). It can even be a simpler design powered by a tractor's hydraulic system.

Each basic type of splitter has its own distinct advantages and disadvantages that determine which is best for any individual.

THE STICKLER

The original screw-type splitter was invented, designed, and first manufactured by one of those great individualists who have done so much for all aspects of our society. Art Stickler of Gunnison, Colorado, made the first screw-type splitter, which he called the Stickler, in his welding shop. It was one of those simple, ingenious ideas that causes many people to wonder why they didn't think of it first. Stickler applied for a patent on the device but was refused,

Photo 11-1—Art Stickler's Splitter

Courtesy Arnold Industries, Inc.

and many companies have since come out with variations, which led Stickler to virtually cease national distribution in the late 1970s. None, says Parp, are as good as Stickler's original design.

The original Stickler was conceived as a threaded cone that could be bolted to the rear wheel of any vehicle. With the rear of the vehicle up on blocks and the transmission in gear, the Stickler revolved with enough torque to split almost any log, almost any kind of wood. You had simply to hold the log against the tip of the screw until it engaged the wood. The Stickler then turned the log until it was stopped by one end hitting either the ground or a frame of some kind. In went the screw, and pop went the log.

The Stickler was the simplest and least expensive of all power splitters, and Stickler had the homesteader and the low-budget firewood dealer in mind when he invented it. For a very modest investment, any old unroadworthy vehicle could be turned into a powerful wood splitter. Or, a person could use a truck to haul in a large supply of round logs, then block the truck up, attach a Stickler, and split enough wood in a short enough time to make a business feasible.

Furthermore, the Stickler was totally maintenance-free, was virtually indestructible, contained no moving parts, never wore out, never needed to be replaced, and actually improved with age and use due to its self-sharpening nature. It was also safe and easy for one person to operate without help. It was even virtually impossible to get your clothing caught on the thing.

The only disadvantage of the Stickler design was that it was somewhat slower than a good hydraulic splitter. It would split a cord of wood per hour, fast enough for most of us, especially considering the savings in investment compared to the cost of a hydraulic splitter.

All of Art Stickler's customers knew that they could depend on the best in materials and manufacturing methods and the optimum designs. Then came the other companies with their national advertising, rushed manufacturing, second-rate materials, and some really goofy designs. Nothing, says Parp, compared favorably to the splitter designed by Stickler himself.

For the homesteader, homeowner, or modest firewood dealer who can't justify the larger investment of a hydraulic splitter, the Stickler is the way to go. Also, Parp doesn't need to mention anything about repairs or maintenance. There aren't any.

If you would like more information about the Stickler splitter, contact Arnold Industries, Inc. (see Appendix C for address). This firm is now producing Sticklers from the original design.

HYDRAULIC SPLITTERS

On the other hand, the fastest and easiest way to split wood is with a good hydraulic splitter. Its disadvantages are that it costs much more than a Stickler, contains moving parts, is less easily moved (but is faster to set up), requires regular maintenance, and is susceptible to occasional mechanical failures that will require repairs.

A number of serious firewood dealers actually manufacture their own hydraulic splitters. Unfortunately, these homemade jobs rarely if ever include some of the important safety and convenience features found on the best commercially built machines.

Illustration 11–1 shows the basic design of a typical hydraulic wood splitter, supplied by Didier Manufacturing of Franksville, Wisconsin. This splitter is self-contained, complete with four-cycle engine, pump, hydraulics, plunger, wedge, towing hitch, and pneumatic tire wheels. When the engine is running, it transmits its power to the pump through a coupling. The pump increases the hydraulic pressure to 2,000 psi and forces the fluid through the pressure line to the control valve.

When the operator places the control valve handle in the forward position, the hydraulic fluid flows under pressure through the cylinder tube to the rear port, which forces the plunger block forward at a constant rate. When the operator places the control valve handle in the reverse position, the fluid is forced through the other cylinder tube to the front port. This causes the plunger to move backward and forces the excess hydraulic fluid through the return line and back into the reservoir, ready to be used for another forward movement of the plunger.

Types and Sizes

Until very recently, most manufacturers of hydraulic splitters concentrated on the professional market. Up to the end of the seventies, most splitters were powerful, heavy machines designed to meet the needs of large-scale firewood dealers, or for use on large farms, ranches, and resorts where wood is split for vacationers and for rental cabins.

The trend now is to manufacture more splitters designed for occasional, lighter use by homeowners and casual firewood dealers. Also, manufacturers are now concentrating on self-contained splitters while making fewer models intended to be used with a tractor's PTO or remote hydraulic system.

The typical small splitter designed for homeowner use is powered by a 5 h.p., four-cycle engine and can handle logs about 18–20 inches long. These splitters usually deliver 7–9 tons of splitting force. This is adequate for almost any need, even fairly constant use by a firewood dealer. A splitter in this power range can occasionally run into logs it can't digest, but only rarely.

Most homeowner splitters are not set up for highway towing. They usually have small, semi-pneumatic, off-the-road-type tires and a simple pin hitch. Except for Didier Model MFD–26, all current homeowner splitters have single-stage pumps that allow a complete hydraulic cycle in about 20–30 seconds or longer. Didier's small-

Illus. 11–1—Basic Design of a Typical Hydraulic Wood Splitter

The engine provides power through coupling to pump. The pump draws oil from the reservoir through the suction line. The pump raises pressure to 2,000 psi, forcing oil to the control valve through the pressure line. With control valve handle forward, oil flows through the control to the rear port through the cylinder tube. The plunger block moves forward. By moving the control handle to the back position, oil flows through the control to the front port through the cylinder tube. The plunger block moves backward. This forces excess oil through the valve return line to the reservoir.

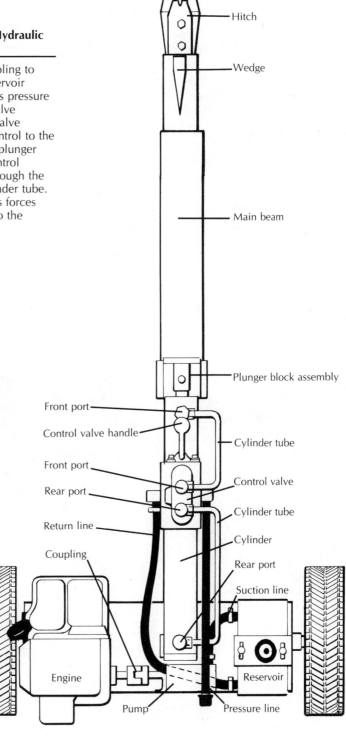

est splitter, the HA–19M, has, at 15 seconds, the fastest single-stage cycle of which Parp knows. The model MFD–26, mentioned above, has a two-stage pump that automatically returns the plunger to the start position. This creates a faster cycle, 12 seconds or less, and allows much more efficient power use.

The typical medium-duty or small professional-quality splitter is powered by a 5–7 h.p. engine and delivers about 10–13 tons of splitting power. This type of splitter may have a single-stage pump that cycles in about 20 or 25 seconds, or it may have a double-stage pump that cuts the cycle time to 12 seconds. These splitters usually handle logs from about 19–25

inches long and of any diameter. Such a splitter will rarely if ever be defeated by any log or type of wood that you can fit onto the loading bed.

Heavy-duty, professional hydraulic splitters can weigh up to 1,000 pounds and are usually powered by engines of 8–10 h.p. or more. One good example is the Didier Model MFX–26. It has a two-stage pump that delivers 20 tons of splitting force in an 11-second cycle with automatic return. It will handle any log up to 24 inches long. Another pro, Amerind-MacKissic's Mighty Mac Model LS2910, has a 10 h.p. cast-iron Kohler engine and a two-stage pump that delivers 18 tons of splitting force in a cycle time of 13 seconds. It will handle logs up to 30 inches

Photo 11–2—The Hydraulic Wood Splitter

A heavy-duty, professional model. Courtesy Didier Manufacturing Co.

long, no matter how tough they are.

Professional splitters should be equipped for highway travel with a good ball hitch, safety chains, taillights, and fully pneumatic highway tires.

Desirable Features on Hydraulic Splitters

Sturdy construction and an efficient design are surely the most desirable features on any hydraulic splitter. The main construction should be around a solid steel ''I'' beam. All engine shrouds and operator controls should be good metal. Plastic parts don't hold up well on a splitter that sees much use.

Each time a splitter is operated, a tremendous hydraulic pressure is applied not only to the log but to parts of the splitter as well. For strength and durability, the hydraulic cylinder should have as strong a shaft with as large a diameter as possible. A 2-inch shaft is probably optimum. The plate, or ram block, on the end of the shaft should be heavy steel and should slide on brass or some similar material. All cylinders, couplings, and controls should be well manufactured for any splitter, not homemade rigs that will fail as soon as pressure builds.

A two-stage pump is a great advantage if you're interested in speed or in the most efficient use of power. A two-stage pump reduces the amount of horsepower needed for any particular splitting job. It operates at high volume and low pressure until it encounters a load that causes it to shift to low volume at high pressure. Thus, it moves the log to the splitter blade faster before shifting over to high power to do the work. Many hydraulic jacks work this way, too.

An auto-cycle hydraulic control valve (ACV) is a very useful option available for most splitters on the market today. This system allows the ram to return to the open position automatically once the control lever is placed in the retract position. Since you don't have to stand there and hold the lever in position, you can use this otherwise

lost time to prepare the next log for splitting.

If you never plan to tow your splitter on the highway, small, standard semipneumatic wheels and a simple pin hitch will do. These are commonly supplied on most homeowner and light-duty machines. However, if you're planning on selling firewood, or if you expect to tow your splitter on the highway for any reason, get large, fully pneumatic wheels, and be sure your model offers plenty of clearance. You should also get a ball-type hitch.

OPERATING A HYDRAULIC WOOD SPLITTER

Hydraulic splitters are rather simple to operate if the machine is in good condition. The four-cycle engine must be checked for proper lubrication prior to starting. For more information on using and maintaining four-cycle engines, see Chapter Three.

Hazards

Until recently, nearly all log splitters were bought and used by professional firewood dealers, resort managers, and ranchers, who were more familiar with such machines than the average person. There were accidents and injuries, but they were few. Now that splitters are becoming widely popular, there are many more reported injuries, and they tend to be quite serious. Severed fingers and broken legs seem to be the most common injuries, usually resulting from carelessness, inattentiveness, and unfamiliarity with the machines. Fires happen on occasion, usually caused by operating a hot splitter in dry brush or by refueling a splitter without allowing it to cool first. Most of these accidents could be avoided if the operators would read their owner's manuals and follow the common safety rules that apply to all gasoline-engine-powered equipment.

With a splitter, the first rule is never to allow any part of your body to get between the plunger and the wedge while the engine is running. This seems so obvious that it's surprising how often it happens. Usually, the operator bends over the loading area of the splitter to retrieve a piece of wood from the other side and somehow engages the operating lever.

There is another serious hazard inherent in all hydraulic splitters that is considerably less obvious. When a hydraulic splitter is in operation, the hydraulic fluid is under tremendous pressure. If a line, connection, or coupling is loose, the fluid can escape with such force that it can actually penetrate the skin. This can cause very serious injuries. These accidents occur most often when an operator attempts to disconnect a hydraulic line without first relieving all pressure, or when an operator applies pressure to a system in which there is a loose connection or a coupling shield missing. Check your splitter for loose connections and broken lines before each use, especially if the machine has been in storage for some time. Also, do not use your hands to search for a suspected small leak in a hydraulic line. The fluid escaping from a small puncture is very hard to see and can shoot into the skin like a needle. The fluid, of course, is highly toxic, especially when introduced into the body. Use a block of wood and wear heavy gloves when trying to locate a possible leak.

Using the Splitter

All horizonal hydraulic splitters are meant to be operated in a level position. Do not start a splitter on a slope or on extremely uneven ground, because of the potential hazards of slipping into the machine and also because the machine works less efficiently. Also, allow the engine to warm up for several minutes before applying hydraulic pressure.

In extremely cold weather or when the splitter has been sitting outside unused in cool weather for a few days, the pump should be disengaged from the engine until the engine is warm. This is usually done by loosening two set screws on the coupling hubs (see Illus. 11–2). With the screws loose, pull the hubs apart until they are just disengaged, then retighten the set screws. Start the engine and allow it to warm. Then *turn it off* and reassemble the coupling hubs, leaving a gap of approximately 1/32 inch on either side of the spider. With some machines you only need to retract the plunger enough to fit in the next log. However, with many machines, it is important to retract the plunger fully in order to develop full power before splitting any wood. Check your owner's manual.

Smaller logs with diameters of 16 inches or less are best centered, one end on the wedge and the other on the plunger, or stop plate in the case of a vertical splitter. Larger logs should be split approximately one-third of the log's cross section at a time.

When a log becomes stuck on the wedge and the plunger cannot push it through, do not attempt to dislodge it with a sledge or similar tool. This is a dangerous practice that can easily damage your machine or hurt you. Instead, force a piece of wedge-shaped wood under the back end of the log to raise it as much as possible.

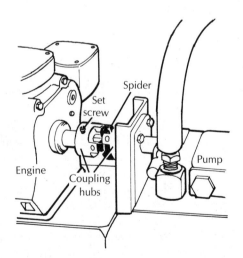

Illus. 11–2—Coupling Hubs of Pump and Engine on a Hydraulic Splitter

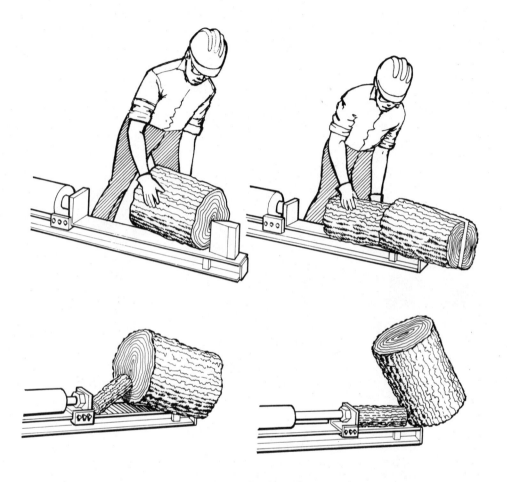

Illus. 11–3—Using a Hydraulic Splitter

Use another log to finish splitting a log half-split.
The second log should be sized to prevent it from
pushing the first log up (lower left), or from sliding
beneath it (lower right).

Do this with increasingly larger pieces of wood
until the plunger will slide under the log. Then
move the plunger fully forward to roll the log
up off of the wedge. Turn the log over, and split
only one-third of a different area of the cross
section.

When a log fails to split completely after
you have moved the plunger fully forward, move
the plunger all the way to the rear, and place a
new log behind the partially split piece. Then
move the plunger forward to finish splitting the
first log, or to split both logs.

Illus. 11–4—Splitting Large Logs

With larger logs, split just one-third of the cross section at a time.

Maintenance

Take extra care to keep a splitter engine clean and well lubricated. Be sure the engine cooling fins and shrouds are free of grease, oil, dirt, and wood dust or sap to prevent over-heating. Check engine oil level every five hours, or more frequently during heavy use. Be sure the oil level is correct for your machine. Take the time to clean around the filler cap. (For four-cycle engine maintenance, see Chapter Three.)

It is important to keep the rails or slide plate of your main beam clean, smooth, and free of nicks and burrs. Clean the beam regularly with solvent to remove tree sap and wood dust. File any nicks or burrs smooth to prevent damage to the side bars. After cleaning or filing, lubricate the top of the main beam with any oil or grease,

provided the lubricant is not itself contaminated.

Splitter wedges are actually designed to cut into the wood. It is occasionally necessary to sharpen a wedge with a file to restore it to its original condition. Do not oversharpen, or the wedge will nick easily. You can use an electric grinder for this job.

Before storing your splitter for any length of time, clean it well, and drain the fuel tank. Follow engine storage suggestions in Chapter Two (also see Index). Additionally, store your splitter with the plunger fully retracted to protect the cylinder rod from rust and damage.

Before each day's use, check all nuts, bolts, screws, and other fasteners to be sure they're tight. Be sure all shrouds are clean and properly in place.

Changing Hydraulic Fluid

Any hydraulic system should be drained and refilled after each 100 hours of use. The following procedure applies to most vertical hydraulic splitters. Refer to Illustration 11–1. **Note**: Never drain any hydraulic system by pumping it dry; this will case severe damage to your machine.

First move the plunger to the fully forward position. Place an empty container under the rear cylinder tube where it connects to the control valve. Then disconnect the rear cylinder tube, and position the tube to drain into the container. Now return the plunger all the way to the rear to drain that end of the cylinder. Reconnect the cylinder tube to the control valve.

Next, remove the hydraulic reservoir cap and the lower suction hose from the hydraulic fluid reservoir or tank. Drain the tank completely, and reconnect the hose with a new hose clamp.

Now place an empty container under the front cylinder tube fitting and disconnect the front cylinder tube. Fill the hydraulic tank with fluid and move the plunger forward about halfway. Again, fill the hydraulic tank, and wait a minute or two. Then move the plunger the rest of the way forward to drain the front of the cylinder completely. Replace the tank cap *loosely*, and reconnect the front cylinder tube.

Now return the plunger all the way to the rear, and again fill the hydraulic fluid tank and replace the cap *loosely*. Move the plunger all the way forward and all the way to the rear two or three times to remove any air from the system. Check the fluid level, and replace the cap tightly. It's ready to split again.

Two Common Problems

Whenever your splitter seems to lack power but the engine is operating normally, or when the plunger seems to move slowly or irregularly, check the hydraulic fluid level. If the tank is full, chances are that air is entering the hydraulic system at one of the connections. Be sure all connections are tight.

If the engine is running normally but there is no hydraulic pressure in the system, it's likely you have a pump problem, or the pump is not being driven due to a coupling failure. Check to see if the coupling hubs have become disconnected. If not, the keys or fasteners inside the pump or in the engine hub are probably broken or missing. If the coupling hubs are disengaged, turn the engine off, and loosen the set screws. Reconnect the coupling and leave a $1/32$-inch gap on either side. Tighten the set screws.

If your problem is broken keys inside the pump, you will have to disassemble the pump and replace the keys, or have the job done by your dealer or a good mechanic.

Safety Rules

1. Keep all children, spectators, and pets at a safe distance from your work area.
2. Never put your hand, foot, or any other part of your body on the log, plunger, or wedge while operating the splitter.
3. Keep to one side, away from the wedge or log, while splitting.
4. Split logs lengthwise with the grain only, never across the grain.
5. Do not place any material other than wood in the splitter.
6. Do not use a sledge or mallet to remove stuck logs.
7. Check all fasteners and shrouds regularly.
8. Do not allow any part of your body to come between the plunger and the wedge or to touch any moving parts while the engine is running.

Parp ends this power tool book the way he began it, stressing always: safety first.

APPENDIX A:
Pumps, Generators, and Electric Motors

PUMPS

Parp's ancient gravity-feed water system was built in 1918 by his neighbor and mentor, Pappy Fairchild. Pappy is still doing fine, thank you, but the water system is quickly failing. It would probably have outlasted Pappy, even, if the Town of Creede hadn't bladed it with bulldozers so often in every "Town Attacks Creek" season of each of those years. Now the 54-inch cypress wood pipe is full of gaping holes, and the precious pressure is lost completely before it reaches the metal stem that enters Parp's bathhouse.

So, the residents of East Willow Canyon, haggard after a vicious winter, are all filling out well permits and sending checks to appropriate bureaucrats for permission to put in individual domestic water systems to replace Pappy's torn-up pipe. Selecting and installing a pump in each new well will probably be the most pleasant aspect of the whole procedure, especially after dealing with all those "gov'ment" agencies.

Now, it isn't far from the rocky bottom of Parp's canyon to the water table underneath, so he's going to use a shallow well pump arrangement. The whole outfit will consist of a pump, a tank, a shallow well ejector (an electric-motor-driven device that produces a vacuum to draw up water and prime the pump), and the necessary plumbing and wiring. And that is a simple list of the basic elements necessary to operate a well. You need a pump to pull the water up,

a tank to hold a certain amount of stored water under pressure (so your pump doesn't have to operate continuously), a device to control the flow (another function of the ejector), some metal or plastic pipes to carry the water, and, of course, some kind of power to drive the pump. In Parp's case, as in most situations these days, the pump has its own electric motor, but the power source could also be a windmill, the hydraulics of a ram pump, or an arm and hand for a manual pump.

The most common type of well pump available today is the electric pump. Gasoline-engine pumps are also very common, but they are rarely used as domestic well pumps because they must be fueled frequently and they make considerably more noise than an electric pump. Gasoline-engine pumps are primarily used in other situations, such as field pumping to clear ditches and swamps.

There are two basic types of domestic wells: the shallow well and the deep well. Wells up to 25 feet deep are called shallow wells, while wells over 25 feet deep are called deep wells. When you choose a pump and tank system for water well use, you must choose either a deep well or a shallow well system. In most cases, the only real differences will be in the ejector and in the plumbing that goes down into the well. Deep wells require a deep well ejector and, usually, a double pipe into the well. Shallow wells require a shallow well ejector and a single pipe into the well. A jet-type pump will operate either system in conjunction with a water system pressure tank.

Jet-type electric water well pumps are generally rated between 1/3–1 1/2 h.p. Parp's shallow well will require only a 1/3 h.p. model. Wells up to 60 feet deep usually require a 1/2 h.p. pump. A 3/4 h.p. pump will work in wells up to about 80 feet deep, and the 1–1 1/2 h.p. size is required if the well is deeper than 80 feet. A jet-type pump is designed to be attached to a plate on the top of the pressure tank. It is never submerged in the well itself.

Submersible Pumps

Domestic wells may also be operated with submersible pumps. These, of course, are designed to be submerged in the well itself and may or may not be used with a pressure tank.

A submersible pump consists of a waterproof electric motor situated at the bottom of the well, and impellers with vanes to drive the water up the pipe. The motor rotates the impellers inside a housing. The vanes, sometimes S-shaped like ship propellers for greater efficiency, draw the water in at one end of the pipe and force it out the other. Submersible pumps are used for deep wells because it is more efficient to run electricity down to the bottom than it is to supply mechanical or water jet power very far from the source of the jet to turn the pump shaft. They also never need to be primed since they are already under water.

The horsepower sizes are the same for submersible pumps as for the jet-type pumps discussed above. Submersible pumps should be placed in cased wells only, and a device called a pitless adapter should be used to connect the vertical drop pipe (the vertical pipe in the well) to the horizontal service pipe. A pitless adapter

prevents well contamination by sealing the connection between the two pipes. All submersible pumps should have built-in automatic overload protection.

Field Pumps

In a rural situation there are many uses for pumps other than for wells. Field pumps are used for irrigation, for watering livestock, and for draining ditches and marshy areas. Field pumps are nearly always powered by four-cycle gasoline engines, although some irrigation installations are best powered by electric motor pumps. Portable field pumps may also be driven from the PTO unit of a tractor (see Index).

Connecting the Field Pump to the Power Source

There are two practical methods of connecting field pumps to gasoline engines, electric motors, or PTO units. The most common is the belt and pulley drive. A flexible coupling direct drive can also be used, provided that the rated rpm of the pump is compatible with the rated rpm output of the power source. If you use a belt and pulley system, you must adjust the system so that the rpm at the pulley on the pump does not exceed the pump's maximum rpm rating. Otherwise, the pump will turn too fast and fail to work correctly. If the power source's rated rpm is less than that of the pump, the pump will operate too slowly and not pump enough water. The motor output power and rpm should be on the manufacturer's tag on its housing. The pump should have a similar metal label permanently affixed with the same rpm information.

Matching motor and pump rpm is best done by using a drive pulley that adjusts the rpm of the power source to match the rated rpm of the pump. To determine the correct diameter of the drive pulley, multiply the rated rpm of the pump by the diameter of the pulley on the pump and divide by the rpm output of the power source. This will give you the correct diameter of the drive pulley that you should use in order to adjust the rpm of the power source to the needs of the pump.

Most pulleys are attached to the shaft by a half-moon key, though some are held in place on a tapered shaft by a nut. If the pulley is fixed (that is, a press fit on the shaft), then you need to match the motor and pump rpm by changing the pulley on the pump. (In order to determine the correct size of the substitute pump pulley, see page 208.)

Note: Whatever drive system you use, be sure to check the label on the pump or your manufacturer's specifications to determine the correct direction of rotation of the pump shaft, and connect your drive system so that the drive shaft of your power source rotates in the same direction.

If you use a belt and pulley system, be sure to use a drive pulley and belt that are the same depth as the pump pulley. Align the pulleys so that the belt is perpendicular to both shafts. A straightedge held perpendicular to the shafts should come up flush against both pulleys. Also, Parp recommends mounting both the pump and the drive source on the same mounting plate whenever possible. Do not overtighten the belt; it should be tensioned so that it gives slightly when you press down at the center of the belt's span.

Connecting a drive unit to a pump slightly out of line requires the use of a flexible coupling. Usually, a flexible coupling consists of a rubberized, heavy fabric disk that has three legs, called a spider connection, on each side. The legs clamp on to the shafts of the engine and pump, and the flexible disk compensates for the misalignment of the shafts. Other couplings work the same way as universal joints in automobiles, though ones used with engines and pumps are much smaller in size.

If you use a direct-drive system, follow these steps when attaching your flexible coupling. Again, be sure that the rpm of the drive shaft matches the recommended rpm of the pump shaft.

To attach a direct drive and flexible coupling:

1. Measure the diameter of the pump shaft and the drive unit shaft.
2. Select the appropriate flexible coupling half for each shaft.
3. Attach both the pump and the drive unit to a common mounting plate or base plate.
4. Measure the distance between the centerline of the pump shaft and the surface of the base plate.
5. Measure the distance between the centerline of the drive shaft and the surface of the base plate.
6. Install mounting blocks as necessary to align the two shafts as closely as possible. The two shafts must be the same distance from the base plate.
7. Place coupling halves over each shaft.
8. Place the spider connection between the two halves of the coupling, and connect them together.
9. Be sure the coupling halves are parallel. Align by placing a straightedge along the side of both coupling halves in two different locations, at right angles to each other. The straightedge should rest squarely on both sides of the coupling halves.
10. Insert a feeler gauge between the coupling faces at four locations, 90° apart. The distance between the faces must be the same at each location.

Using a Field Pump

The following instructions will help insure efficient use of a field pump.

1. Be sure all hose and pipe connections are airtight. Be sure that both the filler cap and the drain plug on the pump are tight.
2. When pumping dirty water, as from a ditch or pond, always use a straining screen on the end of the suction line.
3. Place the pump as close as possible to the liquid you plan to pump.
4. Keep the pump on a solid, level foundation. To prevent the pump from being pulled into the liquid by the strength of the suction, bolt it to a foundation, or tie it down.
5. Be sure the pump is primed with clean water according to the manufacturer's instructions before starting the drive unit. In freezing weather, always drain the pump after use. Drain the pump either by removing the fitted drain plug or by uncoupling the inlet and outlet hoses so that the water runs out to prevent it from freezing in the pump. Also, if you are pumping liquids that when dry could clog the impellers, rinse the pump out with clear water before draining. After priming the pump in freezing weather, slowly rotate the pump shaft by hand to be sure it is not frozen before you start the drive unit.
6. Keep lines and hoses as straight as possible.
7. Make vertical suction lift distance as short as possible. Centrifugal pumps can lift water efficiently only for short distances vertically. Output is greater, therefore, with a shorter lift than a longer lift. Also, any leak in the vacuum on the lift side can cause the pump to lose its prime and stop working altogether.
8. Use suction and discharge lines of as large a diameter as is practical to minimize resistance. Also, for the same reason, use as few connectors, elbows, and adapters as possible.
9. Protect lines from being crushed by trucks or equipment. If the pump is instantly shut off by a crushed suction or discharge line, the pump body can crack.
10. In muddy or silty conditions, protect the suction strainer from clogging by suspending it in a pail or in a bed of rocks.
11. Maintain pump and drive unit in good condition. Follow the manufacturer's instructions that come with the pump for maintenance. Usually, this means keeping the hoses from leaking, the bearings greased, and rocks or other hard objects out of the pump.

Storing Field Pumps

If you plan to store a field pump for more than a few days or in freezing temperatures, first drain the pump thoroughly. If the pump has been used in dirty or muddy conditions, first pump enough clean water to clear the pump of any contaminants. After clearing and draining, leave the filler cap and drain plug removed, and store them in a safe place so they won't be lost. Wipe clean the outside of the pump, and store it in a cool, dry area that is well ventilated but where the temperature is as stable as possible.

GENERATORS

There was a time, not long ago, when most rural American citizens who wanted electric lights had two choices. They could build their own hydroelectric systems, or they could buy a contraption invented by a man named Charles H. Ferguson. Ferguson's invention was a gasoline-engine-powered electric generator called the Homelite. He sold them to farmers all over the country from about 1921 until the time when wires were finally strung everywhere people lived.

We still have the wires, and few people have to produce their own everyday electrical power, but there are times when the wires break, or someone is building a new shack where the power company hasn't yet planted a pole. And, of course, we all know that untimely interruptions of electricity can occur at any time. So, there is still a large need for lightweight gasoline-engine-powered generators.

Most of the gasoline-engine generators are sold today as standby units for emergency use. In the event of a prolonged commercial power failure, a standby generator can be used to operate the refrigerator and freezer to prevent spoiled food, the sump pump to prevent a flooded home or basement, the electrical functions of the furnace to keep the house from getting cold, and lights to keep the house from getting dark. In a really bad storm, it is quite possible to lose the power long enough to leave you sitting in a cold, dark, flooded house with rotting food—unless you have a standby generator.

These small power plants also can help farmers prevent or minimize a disaster by operating milking machines, milk coolers, ventilating fans, pumps, feed augers, incubation systems, and other critical machinery.

Portable generators are also used on construction sites where commercial power is unavailable to operate power tools, pumps, blowers, and emergency or security lighting.

Family campers also use portable generators to operate toasters and to avoid missing episodes of "As the Stomach Turns."

Generators operate along the same electro-magnetic principles as electric motors, and the basic mechanisms are the same. A generator passes the windings of its armature through magnetic fields and then collects the current thus induced. An electric motor uses the electricity to create magnetic fields, which then push and pull on the armature to make it turn. Thus, a generator converts mechanical energy into electrical energy, and an electric motor converts electric energy into mechanical energy. A generator can be run as a motor and vice versa, but for greatest efficiency the wiring and magnets are arranged differently for generators and motors.

Output Range

Available portable gasoline-engine generators range in power output from about 1,000 watts (w.) up to about 20,000 w. Most lightweight consumer models for standby use range from about 1,200–5,000 w. Although most of these units are equipped with standard rope-pull, magneto-ignition starters, others are available with push-button electric starters. It is also possible to wire into the commercial power lines an emergency starting system that will start your generator a few minutes after a power failure occurs. These automatic starting systems are used in hospitals and security installations, but they are also practical for home and farm use where a loss of power presents a serious problem.

A typical 1,200-w. generator weighs about 65 pounds, while a typical 5,000-w. generator weighs about 150 pounds. Most consumer-type, standby generators will operate slightly over one hour before they must be refueled. Most portable generators are powered by four-cycle gasoline engines.

Selecting the Generator Size

To select an emergency standby generator that will serve your needs, add up the total watts of all the power equipment you are likely to operate at one time. Your generator doesn't have to be big enough to light every room and also run every electric appliance in the kitchen. It need only be big enough to operate those items that you must operate to stay safe and comfortable. These should include one or two electric lights, your refrigerator and freezer, your sump pump (if necessary), your emergency radio, and any power tool that you may need in an emergency. To determine your total watts, check the labels on your equipment. A 60-w. light bulb, of course, requires 60 w. If an appliance is labeled in volts and amperes only, multiply the volts times the amperes to determine the watts required. Motorized equipment such as refrigerators or freezers require a surge of power to start their motors. In this case, use the starting load listed on the label to determine the watts required.

If you live at a high altitude, the power output of your generator will be decreased by about 3½ percent for each 1,000 feet above sea level. Take that into account when you determine your emergency needs. Also, add at least 10 percent to your emergency watt allowance to account for engine wear, slight contaminants in your fuel, and similar factors.

The average watts requirements of some typical power equipment are listed below. If possible, determine your needs for watts from your equipment. This table should be used only as a substitute for an unavailable official source of watts information.

Storing a Standby Generator

A standby generator should be stored in ready-to-use condition, fully fueled and ready to connect to your emergency power circuit. The unit should be stored in a weatherproof, ventilated container designed especially for this purpose. About once each year you should remove the generator from its container, drain the fuel tank, refill with fresh fuel, and check the oil level. Parp recommends starting and using

Domestic Equipment	Watts Required
Refrigerator	400–500
Freezer	300–400
Furnace fan and starting system	800–1,200
Oil furnace	200–300
Sump pump	300–500
Well pump	350–600
Radio	50–100
Coffeepot	700–900
Frying pan	1,000–1,200
Electric heater	1,100–1,300
Lights for three rooms	200–400
Electric range, one element only	1,200–1,400
Water heater	2,500–3,500
Construction Equipment	**Watts Required**
Circular saw	1,000–2,000
½-inch drill	700–800
Air compressor	1,800–2,250
Belt sander	900–1,100
Impact wrench	400–600

the generator four times a year, at the start of each new season, to be sure it is always available in an emergency. Before starting a generator that has been stored in a container, lift the container cover, and wait several minutes to allow any gasoline fumes to escape. Be sure the ventilation louvers are kept clean and free of leaves, grass, and other obstructions at all times. The generator container should be kept at least 12 inches away from the outside wall of any building to allow adequate air circulation.

Desirable Features for Construction Generators

Portable generators for use on construction sites are generally larger in both size and output than consumer-type standby generators. Most construction-type generators range from 3,500–7,500 w., with a few 20,000-w. models for special needs (20,000-w. generators are driven by separate gasoline engines or by tractor PTO units). The average construction generator puts out about 5,000 w. Although most generators have 120-volt (v.) circuits only, several construction generators are available with both 120-v. and 240-v. outlets.

Construction generators should be powered by industrial-grade, four-cycle engines designed for continuous duty. The control panel should be an industrial type with at least four, but preferably six, outlets. It should incorporate circuit-breaker overload protection rather than fuses. A lift hook makes the handling of heavier models easier, and any construction generator should be protected by a wraparound industrial cradle. Whenever a generator is used in the woods, it should be equipped with a United States Forest Service-approved, spark-arrester-type muffler. When not in use, the generator should be protected by a weatherproof cover. It is possible to buy conversion kits to allow the use of either natural gas or liquid petroleum gas from large tanks instead of gasoline to avoid

frequent refueling. A wheel dolly kit is also a handy accessory for any construction generator.

Maintenance

Other than keeping the unit clean and ready for use, as described under Storing a Standby Generator, and keeping the container ventilation louvers free of obstructions, there is no special maintenance required for generators beyond the normal maintenance recommended for all four-cycle engines (see Index).

ELECTRIC MOTORS

This book has dealt primarily with gasoline-engine-powered backyard tools that are designed to handle fairly specific jobs, such as cutting wood, mowing grass, or turning small limbs into compost. Any of these tools might be found in almost any homeowner's shed, whether urban, suburban, or rural. Most homeowners find that most of their backyard tool requirements are met by these and similar appliances.

In a truly rural or homesteading situation, however, many people find that they have needs that are not met by commonly available power tools. Ask any farmer. From ventilating fans in barns and chicken coops to elevators, forage blowers, and manure agitators, the remote homesteader often must design and build very specialized power tools for specific, individual installations. Often, the best and most efficient power for such applications comes from small electric motors. For this reason, Parp offers this introduction to the types and uses of various electric motor designs.

Types of Electric Motors

The classification of electric motors depends upon the type of current supplied by power companies. Most utilities provide residences with single-phase alternating current (a.c.), so called because the electricity moves in wave form first in one direction, then reverses itself. (Direct current, or d.c., moves in one direction only.) The complete back-and-forth movement of a single-phase wave of a.c. occurs in what is called a cycle. Single-phase a.c. produces one wave per cycle, called a sine wave after a similarly shaped wave in trigonometry. The other type of current available is known as polyphase, or multiphase, which signifies that several sine waves of a.c. are being delivered during a cycle.

Single-phase motors consist of a single set of coils in its winding, sufficient to produce magnetomotive force from the a.c. Polyphase motors have more than one winding and two or three transformers and secondary wires that accommodate the multiphase current to produce corresponding waves of alternating magnetomotive energy.

Single-phase motors are by far the most common, and there are several different types of single-phase motors for a wide variety of applications, discussed below. Single-phase motors are usually designed to produce a fraction of a horsepower, such as $\frac{1}{10}$–$\frac{1}{2}$ h.p. Almost all home and farm electrical appliances and tools are driven by small, inexpensive, single-phase motors.

Polyphase motors are available with two phases (two separate windings) or several phases, but the most common polyphase design is the three-phase motor. Other polyphase designs are not likely to be encountered in domestic use. It is important to know that single-phase motors can be operated on single-phase power only, while three-phase motors can be operated either on three-phase power or on single-phase power if the motor is operated through a phase converter (see page 212).

In choosing an electric motor for a particular purpose, there are two basic considerations. The first is the amount and type of electrical power that enters at the source. You have little or no control over this factor, so you must choose a motor that is compatible with the power that enters your home or farm. Domestic electrical service is usually rated at 120 or 240 v., 60 Hertz, and single-phase. This is compatible with motors or appliances rated at 115 or 230 v. (The reasons for this apparent discrepancy in voltage have always escaped poor, thick Parp.) In any case, single-phase motors up to about 1 h.p. can be operated at 115 (120?) v. Larger motors should be operated on 230 (240?) v.

Three-phase power is available in some areas. Three-phase power allows the use of three-phase motors rated at over 2 h.p. These motors are less expensive than comparable single-phase motors. There are two different types of three-phase power. These are the wye and the delta systems, designations that denote the circuitry of the windings designed to accommodate the various phases, poles, and other considerations. The reader should know that a three-phase motor chosen for use with a three-phase system must match the system by type—that is, either a wye-type or a delta-type motor, according to the type of power available. You can find this out by consulting your local power company.

Motor Torque

As discussed, the first consideration in using an electric motor is the power available. The next consideration is the other end of the motor—that is, the size of motor required for the work load at hand, in order to efficiently use the mechanical energy produced by the motor.

When electrical energy enters the motor, it is converted into mechanical energy in the form of a turning shaft. This shaft is then connected to the appliance that you wish to operate. This is the work load that is placed on the motor. The turning force that is available from the turning shaft is known as torque. Some appliances require relatively little torque in order to begin functioning. Others require a great deal of torque. A load that requires relatively little torque is said to require low starting torque, while a load that is much harder to start is said to require high starting torque. In choosing an electric motor for any particular application, you must consider the starting torque required by the load as well as the torque necessary to bring the appliance up to its full operating speed.

Generally, once the appliance is operating, less torque is required to keep it operating at the proper speed. Different types of motors produce different combinations of starting torque and running speed. Therefore, the factors that must be considered in selecting a motor for an application include the type and amount of available power, the torque required to start the load, and the operating speed of the motor under full load (full-load torque). The power that the motor produces is proportional to the running speed and the required starting torque, and it is measured in horsepower. The horsepower required to start and operate the appliance determines the size of the motor that must be selected. If the motor is too large, it will be inefficient in terms of both the initial cost and the operating expense. If it is too small, it will be overloaded and will burn out quickly.

Overload Check

The best method for checking for overload on an in-use motor is to measure the current pulled by the motor. An ammeter is used to make this measurement. An ammeter records the number of amperes (amp.), the unit of measure for the amount of current flowing, drawn by the motor. A clamp-type ammeter is the best type to use in most situations. This tool clamps over each of the wires connected to the motor. The readings should be within the ratings listed on the motor nameplate.

Single-phase motors on 110 v. should draw the following currents: ¼ h.p., 4.8 amp.; ½ h.p., 7 amp.; 1 h.p., 11 amp. On 220 v., single-phase motors should draw half as many amperes because of the doubled voltage. A three-phase motor draws less power than single-phase motors. Therefore, a ½ h.p., three-phase motor should draw 5 amp. instead of the 7 amp. of a single-phase motor. If current drawn is higher than the rating on the motor's nameplate, either the motor is overloaded, the voltage is low, or some mechanical problem in the motor, such as too much friction between the bearings, is causing the malfunction.

Operating Conditions

When you choose an electric motor, you should consider the conditions in which it will be operating. If the motor will be exposed to the weather, it must be protected by an enclosure. Do not attempt to manufacture your own enclosure for a motor that is designed to operate fully exposed. An enclosure for such a motor will likely interfere with the air circulation needed to cool the motor. Buy a motor that has its own proper enclosure and that is approved for the intended application. For example, farmers often use electric motors in buildings that house feed or flour mills. Feed and flour mills can produce a highly explosive dust that can be ignited by a poorly selected motor. The selected motor should be one that is enclosed and is specifically approved for this type of environment.

Bearings

Another factor to consider in choosing a motor is the type of bearings used in the motor. These may be either sleeve bearings or ball bearings. Each type has its advantages and disadvantages. Sleeve bearings make much less noise and cost considerably less than ball bearings, but they are less durable and require more frequent maintenance or replacement. Sleeve bearing motors must usually operate in a predetermined position, while ball bearing motors can operate in any position. Most sleeve bearing motors are lubricated from an oil reservoir that must be at the bottom of the motor. Enclosed motors designed for use in wet or dusty conditions are usually of the ball bearing type.

Duty Types

Electric motors are designed for two different kinds of duty, either limited or continuous. Continuous-duty motors are used in fans and in any other appliance in which the motor runs for more than a few minutes at a time. Since they are designed to run without overheating while handling their rated load on a continuous basis, they will deliver their rated power until they fail mechanically, something that with proper maintenance shouldn't happen for a long time.

Limited-duty motors deliver a rated power for a specified amount of time and cannot be operated continuously at the rated load. An appliance such as a blender is run for short periods of time and then is shut off before it has time to overheat. These motors are less expensive than continuous-duty motors, but they should be used in only specific applications in which continuous power is not required. Motors used for most general purposes should be of the continuous-duty type.

Motor Installation

After you've determined the correct motor for an application, you must install the motor and properly connect it to your power source. The installation and wiring should conform at least to the National Electrical Code (N.E.C.) and preferably to any local codes that you might encounter (they are often more stringent than the N.E.C.). To obtain a copy of the N.E.C., check your local bookstore, or write to the National Fire Protection Association, 470 Atlantic Ave., Boston, MA 02210.

Note: Parp says all electric motors and appliances and circuits must be properly grounded to avoid the hazards of fire and shock. Parp recommends that you employ a master electrician to install any electric motor.

Electric motors should always be securely mounted on a smooth, solid surface and fastened down with mounting bolts. If the motor is not level and secure, it may become loose or misaligned during operation, thus placing a strain on the frame and bearings that can lead to noisy operation, vibration, overheating, and rapid wear. Whenever possible, motors should be located in a conveniently accessible place, but out of the way, and protected as much as possible from dirt, dust, excessive heat and moisture, and surfaces or materials that can abrade the frame as it vibrates normally during operation.

Connecting the Motor to the Load

There are three common methods of connecting electric motors to loads. These methods are direct drive, belt and pulley, and chain and sprocket. Use direct drive only when the motor and the appliance are designed to operate at the same speed as indicated by the ratings on the nameplate of the motor and the manufacturer's specifications for the appliance or equipment. Align the motor shaft and the driven shaft of the appliance as carefully as possible, and join them with a flexible coupling. (See page 201 for tips on installing a flexible coupling.)

The belt and pulley system is the easiest and most common method of connecting a motor to a load. The trick here is to determine the correct size of pulley to use on the driven equipment in order to properly reduce the output speed of the motor so that it matches the requirements of the appliance. To do this, multiply the speed of the motor (stated on the nameplate) by the diameter of the motor pulley, then divide by the correct running speed of the driven equipment as specified by the manufacturer. (Note that most common electric motors operate at about 1,800 rpm and that almost all appliances are designed to run much slower than that.)

For example, if your load should run at 400 rpm and your motor operates at 1,800 rpm and is supplied with a 5-inch motor pulley, the formula is as follows:

$$\frac{1800 \times 5}{400} = 22\frac{1}{2} \text{ inches}$$

Thus, in this example, you will need to use an equipment pulley with a diameter of 22½ inches to properly reduce the motor output speed to match the speed required by the equipment. When using the belt and pulley method, be sure to align the motor with the equipment so that the belt is perpendicular to both the motor shaft and the equipment shaft. (If the fixed pulley is on the equipment, see page 200 to determine the correct motor pulley size.)

A chain and sprocket connection is similar to a belt and pulley connection, but it provides positive drive (a belt system always involves some amount of slipping) for equipment that requires greater efficiency and, sometimes, a higher torque than that transmitted by a belt. Alignment and sprocket size requirements are similarly equated. For example, the 1,800 rpm motor with 10 teeth on its sprocket will need 45 teeth on the equipment sprocket of a 400 rpm appliance:

$$\frac{1800 \times 10}{400} = 45 \text{ teeth}$$

With either the belt and pulley or the chain and sprocket systems, the motor should be mounted so that it can be moved to adjust the tension as necessary. You can buy a slotted motor mounting base for this purpose. (See page 201 for correct belt tension.)

Single-Phase Electric Motors

The most common type of electric motor is the single-phase design. There are seven types of a.c., single-phase motors and several sub-types. They differ chiefly in the amount of starting torque that they develop and in the amount of current required to start them working. The choice of a particular motor for a specific application depends on the starting requirements of the equipment in question and the maximum current that will be drawn in use. The accompanying Single-Phase Electric Motor Chart lists the various types of single-phase motors and some suggested applications. This is followed by comments on each of the most common single-phase motor types.

Table A-1: Single-Phase Electric Motor Chart

Type	Horsepower	Best For	Starting Current	Comments	Recommended Applications
Split-phase	½₀–½	Easy-to-start applications	High	Inexpensive. Simple construction. Constant speeds.	Centrifugal pumps, fans, sumps
Capacitor-start	⅛–10	Hard-to-start applications	Medium	Simple, long-lasting design. Constant speeds.	Compressors, conveyors, grain augers
Two-value capacitor	2–20	Hard-to-start applications	Medium	Larger design requires more space. Simple, durable. Low line current.	Elevators, silo unloaders, barn cleaners

[Continued on next page]

Table A–1—*Continued*

Type	Horsepower	Best For	Starting Current	Comments	Recommended Applications
Permanent-split capacitor	1/20–1	Easy-to-start applications	Low. Two to four times the full-load current.	Inexpensive. No start winding switch. Reduce speed by lowering voltage.	Fans and blowers
Shaded-pole	1/250–1/2	Easy-to-start applications	Medium	Light-duty only. Less efficient.	Small blowers, fans, some appliances
Wound-rotor	1/6–10	Very hard-to-start applications	Low	Running current varies slightly with load. Large for power output.	Conveyors, deep-well pumps, hoists, bucket elevators
Universal, or series	1/150–2	Hard-to-start applications	High	Small, efficient size for power output. High speed. Usually connected directly to the load. Speed changes with load.	Portable tools and kitchen appliances
Synchronous	Very light	Light loads	N/A	Constant speed.	Clocks and timers
Soft-start	10–75	Easy-to-start applications	Low	Best for large loads requiring low starting torque.	Forage blowers, irrigation pumps, manure agitators

Split-Phase Motors

Split-phase motors are the most common electric motors, especially for farming requirements. They're called split-phase motors because they have two sets of windings, one for starting the motor and the other for running it. They are inexpensive and fairly efficient, although they produce only small amounts of power, about 1/3 h.p. on the average. They also produce very low starting torque, so they must be used only with easy-to-start loads, such as ventilating fans and centrifugal pumps.

Capacitor-Start Motors

The capacitor-start motor is very similar in design to the split-phase motor except that it has a capacitor (condenser) placed in series with the starting winding. The capacitor allows the voltage to build up to a high starting torque, up to twice that of a split-phase motor with about a third less current. For this reason the capacitor-start design is best used on such hard-to-start machines as compressors, conveyors, water pumps, and other frequent start/stop, motor-powered equipment that starts under full load. The efficiency of capacitor-start motors is significantly reduced in cold weather, however, so a larger one may be necessary for hard-starting appliances in colder climates.

Two-Value Capacitor Motors

These motors are similar to the capacitor-start motors except that a small capacitor remains in series with the starting winding while the motor is running. This is more efficient than the simple capacitor-start motors because the former can operate on lower line current while still producing a somewhat higher starting torque. The current required to start this type of motor is about the same as that for the capacitor-start motor, but the two-value type can handle even harder-to-start appliances, such as elevators and silo unloaders.

Permanent-Split Capacitor Motors

This design uses the same capacitance (a circuit's resistance to changes in voltage) for both starting and running. This results in a lower starting torque, so we're back to the easy-to-start applications such as fans and blowers. The advantage here is that no starting mechanism is used, so the motor speed can be adapted by lowering the effective supply of voltage to reduce the operating speed of the motor.

Shaded-Pole Motors

These low-cost electric motors have very low starting torque, but they are also much less efficient than the other designs discussed here. They should be used only with very light, easy-to-start loads such as small blowers or fans.

Wound-Rotor Motors

These are single-phase motors with a stator winding that connects to the power source and a rotor winding connected to a commutator. Their advantages are that their running current changes very little with variations in the load and that they use a low current to start heavy loads. These motors are more expensive than other designs and require more maintenance because of brush and commutator wear. However, they are by far the best design for extremely hard-to-start applications such as deep-well pumps and bucket elevators, which also place varying loads on the motor during operation. There are various wound-rotor designs for specific applications.

Universal, or Series, Motors

A universal, or series, motor is an unusually high-speed electric motor capable of operating on either a.c. or d.c. Universal motors are used in portable tools and appliances, including sprayers, sanders, drills, grinders, and vacuum cleaners. These tools require a high starting torque, quick acceleration, and the excellent power-to-size ratio offered almost exclusively by the universal design. A universal motor should never be operated without a load. They also should not be used to power equipment such as a pump or hoist, which may suddenly drop in load; the motor will overspeed when not under load, and damage is likely to result.

Synchronous Motors

The most common uses for the synchronous motor are to operate clocks, timers, and other very light loads. This is because this type of motor operates at a very constant speed that is predetermined by the design and otherwise is affected only by the frequency of the a.c. line voltage. Synchronous motors should never be used with hard-to-start or hard-to-run loads.

211

Soft-Start Motors

These motors are used with large loads that would otherwise require a starting current too high for a single-phase power line. The soft-start design operates on a reduced starting current of 1½–2 times the normal running current, a very low requirement that allows a very large motor to be operated on a single-phase power line. However, this results in a lower starting torque, often only half of the full running load torque, so these motors are useful only on easy-starting loads that, nevertheless, require the running power of a large motor. The best applications of the soft-start design are on irrigation pumps (110–120 a.c.), crop dryer fans, stationary power saws, forage blowers, and manure agitators. Other than for farm and homestead use, there are few suitable domestic applications for these large motor designs.

Three-Phase Electric Motors

Three-phase electric motors have one major advantage over the simpler single-phase motors discussed above: they do not require a separate auxiliary winding switch or a starting and running capacitor. Since these aspects of single-phase motors are frequently the causes of motor failure, three-phase motors are generally much more dependable and durable. Also, three-phase motors can be much more powerful, ranging all the way from ½–400 h.p.

Phase Converters

The three-phase electric motor is often the best power source for farm applications such as large irrigation pumps, crop dryers, feeding systems, and grain processing systems. Unfortunately, single-phase power is still the only power available in most of rural North America, and three-phase power is required for three-phase motors, unless the motor is used in combination with a phase converter. Phase converters make it possible to operate three-phase motors on single-phase power lines.

The two basic types of phase converters are the static converter and the rotary converter. Each has its own advantage, and a master electrician should always be consulted regarding any new application of a three-phase motor combined with a converter. Besides advising you upon the correct choice of either the static or the rotary converter, only a master electrician is qualified to determine the best combination of motor and converter for each particular application in order to avoid motor damage and a dangerous system overload. If the currents in each phase are too great for the motor rating, the motor will be damaged. Also, the converter must be balanced for the load under which the motor will operate, or else the motor will not run smoothly. When a combination of two or more three-phase motors is operated on the same phase converter, the converter should be of the rotary type. Be sure that your electrical consultant is familiar with these systems and with three-phase motor applications. Not every electrician is an expert in this area.

Note that for both types of converters the starting torque of the three-phase motor can usually be reduced to about 60–75 percent of the normal requirement. Again, your electrician can determine the exact torque reduction, but the result in a balanced system is that the motor-starting current is reduced at the same time. This means that the motor can have more power than a single-phase motor used in the same application, and the end result is the same as the advantage of having a soft-start motor.

Although a three-phase motor by itself is usually less expensive than a comparable single-phase motor, the total initial cost of a three-phase motor operated on single-phase power will be increased by the converter. This higher initial cost may be justified, however, because a three-phase system is usually more efficient and durable in the long run. Also, more than one three-phase motor can be placed on the same phase converter, provided the converter is the rotary type.

Maintaining Electric Motors

Electric motors that are correctly chosen and installed usually require far less attention than other types of equipment, especially gasoline engines, and this is the chief advantage of the electric motor. Motors that are worn out can be rewound and completely rebuilt, but this is not a job for the average home mechanic and is usually not justified, because a new motor costs about the same as having a motor rebuilt. Short of rewinding it yourself, the following are the only maintenance and repair procedures that are practical when compared with the relatively low cost of replacing the motor. (Large, expensive motors for special applications may be an exception, and having one of these rewound and rebuilt may be the best thing to do when the motor wears out.)

To keep your electric motors running efficiently and safely, perform the following service procedures at least once a year, or more often if the motor operates in adverse conditions, such as excessive heat (air temperature averages above 90°F), cold (air temperature averages below 30°F), or in an extremely dusty or dirty location. **Caution**: Disconnect power before servicing any electric motor.

1. Clean the motor—Remove dirt, dust, and grease from the surface of the motor and from the motor's air cooling passages. This helps prevent overheating.
2. Check shaft turn and bearings—Be sure the motor shaft turns as freely as it did when it was new. If the shaft turns with difficulty, the bearings may be worn, overtight, or misaligned. If the shaft moves from side to side or in and out, the bearings are worn, and you should have them replaced. Worn bearings will cause the motor to draw higher currents and develop less starting torque, which will soon result in motor or equipment damage.
3. Check wiring—Look for frayed and worn wiring and for exposed bare places. Some damage may be repaired with a moderate amount of good quality electrical tape on 115-v. units only. If wear is extensive or if the unit uses 230 v., replace all worn wires. Use the same type and size wire as originally supplied.
4. Clean starting-switch contacts—Many motors have a starting switch. The contacts of these switches should be very carefully polished once a year with a very fine sandpaper. Do not use emery cloth.
5. Check pulleys and belts—Belts should be checked for proper tension whenever you service a motor. Any worn belt should be replaced, especially if the motor is used to drive important equipment such as feeders. Adjust belts so that they give $\frac{1}{64}$ inch for each inch of span when you press down in the center of the belt's span. Check to be sure the belt pulleys are secure on their shafts. Align belts perpendicular to both the motor shaft and the driven shaft.
6. Lubricate the motor—Whenever possible, follow the manufacturer's lubrication recommendations exactly. Too much oil is as bad as too little, and it can be worse. If you don't have a manual for a particular motor, look for lubrication instructions on the motor itself. Apply only a drop or two of light machine oil to each indicated lubrication point.

APPENDIX B:
Engine Troubleshooting Charts

Troubleshooting is simply the detective process of logically determining the most likely cause and remedy of any particular problem. You start with the superficial indications, decide what clues these give you, and proceed to identify the most likely culprit causing the problem. The important thing is to proceed logically. In mechanics, this means starting with the simplest and most obvious possible cause of the difficulty at hand and eliminating the possibilities, one by one, until you reach a list of probables, *the* probable, and then the certainty.

Even if you never want to repair anything, and no sane person could blame you for that, learning to troubleshoot accurately can save you a great deal of money. Most mechanics really are conscientious and honest, but there's always one who'll charge you for a tune-up even though the problem was a turned-off ignition switch, an empty fuel tank, or a clogged air filter. If you have a pretty fair understanding of your engine and can determine the most likely problem through troubleshooting, you won't be fooled easily by an ambitious repair person. You may even find yourself holding a wrench, while beaming at an engine that runs again, with little effort on your part.

Note: Parp says if your engine is still under a warranty when a problem develops, don't think twice. Head straight for your dealer. Well, maybe check the switch and the fuel supply first.

HOW TO USE THE TROUBLESHOOTING CHARTS

The first thing to do is to determine whether your particular engine is a two-cycle or a four-cycle engine. The easiest way to do so is to look for an oil filter or a separate oil tank, which are present only on four-cycle engines. (In a two-cycle engine, the oil is mixed right in with the gasoline in the fuel tank, eliminating the need for a separate oil tank.) Another method that might prove useful to you is to check for valves on your engine—they are usually present only on four-cycle engines.

Once you have determined what type of engine you have, you will be able to refer to the appropriate chart for either two-cycle or four-cycle engines. The charts that follow list some common engine problems, and for each problem there is a variety of possible causes and their remedies. The simplest, most likely causes and remedies are listed first on the charts, followed by those that are more complex and somewhat less likely to occur. When trying to find the cause of a particular problem, you should start at the top and progress down the list until you reach a solution.

For example, the first engine problem listed on the Complete Two-Cycle Engine Trouble-shooting Chart is "Engine Won't Start or Is Hard to Start." The most obvious cause of this problem is that the ignition switch is turned OFF, a situation that is readily corrected. Try the easiest, most likely remedies before you decide to overhaul your engine.

In addition to the two charts dealing with the major types of engines, Parp has included a troubleshooting chart designed for those readers who own small tractors; because of the many diverse tasks that tractors help you perform, they deserve special care and maintenance. The chart will help you keep yours in tip-top shape.

Finally, these charts are designed to be used hand in hand with Parp's text. For each remedy (except those that are very simple to do, such as turning the ignition switch ON) you will find a page number referring back to the part of the book that covers the particular repair or adjustment you need to perform.

Table B–1: Parp's Complete Two-Cycle Engine Troubleshooting Chart

Problem: Engine Won't Start or Is Hard to Start

Possible Cause	Remedy
Ignition switch turned OFF	Turn ignition switch ON
Fuel level low	Fill fuel tank
Failure to choke cold engine	Close choke
Choke closed on warm engine	Open choke
Closed fuel shut-off valve	Open fuel shut-off valve
Clogged fuel filter	Clean or replace fuel filter (p. 22)
Clogged fuel tank cap vent	Open or clean fuel tank cap vent
Fuel line blocked or constricted	Blow fuel line clear with compressed air, or replace with new line (pp. 22, 63)
Flooded engine	Close fuel shut-off valve, if featured Remove spark plug, and pull starter cord several times to clear cylinder Clean, dry, regap, and reinstall plug (p. 25) Open fuel shut-off valve, if featured; open choke and throttle; and start engine
Carburetor out of adjustment	Adjust carburetor (p. 19)
Incorrect fuel mixture	Drain tank, and refill with correct mixture (p. 18)
Fuel contaminated by ice, water, or dirt	Drain tank, blow fuel lines clear with compressed air, and clean carburetor and fuel pump (p. 22) Clean or replace fuel filter (p. 22) Refill with fresh fuel (p. 23)
Throttle or choke linkage damaged or jammed	Clean, adjust, or replace linkage (p. 68)
Spark plug fouled or defective	Clean and regap or replace spark plug (p. 25)
Spark plug cable loose, broken, or oil-soaked	Repair and tighten, or replace spark plug cable (p. 27)
Clogged fuel pump	Clean or rebuild fuel pump (p. 64) Check carburetor (p. 19)
Defective fuel pump diaphragm	Replace fuel pump diaphragm (p. 64) Rebuild carburetor if necessary (p. 65)

[Continued on next page]

Table B–1—*Continued*

Problem: Engine Won't Start or Is Hard to Start—*Continued*

Possible Cause	Remedy
Fatigued reed valve	Replace reed valve (p. 6)
Carburetor needles, jets, gaskets, or diaphragms damaged or leaking	Clean and rebuild or replace carburetor (p. 65)
Defective carburetor or cylinder head gasket	Replace defective gasket (p. 77)
Faulty ignition switch	Repair or replace ignition switch (p. 27)
Loose crankcase fasteners	Tighten crankcase fasteners
Defective crankcase seals	Replace defective seals (p. 76)
Damaged flywheel half-moon key	Replace half-moon key (p. 29)
Short in high-tension wire	Replace high-tension wire (p. 27)
Loose ground connection	Tighten ground connection (p. 27)
Fouled breaker points	Clean and set points Search for cause of fouling (p. 31)
Breaker points assembly loose or defective	Reset points and tighten assembly, or replace (p. 31)
Bad condenser	Replace condenser (p. 32)
Breaker points bent, worn, burned, or pitted	Replace and set breaker points assembly (p. 31) Replace condenser if points are burned (p. 32)
Incorrect armature air gap	Adjust armature air gap (p. 34)
Magneto wiring loose or defective	Tighten connections or replace magneto leads (p. 28)
Magneto coil damaged or defective	Repair or replace magneto coil (p. 28)
Incorrect ignition timing	Adjust ignition timing (p. 33)
Poor compression	Replace head gasket (p. 77) Overhaul engine (p. 83)

Table B–1—*Continued*

Problem: Engine Runs Unevenly

Possible Cause	Remedy
Carburetor out of adjustment	Adjust carburetor (p. 19)
Fuel line clogged or contaminated	Blow fuel line clear with compressed air Drain and refill tank with fresh fuel (p. 23)
Carburetor clogged or contaminated	Drain and refill fuel system May be necessary to clean or rebuild carburetor (pp. 23, 65)
Spark plug fouled or defective	Clean and regap or replace spark plug (p. 25)
Incorrect spark plug gap	Regap spark plug (p. 25)
Reed valve clogged or fatigued	Clean or replace reed valve (p. 6)
Defective crankcase seals	Replace defective seals (p. 76)
Defective cylinder head gasket	Replace defective gasket (p. 77)
Incorrect breaker points adjustment	Adjust or replace breaker points assembly (p. 31)
Breaker points bent, worn, burned, or pitted	Replace and set breaker points assembly Replace condenser if points are burned (p. 32)
Bad condenser	Replace condenser (p. 32)
Magneto coil damaged or defective	Replace magneto coil (p. 28)
Incorrect ignition timing	Adjust ignition timing (p. 33)

Problem: Engine Does Not Turn Over

Possible Cause	Remedy
Defective starter	Repair or replace starter (p. 23)
Damaged flywheel half-moon key	Replace half-moon key Check for flywheel damage (p. 29)
Debris caught behind flywheel or attached to flywheel magnets	Remove flywheel, dispose of debris, and reset flywheel Check flywheel and half-moon key for damage Check ignition timing (p. 29)

[*Continued on next page*]

Table B–1—*Continued*

Problem: Engine Does Not Turn Over—*Continued*

Possible Cause	Remedy
Debris caught between flywheel and armature	Remove debris Check for damage (p. 29)
Broken piston rings	Replace piston rings Repair cylinder damage Overhaul engine, if necessary (p. 83)
Bent crankshaft	Replace crankshaft Overhaul engine (p. 83)
Damaged connecting rod	Overhaul engine (p. 83)
Engine seized by extensive mechanical damage	Overhaul engine or replace machine (p. 83)

Problem: Engine Runs Poorly at All Speeds, Lacks Power

Possible Cause	Remedy
Low fuel level	Fill fuel tank
Fuel foaming in tank	Fill fuel tank
Fuel tank cap vent partially clogged	Open or clean fuel tank cap vent
Incorrect fuel mixture, or fuel stale or contaminated	Drain fuel system, and refill with fresh, correctly mixed and measured fuel mixture (p. 18) Clean and regap spark plug (p. 25) Clean or replace fuel filter (p. 23) May be necessary to clean and/or rebuild carburetor (pp. 23, 65)
Air or fuel dirty or contaminated	Clean or replace air or fuel filter (pp. 20, 22)
Fuel line vapor lock	Allow engine to cool Clean and check cooling and exhaust systems (pp. 15, 34)
Carburetor out of adjustment	Adjust carburetor (p. 19)
Throttle linkage bent, loose, or damaged	Repair, clean, and oil throttle linkage, or replace (p. 65)

Table B–1—*Continued*

Problem: Engine Runs Poorly at All Speeds, Lacks Power—*Continued*

Possible Cause	Remedy
Defective fuel pump diaphragm	Replace fuel diaphragm Rebuild carburetor if necessary (p. 65)
Incorrect spark plug gap	Regap spark plug (p. 25)
Spark plug worn, defective, or wrong type or size	Replace spark plug (p. 25)
Muffler or exhaust ports clogged with carbon or dirt	Clean muffler or exhaust ports (p. 34)
Reed valve clogged or fatigued	Clean or replace reed valve (p. 6)
Leaking around cylinder head gasket	Check cylinder head torque Replace defective gasket (p. 77)
Air leak at carburetor gasket	Replace carburetor gasket (p. 65)
Incorrect breaker points adjustment	Adjust and tighten breaker points assembly (p. 31)
Breaker points bent, worn, burned, or pitted	Replace and set breaker points assembly Replace condenser if points are burned (p. 32)
Loose magneto coil connection	Tighten magneto coil connection (p. 28)
Magneto coil damaged or defective	Replace magneto coil (p. 28)
Bad condenser—opens with heat or vibration	Replace condenser (p. 32)
Incorrect ignition timing	Adjust ignition timing (p. 33)
Defective crankcase seals	Replace defective seals (p. 76)
Worn or damaged piston or piston rings	Replace worn or damaged piston or piston rings Repair cylinder damage (p. 83)
Poor compression	Repair or replace worn or damaged parts Replace head gasket Overhaul engine (p. 83)
Connecting rod worn or damaged	Overhaul engine (p. 83)
Cracked crankcase casting	Weld to repair, or replace entire machine

[*Continued on next page*]

Table B–1—*Continued*

Problem: Engine Sluggish, Won't Run Full Speed

Possible Cause	Remedy
Clogged air filter	Clean or replace air filter (p. 19)
Clogged fuel filter	Clean or replace fuel filter (p. 22)
Fuel tank cap vent partially clogged	Clean fuel tank cap vent Replace fuel tank cap if necessary (p. 4)
Sticking choke	Adjust choke, or adjust or replace choke linkage (p. 68)
Fuel line clogged or contaminated	Blow fuel line clear with compressed air Drain and refill tank with fresh fuel (p. 22)
Muffler or exhaust ports clogged with carbon or dirt	Clean muffler or exhaust ports (p. 34)
Carburetor out of adjustment	Adjust carburetor (p. 19)
Throttle linkage bent, loose, or damaged	Repair, clean, and oil throttle linkage, or replace (p. 65)
Loose carburetor	Tighten carburetor Check carburetor gasket, and replace if necessary (p. 65)
Tiny holes in fuel lines	Replace fuel lines (p. 63)
Defective reed valve	Replace reed valve (p. 6)
Carburetor needles, jets, or gaskets worn or clogged	Rebuild or replace carburetor (p. 65)
Worn piston rings	Replace piston rings Overhaul engine (p. 83)
Engine and systems poorly maintained	Tune up engine and systems as necessary

Table B–1—*Continued*

Problem: Engine Stalls Frequently

Possible Cause	Remedy
High-speed carburetor needle set too lean	Adjust high-speed carburetor needle (p. 19)
Low fuel level	Fill fuel tank
Overheating engine	Stop and cool engine Clean air cooling system Check work-performing attachment for loose, worn, or dull parts Clean cooling fins
Choke partially closed	Open choke
Clogged air filter	Clean or replace air filter (p. 19)
Clogged fuel filter	Clean or replace fuel filter (p. 22)
Contaminated fuel, or dirt or water in fuel lines	Drain fuel system Blow fuel lines clear with compressed air (p. 22) Refill with fresh fuel (p. 23) Clean or replace fuel filter (p. 22)
Jammed throttle plate, or throttle linkage bent or damaged	Repair or replace throttle plate or linkage (p. 65)
Spark plug defective or incorrectly gapped	Replace or clean and regap spark plug (p. 25)
Ignition wires or connections loose or defective	Tighten ignition connections Replace ignition leads as necessary (p. 27)
Defective fuel pump	Rebuild fuel pump
Reed valve clogged or defective	Clean or replace reed valve (p. 23)
Carburetor dirty or defective	Clean or rebuild carburetor (p. 65)
Breaker points assembly loose or defective	Reset points and tighten assembly, or replace (p. 31)
Incorrect breaker points gap	Regap by adjusting breaker points assembly (p. 31)
Bad condenser	Replace condenser (p. 32)

[Continued on next page]

Table B–1—*Continued*

Problem: Engine Runs Unevenly, Power Surges*

Possible Cause	Remedy
Low fuel level	Fill fuel tank
Clogged fuel tank cap vent	Clean fuel tank cap vent Replace fuel cap if necessary (p. 4)
Fuel stale or contaminated	Drain fuel system, and refill with fresh fuel (p. 23)
Clogged air filter	Clean or replace air filter (p. 19)
Clogged fuel filter	Clean or replace fuel filter (p. 22)
Carburetor out of adjustment	Adjust carburetor (p. 19)
Throttle linkage bent, loose, or damaged	Repair, clean, and oil throttle linkage, or replace (p. 65)
Electrical leads or connections shorting or loose	Check and tighten all electrical leads and connections Replace damaged parts (p. 27)
Defective reed valve	Replace reed valve (p. 6)
Defective fuel pump	Rebuild fuel pump (p. 64)
Defective carburetor	Rebuild or replace carburetor (p. 65)

Overloaded engine	Ease up on use of work-performing attachment
	Practice general maintenance on work-performing
	   attachment
	Check for proper lubrication and loose, worn, or dull
	   parts

Overheating engine	Clean air cooling system (p. 15)
Breaker points assembly loose or defective	Adjust and tighten or replace breaker points assembly (p. 31)
Incorrect armature air gap	Adjust armature air gap (p. 34)
Bad condenser	Replace condenser (p. 32)

*Note: Whenever you notice engine power surges, discontinue operation until the problem is discovered and corrected. Continued operation is likely to cause severe engine damage.

Table B–1—*Continued*

Problem: Excessive Engine Noise or Engine Knocks

Possible Cause	Remedy
Combustion chamber and cylinder clogged with carbon	Overhaul engine Clean carbon deposits from cylinder, cylinder head, piston, and piston head (p. 83)
Debris caught behind flywheel or attached to flywheel magnets	Remove flywheel, dispose of debris, and reset flywheel Check flywheel and half-moon key for damage Check ignition timing (p. 33)
Blower fan or other air cooling system parts broken or bent	Check and repair air cooling system (p. 15)
Flywheel or half-moon key loose or damaged	Repair or replace flywheel Replace half-moon key (p. 29)
Incorrect spark plug	Replace with correct spark plug (p. 25)
Incorrect ignition timing	Adjust ignition timing (p. 33)
Connecting rod and bearings loose, worn, or damaged	Replace connecting rod and bearings Overhaul engine if necessary (p. 83)
Cylinder worn or damaged	Repair or replace cylinder Overhaul engine (p. 83)

Problem: Excessive Vibration

Possible Cause	Remedy
Loose work-performing attachment or engine mounts	Tighten work-performing attachment or engine mounts Perform general work-performing maintenance; clean, align, tighten, and sharpen Check for stripped threads (p. 77)
Flywheel or half-moon key loose or damaged	Repair or replace flywheel Replace half-moon key (p. 29)
Unbalanced work-performing attachment	Check for worn or damaged accessory blades or parts (bent chain saw bar, broken mower blade, etc.)
Main bearings worn or damaged	Replace worn main bearings (p. 77)
Crankshaft bent or damaged	Replace crankshaft and bearings or engine (p. 77, 83)

[*Continued on next page*]

225

Table B–1—*Continued*

Problem: Engine Overheats

Possible Cause	Remedy
Engine cylinder fins dirty or clogged	Clean cylinder fins (p. 15)
Air cooling system clogged or damaged	Clean air cooling system (p. 15) Repair or replace bent, damaged, or missing shrouds or other parts
Fuel line vapor lock	Allow engine to cool Clean and check cooling and exhaust systems (pp. 15, 34)
Oil in fuel mixture insufficient or incorrect	Drain fuel system Refill with correct fuel/oil mixture (p. 18)
Muffler or exhaust ports clogged with carbon or dirt	Clean muffler or exhaust ports (p. 34)
Clogged air filter	Clean or replace filter (p. 19)
Overloaded engine	Ease up on use of work-performing attachment Practice general maintenance on work-performing attachment Check for proper lubrication and loose, worn, or dull parts
High-speed carburetor needle set too lean	Adjust high-speed carburetor needle (p. 19)
Defective spark plug	Replace spark plug (p. 25)
Loose carburetor	Tighten carburetor Check carburetor gasket, and replace if necessary (p. 65)
Carburetor dirty or defective	Clean or rebuild carburetor (p. 65)
Defective carburetor gasket	Replace carburetor gasket (p. 65)
Blower fan or flywheel loose or damaged	Tighten or replace blower fan or flywheel (p. 29)
Incorrect breaker points gap	Regap by adjusting breaker points assembly (p. 31)
Bad condenser	Replace condenser (p. 32)
Incorrect ignition timing	Adjust ignition timing (p. 33)
Combustion chamber and cylinder clogged with carbon	Overhaul engine Clean carbon deposits from cylinder, cylinder head, piston, and piston head (p. 83)

Table B–2: Parp's Complete Four-Cycle Engine Troubleshooting Chart

Problem: Engine Won't Start or Is Hard to Start

Possible Cause	Remedy
Ignition switch turned OFF	Turn ignition switch ON
Low fuel level	Fill fuel tank
Failure to choke cold engine	Close choke
Choke closed on warm engine	Open choke
Closed fuel shut-off valve	Open fuel shut-off valve (p. 43)
Fuel line vapor lock	Allow engine to cool Check and clean crankcase breather and air cooling system (pp. 15, 58)
Low battery power, or connections loose or corroded	Recharge battery, or clean and tighten connections (p. 58)
Clogged fuel filter	Clean or replace fuel filter (p. 43)
Clogged fuel tank filter screen	Clean fuel tank filter screen (p. 22)
Clogged fuel tank cap vent	Open or clean fuel tank cap vent
Fuel line blocked or constricted	Blow fuel clear with compressed air, or replace with new line (pp. 22, 63)
Flooded engine	Close fuel shut-off valve, if featured Remove spark plug, and turn engine over to clear cylinder Clean, dry, regap, and reinstall spark plug Open shut-off valve, if featured; open choke and throttle; and start engine (pp. 25, 43)
Carburetor out of adjustment	Adjust carburetor (p. 19)
Fuel stale or contaminated	Drain fuel tank and carburetor Blow fuel lines clear with compressed air, and refill tank with fresh fuel (p. 57)
Throttle or choke linkage damaged or jammed	Clean, adjust, or replace linkage (p. 68)
Spark plug fouled or defective	Clean and regap or replace spark plug (p. 25)
Spark plug cable loose, broken, or oil-soaked	Repair and tighten, or replace spark plug cable (p. 27)
Clogged fuel pump	Clean or rebuild fuel pump (p. 64) Check carburetor (p. 65)

[Continued on next page]

Table B–2—*Continued*

Problem: Engine Won't Start or Is Hard to Start—*Continued*

Possible Cause	Remedy
Defective fuel pump diaphragm	Replace fuel pump diaphragm (p. 64) Rebuild carburetor if necessary (p. 65)
Carburetor needles, jets, gaskets, diaphragms, or valves defective	Clean and rebuild or replace carburetor (pp. 23, 65)
Defective carburetor or cylinder head gasket	Replace defective gasket (p. 76)
Governor defective or jammed	Check governor linkage Replace defective parts, or have governor repaired (p. 58)
Faulty ignition switch	Repair or replace ignition switch (p. 27)
Crankcase or cylinder head fasteners loose	Tighten loose fasteners Check gaskets (p. 77)
Leaking valves	Clean valve heads and seats Replace valves, if necessary (pp. 58, 77)
Defective crankcase seals	Replace defective seals (p. 76)
Damaged flywheel half-moon key	Replace half-moon key (p. 29)
Short in high-tension wire	Replace high-tension wire (p. 27)
Loose ground connection	Tighten ground connection (p. 27)
Fouled breaker points	Clean and set points Search for cause of fouling (p. 31)
Breaker points assembly loose or defective	Reset points and tighten assembly, or replace (p. 31)
Bad condenser	Replace condenser (p. 32)
Breaker points bent, worn, burned, pitted, or incorrectly set	Replace or regap points Service ignition switch Replace condenser if points are burned (pp. 31, 32)
Incorrect armature air gap	Adjust armature air gap (p. 34)
Magneto wiring loose or defective	Tighten connections or replace magneto leads (p. 28)
Damaged or defective magneto coil	Repair or replace magneto coil (p. 28)
Defective starter	Repair or replace starter (pp. 23, 53)
Defective voltage regulator	Repair or replace voltage regulator

Table B–2—*Continued*

Problem: Engine Won't Start or Is Hard to Start—*Continued*

Possible Cause	Remedy
Incorrect ignition timing	Adjust ignition timing (p. 33)
Poor compression	Replace head gasket Overhaul engine (pp. 77, 83)

Problem: Engine Runs Unevenly

Possible Cause	Remedy
Carburetor out of adjustment	Adjust carburetor (p. 19)
Fuel line clogged or contaminated	Blow out fuel line with compressed air Drain and refill fuel system (p. 57)
Carburetor clogged or contaminated	Drain and refill fuel system (p. 57) May be necessary to clean or rebuild carburetor (pp. 23, 65) Replace fuel filter (p. 43)
Spark plug worn, defective, or wrong size or type	Replace spark plug (p. 25)
Incorrect spark plug gap	Regap spark plug (p. 25)
Clogged crankcase breather	Clean crankcase breather (p. 58)
Defective crankcase seals	Replace defective seals (p. 76)
Defective cylinder head gasket	Replace defective gasket (p. 77)
Incorrect breaker points adjustment	Adjust or replace breaker points assembly (p. 31)
Breaker points bent, worn, burned, or pitted	Replace and set breaker points assembly Replace condenser if points are burned (p. 32)
Bad condenser	Replace condenser (p. 32)
Magneto coil damaged or defective	Replace magneto coil (p. 28)
Incorrect ignition timing	Adjust ignition timing (p. 33)
Defective valve spring	Replace worn valve spring (p. 77)

[Continued on next page]

Table B–2—*Continued*

Problem: Engine Runs Unevenly—*Continued*

Possible Cause	Remedy
Incorrect valve-to-tappet clearance	Adjust valve-to-tappet clearance (p. 59)
Poor compression	Replace head gasket Grind or replace valves Overhaul engine (p. 77)

Problem: Engine Does Not Turn Over

Possible Cause	Remedy
Battery dead or disconnected	Check, clean, and tighten battery connections Recharge battery (p. 58)
Defective starter motor	Repair or replace starter motor (p. 54)
Damaged flywheel half-moon key	Replace half-moon key Check for flywheel damage (p. 29)
Debris caught behind flywheel or attached to flywheel magnets	Remove flywheel and dispose of debris Check flywheel and half-moon key for damage (p. 29)
Debris caught between flywheel and armature	Check ignition timing Remove debris Check for damage (p. 29)
Frozen valves	Replace valves Overhaul engine (p. 77)
Broken piston rings	Replace piston rings Repair cylinder damage Overhaul engine, if necessary (p. 83)
Bent crankshaft	Replace crankshaft Overhaul engine (p. 83)
Damaged connecting rod	Overhaul engine (p. 83)
Engine seized by extensive mechanical damage	Overhaul engine or replace machine (p. 83)

Table B–2—*Continued*

Problem: Engine Runs Poorly at All Speeds, Lacks Power

Possible Cause	Remedy
Low fuel level	Fill fuel tank
Fuel foaming in tank	Fill fuel tank
Choke partially closed	Open choke, or clean or repair choke linkage
Fuel tank cap vent partially clogged	Clean fuel tank cap vent
Fuel stale or contaminated	Drain fuel tank and carburetor Blow fuel lines clear with compressed air, and refill tank with fresh fuel (p. 57)
Air or fuel filter dirty or contaminated	Clean or replace air or fuel filter (pp. 43, 50)
Fuel line vapor lock	Allow engine to cool Clean air cleaning system (p. 50)
Carburetor out of adjustment	Adjust carburetor (p. 19)
Lubrication improper or inadequate	Check and fill oil to proper level, or drain crankcase and fill with correct oil (p. 57)
Overloaded engine	Ease up on use of work-performing attachment Practice general maintenance on work-performing attachment Check for proper lubrication, and loose, worn, or dull parts
Defective governor, or linkage loose, bent, or sticking	Repair or replace governor, and clean, tighten, and lubricate linkage Repair or replace linkage if necessary (p. 58)
Throttle linkage bent, loose, or damaged	Repair, clean, and oil throttle linkage, or replace (p. 67)
Fuel pump clogged or defective	Clean or rebuild fuel pump (p. 64)
Incorrect spark plug or spark plug gap	Replace or regap spark plug (p. 25)
Muffler or exhaust ports clogged with carbon or dirt	Clean muffler or exhaust ports (p. 34)
Leaking around cylinder head gasket	Check cylinder heat torque Replace defective gasket (p. 77)
Air leak at carburetor gasket	Replace carburetor gasket (p. 65)
Defective carburetor	Rebuild or replace carburetor (p. 65)

[*Continued on next page*]

Table B–2—*Continued*

Problem: Engine Runs Poorly at All Speeds, Lacks Power—*Continued*

Possible Cause	Remedy
Leaking intake valve or sticking exhaust valve	Clean, repair, or replace valves and valve seats (pp. 59, 77)
Defective generator or voltage regulator	Repair or replace generator or voltage regulator (p. 55)
Incorrect breaker points adjustment	Adjust and tighten breaker points assembly (p. 31)
Breaker points bent, worn, burned, or pitted	Replace and set breaker points assembly Replace condenser if points are burned (p. 32)
Loose magneto coil connection	Tighten magneto coil connection (p. 28)
Magneto coil damaged or defective	Replace magneto coil (p. 28)
Bad condenser	Replace condenser (p. 32)
Incorrect ignition timing	Adjust ignition timing (p. 33)
Defective crankcase seals	Replace defective seals (p. 76)
Cracked intake manifold	Replace intake manifold (p. 50)
Worn piston or piston rings	Replace worn piston or piston rings Repair cylinder damage (p. 83)
Cracked crankcase casting	Weld to repair, or replace entire machine
Connecting rod or crankshaft worn or damaged	Overhaul engine (p. 83)

Problem: Engine Sluggish, Won't Run Full Speed

Possible Cause	Remedy
Clogged air filter	Clean air cleaner (p. 50)
Clogged fuel filter	Clean or replace fuel filter (p. 43)
Clogged fuel tank cap vent	Clean fuel tank cap vent
Choke partially closed	Open choke, or clean or repair choke linkage

Table B–2—*Continued*

Problem: Engine Sluggish, Won't Run Full Speed—*Continued*

Possible Cause	Remedy
Fuel shut-off valve partially closed	Open fuel shut-off valve (p. 43)
Fuel line clogged or contaminated	Blow fuel line clear with compressed air Drain and refill tank with fresh fuel (p. 57)
Carburetor out of adjustment	Adjust carburetor (p. 19)
Throttle linkage bent, loose, or damaged	Repair, clean, and oil throttle linkage, or replace (p. 67)
Governor linkage bent or jammed	Clean and repair, or replace governor linkage (p. 58)
Loose carburetor	Tighten carburetor, check carburetor for gasket, and replace if necessary (p. 65)
Tiny holes in fuel lines	Replace fuel lines (p. 63)
Overloaded engine	Ease up on use of work-performing attachment Practice general maintenance on work-performing attachment Check for proper lubrication and loose, worn, or dull parts
Leaking intake valve or sticking exhaust valve	Clean, repair, or replace valves and valve seats (pp. 58, 77)
Defective carburetor	Rebuild or replace carburetor (p. 65)
Worn piston rings	Replace piston rings Overhaul engine (p. 83)
Engine and systems poorly maintained	Tune up engine and systems as necessary

Problem: Engine Stalls Frequently

Possible Cause	Remedy
High-speed carburetor needle set too lean	Adjust high-speed carburetor needle (p. 19)
Low fuel level	Fill fuel tank

[Continued on next page]

Table B–2—*Continued*

Problem: Engine Stalls Frequently—*Continued*

Possible Cause	Remedy
Overheating engine	Stop and cool engine Clean air cooling system (p. 15) Check work-performing attachment for loose, worn, or dull parts Clean crankcase breather Clean cooling fins (p. 15)
Choke partially closed	Open choke, or clean or repair choke linkage
Clogged air filter	Clean air cleaner (p. 50)
Clogged fuel filter	Clean or replace fuel filter (p. 43)
Clogged fuel tank filter screen	Clean fuel tank filter screen (p. 22)
Clogged fuel tank cap vent	Clean fuel tank cap vent
Fuel stale or contaminated	Drain fuel tank and carburetor Blow fuel lines clear with compressed air, and refill tank with fresh fuel Clean or replace fuel filter (pp. 43, 57)
Clogged crankcase breather	Clean crankcase breather (p. 58)
Defective governor	Repair or replace governor (p. 58)
Jammed throttle plate, or throttle linkage bent or damaged	Repair or replace throttle plate or linkage (p. 67)
Ignition wires or connections loose or defective	Tighten ignition connections Recheck Replace ignition leads as necessary (p. 27)
Defective spark plug	Replace spark plug
Defective fuel pump	Rebuild fuel pump (p. 64)
Leaking intake valve or sticking exhaust valve	Clean, repair, or replace valves and valve seats (pp. 58, 77)
Carburetor dirty or defective	Clean or rebuild carburetor (p. 65)
Breaker points assembly loose or defective	Reset points and tighten assembly, or replace (p. 31)
Incorrect breaker points gap	Regap by adjusting breaker points assembly (p. 31)
Bad condenser	Replace condenser (p. 32)

Table B–2—*Continued*

Problem: Engine Runs Unevenly, Power Surges*

Possible Cause	Remedy
Low fuel level	Fill fuel tank
Clogged fuel tank cap vent	Clean fuel tank cap vent Replace fuel cap if necessary
Fuel stale or contaminated	Drain fuel system, and refill with fresh fuel (p. 57)
Clogged air cleaner	Clean air cleaner (p. 50)
Clogged fuel filter	Clean or replace fuel filter (p. 43)
Carburetor out of adjustment	Adjust carburetor (p. 19)
Clogged crankcase breather	Clean crankcase breather (p. 58)
Throttle linkage bent, loose, or damaged	Repair, clean, and oil throttle linkage, or replace (p. 67)
Electrical leads or connections shorting or loose	Check and tighten all electrical leads and connections Replace damaged parts (p. 27)
Intake manifold loose or cracked	Tighten loose or replace cracked intake manifold (p. 50)
Defective spark plug	Replace spark plug

Defective governor, or linkage loose, bent,
  or sticking
	Repair or replace governor, and clean, tighten, and
	  lubricate linkage
	Repair or replace linkage if necessary (p. 58)

Faulty cooling system—dirty cooling fins or damaged flywheel or blower fan	Clean air cooling system Check flywheel or blower fan Repair or replace as necessary (pp. 15, 29)
Defective fuel pump	Rebuild fuel pump (p. 64)
Sticking exhaust valve	Clean or repair valves and valve seats (pp. 58, 77)
Defective carburetor	Rebuild or replace carburetor (p. 65)
Breaker points assembly loose or defective	Reset points and tighten assembly, or replace (p. 31)
Incorrect armature air gap	Adjust armature air gap (p. 34)

***Note:** Whenever you notice engine power surges, discontinue operation until the problem is discovered and corrected. Continued operation is likely to cause severe engine damage.

[*Continued on next page*]

Table B–2—*Continued*

Problem: Engine Runs Unevenly, Power Surges*—*Continued*

Possible Cause	Remedy
Bad condenser	Replace condenser (p. 32)
Flywheel or magnetic ring magnets weak	Replace flywheel or magnetic ring (p. 29)
Defective connecting rod	Replace connecting rod Probably necessary to overhaul engine (p. 83)

Problem: Engine Uses or Loses Oil

Possible Cause	Remedy
Incorrect oil type, or oil exhausted or contaminated	Drain crankcase, and refill with recommended oil (p. 57)
Oil level too high	Reduce oil level Check when engine is cold
Loose oil filler cap	Tighten or replace oil filler cap and gasket
Clogged oil passages	Clean oil pressure system (p. 41)
Clogged crankcase breather	Clean crankcase breather (p. 58)
Crankcase breather loose or incorrectly installed	Remove and install correctly, or tighten (p. 57)
Defective governor—engine running too fast	Repair or replace governor, linkage, or spring (p. 58)
Overloaded engine	Ease up on use of work-performing attachment Perform general maintenance on work-performing attachment Check for proper lubrication and loose, worn, or dull parts
Defective crankcase breather	Replace crankcase breather (p. 57)
Defective crankcase gaskets or seals	Replace defective gaskets or seals (p. 77)
Clogged breather oil return passage	Clear breather oil return passage
Defective oil pump	Rebuild or replace oil pump

Table B–2—*Continued*

Problem: Engine Uses or Loses Oil—*Continued*

Possible Cause	Remedy
Worn valves or valve guides	Replace valves, or repair valve guides and install oversize valves (p. 77)
Worn piston rings	Replace piston rings (p. 83)
Crankshaft bent or damaged	Replace crankshaft and oil seals Overhaul engine (p. 83)

Problem: Excessive Engine Noise or Engine Knocks

Possible Cause	Remedy
Combustion chamber and cylinder clogged with carbon	Overhaul engine (p. 83) Clean carbon deposits from cylinder, cylinder head, piston, and piston head (p. 84)
Fuel stale, improper, or of low quality	Drain fuel system, and refill with fresh, good-quality fuel (p. 57)
Debris caught behind flywheel or attached to flywheel magnets	Remove flywheel, dispose of debris, and reset flywheel Check flywheel and half-moon key for damage (p. 29)
Blower fan or shroud bent or damaged	Replace damaged parts
Loose air cooling shrouds	Tighten shrouds Check for missing fasteners
Flywheel or half-moon key loose or damaged	Repair or replace flywheel Replace half-moon key (p. 29)
Incorrect ignition timing	Adjust ignition timing (p. 33)
Defective starter	Repair or replace starter (p. 23)
Loose valves or worn valve guides	Replace valves, or repair valve guides and install oversize valves (p. 77)
Cylinder worn or damaged	Repair or replace cylinder Overhaul engine (p. 83)

[Continued on next page]

Table B–2—*Continued*

Problem: Excessive Vibration

Possible Cause	Remedy
Loose work-performing attachment or engine mounts	Tighten work-performing attachment or engine mounts Perform general work-performing attachment maintenance: clean, align, tighten, and sharpen Check for stripped threads (p. 77)
Defective governor—engine running too fast	Repair or replace governor, linkage, or spring (p. 58)
Flywheel or half-moon key loose or damaged	Repair or replace flywheel Replace half-moon key (p. 29)
Unbalanced work-performing attachment	Check for worn or damaged accessory blades or parts (bent chain saw bar, broken mower blade, etc.)
Main bearings worn or damaged	Replace worn main bearings (p. 77)
Crankshaft or Power Take-Off (PTO) extension bent or damaged	Replace crankshaft and bearings (p. 83)

Problem: Engine Overheats

Possible Cause	Remedy
Engine cylinder fins dirty or clogged	Clean cylinder fins (p. 15)
Air cooling system clogged or damaged	Clean air cooling system Repair or replace bent, damaged, or missing shrouds or other parts (p. 15)
Fuel line vapor lock	Allow engine to cool Clean and check cooling and exhaust systems (pp. 15, 34)
Incorrect oil or oil level	Use recommended oil Check oil level with engine cold Change oil frequently (p. 58)
Muffler or exhaust ports clogged with carbon or dirt	Clean muffler or exhaust ports (p. 34)
Clogged air filter or crankcase breather	Clean air filter or crankcase breather (pp. 50, 58)

Table B–2—*Continued*

Problem: Engine Overheats—*Continued*

Possible Cause	Remedy
Overloaded engine	Ease up on use of work-performing attachment Perform general maintenance on work-performing attachment Check for proper lubrication and loose, worn, or dull parts
Carburetor out of adjustment—set too lean	Adjust carburetor with engine hot and air filter clean (p. 19)
Defective governor—engine running too fast	Repair or replace governor, linkage, or spring (p. 58)
Loose carburetor	Tighten carburetor mounts Check carburetor gasket, and replace if necessary (p. 65)
Exhaust manifold loose or damaged	Tighten or replace exhaust manifold (p. 56)
Defective spark plug	Replace spark plug (p. 25)
Sticking exhaust valve	Free exhaust valve and valve seat (p. 77)
Carburetor clogged or damaged	Rebuild carburetor (p. 65)
Defective carburetor gasket	Replace carburetor gasket (p. 65)
Blower fan or flywheel loose or damaged	Tighten or replace blower fan or flywheel (p. 29)
Incorrect breaker points adjustment	Adjust breaker points gap (p. 31)
Bad condenser	Replace condenser (p. 32)
Incorrect ignition timing	Adjust ignition timing (p. 33)
Combustion chamber and cylinder clogged with carbon	Overhaul engine (p. 83) Clean carbon deposits from cylinder, cylinder head, piston, and piston head (p. 81)

Table B-3: Small Tractors: Troubleshooting Chart

Most tractor troubles are related to poor maintenance and are often easily corrected by following a maintenance procedure. If you follow a recommended maintenance schedule regularly, you'll have a minimum of the troubles mentioned below. If not, this troubleshooting chart may help you to remember some important service you forgot.

Problem	Possible Cause(s)	Remedy
Starter motor does not run	Hydrostatic control lever not in NEUTRAL	Put lever in NEUTRAL
	Electric clutch or PTO switches in ON position	Turn switches OFF
	Dead battery	Charge or replace battery
	Safety switch not activated	Activate switch
	Defective wiring or connections	Clean and replace as necessary (p. 27)
Starter runs, but engine will not start	Out of fuel	Refill fuel tank
	Flooded engine	Push choke in, and attempt to start
	Clogged fuel filter	Replace fuel filter (p. 156)
	Fuel stale or contaminated	Replace fuel
	Defective spark plug	Replace spark plug (p. 25)
	Worn points	Replace and adjust points (p. 31)
	Contaminated breaker box	Clean and adjust breaker box (p. 31)
	Poor ignition timing	Reset ignition timing (p. 33)
Engine cranks too slowly to start	Incorrect engine oil (too heavy)	Drain and replace with correct oil
Engine is hard to start	Fuel mixture too rich	Push choke in
	Clogged air filter	Clean air filter (p. 155)
	Defective spark plug	Replace spark plug (p. 25)
	Carburetor out of adjustment	Adjust carburetor (p. 19)
	Ignition points dirty or out of adjustment	Service ignition points (p. 31)
	Poor ignition timing	Reset ignition timing (p. 33)
Engine knocks	Low oil level	Add oil
	Incorrect oil	Drain and replace with correct oil
	Incorrect fuel	Drain and replace with correct fuel
	Poor ignition timing	Reset ignition timing (p. 33)
	Intake or exhaust valve lifter out of adjustment or defective	Adjust or replace valve lifter (p. 83)

Table B–3—*Continued*

Problem	Possible Cause(s)	Remedy
Exhaust is black or smoky	Choke partially closed	Open choke, or adjust choke control or plate as necessary
	Clogged air filter	Clean air filter (p. 155)
	Carburetor out of adjustment	Adjust carburetor (p. 19)
Oil is contaminating breaker box	Clogged crankcase breather assembly	Clean breather assembly (p. 156)
	Loose breaker box screws	Tighten breaker box screws
Excessive oil consumption	Engine running too hot	Clean engine fins and blower screen (p. 156)
	Too much oil in crankcase	Remove oil to attain correct oil level
	Incorrect oil	Drain and replace with correct oil
	Oil leaking at engine seals or around dipstick	Repair as necessary (p. 57)
	Worn piston rings and valve guides	Overhaul engine (p. 83)
Oil pressure indicator or lamp indicates low pressure after engine starts	Low oil level	Replace oil filter
	Clogged oil filter	Add oil
	Incorrect oil	Drain and replace with correct oil
	Faulty indicator	Repair indicator
	Worn bearings	Overhaul engine (p. 83)
Hot lamp or indicator shows overheated engine or transmission	Operating tractor in wrong gear	Clean oil cooler (p. 153)
	Dirty transmission oil cooler	Shift to a lower gear
	Fuel mixture too lean	Adjust carburetor (p. 19)
Engine runs, but tractor will not drive or lacks power	Transmission in NEUTRAL	Place in gear
	Foot or parking brakes locked	Release
	Cold transmission oil	Allow oil to warm
	Low transmission oil level	Add oil
	Carburetor dirty or out of adjustment	Service carburetor (pp. 22, 65)
	Carbon buildup	Remove and clean cylinder heads and exhaust system (pp. 34, 77)
	Drive belt slips	See next entry

[*Continued on next page*]

Table B–3—*Continued*

Problem	Possible Cause(s)	Remedy
Drive belt slips or clutch fails	Pulleys or belt greasy or oily Incorrect clutch tension	Clear pulleys or belt Have professional adjust as necessary
Tractor creeps with control in NEUTRAL	Idle speed too high Transmission NEUTRAL setting out of adjustment	Adjust carburetor (p. 19) Have professional adjust as necessary
Battery will not accept charge	Battery connections loose or dirty Dead battery Defective battery cables Defective alternator or generator	Clean and tighten, then recharge (p. 58) Replace battery Replace battery cables Repair or replace alternator or generator
Tractor handles poorly	Driving too fast Incorrect tire pressure Wheels slip Steering system requires lubrication Steering linkage loose or defective	Decrease speed Correct tire pressure Use wheel weights (p. 145) Lubricate steering system Tighten or replace as necessary
Engine runs too fast or too slow	Carburetor out of adjustment Governor linkage loose or dirty	Adjust carburetor (p. 19) Clean and tighten linkage (p. 156)
Electric PTO clutch won't operate	Broken or loose wires Open circuit breaker PTO clutch out of adjustment	Replace or repair wires If it fails to reset automatically, close it manually, or have professional adjust it Have professional adjust clutch

Table B–3—Continued

Problem	Possible Cause(s)	Remedy
Tractor stops suddenly	Out of fuel	Refill fuel tank
	Engine overloaded	Reduce load, or shift to a lower gear
	Fuel line dirty or defective	Blow out fuel line with compressed air, or replace as necessary (pp. 23, 63)
	Ignition switch shut off or electrical failure	Turn on switch, check for spark, and troubleshoot ignition system
Excessive fuel consumption	Clogged air filter	Clean air filter (p. 155)
	Incorrect fuel	Drain and replace with correct fuel
	Defective spark plug	Replace spark plug (p. 25)
	Poor compression	Service valves or overhaul engine (pp. 59, 83)

Appendix C:
Useful Addresses

Arnold Industries, Inc.
P.O. Box 2790
Toledo, OH 43606

Manufacturers and marketers of Stickler splitters of original design

Bailey's, Inc.
P.O. Box 550
Laytonville, CA 95454

Mail-order suppliers of tools, accessories, and safety clothing

Brookstone Co.
Vose Farm Rd.
Peterborough, NH 03458

Mail-order suppliers of hard-to-find tools and accessories

Engine Service Assn.
710 N. Plankinton Ave.
Milwaukee, WI 53203

Association for professional small-engine mechanics

Forestry Suppliers, Inc.
205 W. Rankin St.
Jackson, MS 39202

Mail-order suppliers of forestry tools and equipment

Gamń Enterprises
11427 Darmstadt Rd.
Evansville, IN 47711

Manufacturers of Gamń sharpeners for saw chains

Heli-Coil Products
1564 Shelter Rock Ln.
Danbury, CT 06810

Manufacturers of thread repair kits for small engines

Intertec Publishing Corp.
Technical Publication Division
1014 Wyandotte St.
Kansas City, MO 64105

Publishers of technical service manuals for power tools

Kemp Co.
3175 Oregon Pike
Leola, PA 17540

Manufacturers of composters, shredders, and chippers

Kwik-Way Mfg. Co.
500 57th St.
Marion, IA 52302

Manufacturers of tools and equipment for small-engine mechanics

Loctite Corp.
999 N. Mountain Rd.
Newington, CT 06111

Manufacturers of thread-locking compounds

McDonough Power Equipment McDonough, GA 30253	Manufacturers of Snapper lawn mowers, rider mowers, tractors, tillers, and snow blowers
Oregon Saw Chain Division Omark Industries 9701 S.E. McLoughlin Blvd. Portland, OR 97222	Manufacturers of saw chain, repair tools, and accessories
Permatex Co., Inc. P.O. Box 1350 West Palm Beach, FL 33402	Manufacturers of gasket sealers
Spencer Production Co. P.O. Box 224 Pullman, WA 99163	Manufacturers of logger's tape, wedges, and logging supplies
U.S. General Supply 100 General Pl. Jericho, NY 11753	Mail-order suppliers of mechanics' hand and power tools
J. C. Whitney Co. 1917–19 Archer Ave. P.O. Box 8410 Chicago, IL 60680	Mail-order suppliers of mechanics' hand and power tools
Zip Penn, Inc. 2008 E. 33d St. P.O. Box 179 Erie, PA 16512	Mail-order suppliers of chain saw tools and accessories

Index

F

G

O

P